Sunset

Southern California

—— TRAVEL GUIDE ——

By the Editors of Sunset Books
and Sunset Magazine

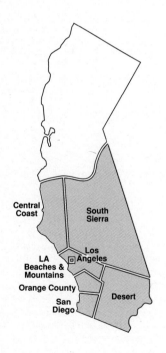

Sunset Publishing Corporation
Menlo Park, California

Research and Text
Barbara J. Braasch

Book Editor
Phyllis Elving

Coordinating Editor
Suzanne Normand Mathison

Design
Cynthia Hanson
Kathy Avanzino Barone

Maps
Eureka Cartography

Our thanks...

to the many people and organizations
who assisted in the preparation of
this travel guide. Special appreciation
goes to city and county visitor
bureaus, chambers of commerce, and
other visitor service agencies
throughout Southern California.

We would also like to thank
Joan Beth Erickson for her editorial
contributions to this manuscript and
Lois Lovejoy for her illustration of the
California poppy.

Photographers

Carr Clifton: 91; **Betty Crowell:** 15,
114; **Jeff Gnass Photography:** 98;
Cliff Hollenbeck Photography: 2,
75, 122; **Dave G. Houser:** 23, 51, 83,
119; **Dennis Junor:** 54; **Marie Mainz:**
35, 46; **David Muench:** 59, 78, 86;
Marc Muench: 62, 127; **Chuck Place
Photography:** 31, 67, 111; **David
Ryan/Photo 20-20:** 94; **Jonathan
Selig/Photo 20-20:** 18, 26; **Larry
Ulrich Photography:** 10, 38, 43, 70,
103, 106.

Cover: Colorful toyon boughs frame
Avalon Harbor, largest anchorage on
Santa Catalina Island. Cover design
by Susan Bryant. Photography by Jeff
Gnass Photography.

Editorial Director, Sunset Books
Kenneth Winchester

Second Printing December 1994

Disney-inspired paraphernalia, like these suspenders, make the ultimate Southern California souvenir.

Contents

Exploring the Southland

*W*acky, wild, and mostly wonderful, Southern California has long been a land of dreams for both vacationers and would-be residents. What is it that draws them? Certainly weather, lifestyle, and one-of-a-kind attractions are prime factors.

Mellowed by a fine subtropical climate, Southern Californians have adopted a more casual—and often innovative—way of life, in the process becoming trendsetters in food, fashion, architecture, and entertainment. And no other single geographical area offers such a combination of natural and man-made attractions, from lofty Sierra peaks and miles of dramatic coastline to the make-believe worlds of Hollywood and Disneyland.

The Southland's popularity has created many of its problems—sprawling cities, crowded freeways, and that coined-for-L.A. word, smog. Nature too throws evil curves—wildfires, floods, and an occasional earthquake. But to visitor and resident alike, the region's allure more than compensates for its disadvantages.

Contents

Agencies listed on the first page of each chapter in this book can provide information about accommodations and attractions in their locales. Contact the following office for general information about traveling in California.

California Office of Tourism
801 K St., Suite 1600
Sacramento, CA 95814
(800) 862-2543 *(for maps and brochures)*

Southern California's image as a carefree, sun-splashed haven was propelled into the national consciousness more than a century ago. A massive advertising campaign by the Southern Pacific and Santa Fe railroads attracted thousands of newcomers in the 1880s with visions of swimming in the blue Pacific, picking oranges from acres of fruit-filled groves, and enjoying shirt-sleeve fun in the snow. Such variety still exists, though it's harder these days to locate a beachside parking lot, find a nearby orange grove, or negotiate bumper-to-bumper mountain roads.

In fact, it's difficult to imagine anyplace with more to offer the visitor. Large cities, with all their cultural and commercial possibilities, add overlays to the landscape between ocean and mountains. Yet the wilderness is close at hand; high bluffs shelter secluded Pacific coves, waterfalls cascade down mountain reaches, and desert badlands stretch for miles in sand and silence.

The lowest point in the western hemisphere (Death Valley's Badwater) is here, not all that far away from the nation's highest point outside of Alaska (Mount Whitney in the Sierra Nevada). Desert resorts offer a wealth of recreational activities, and a fringe of beaches is dotted with bronzed beauties and wave-borne surfers.

Land of entertainment

Southern California sets the pace for the rest of the country in entertainment. Hollywood, Sunset Boulevard, Disneyland, and the Rose Bowl—these are bywords nationwide. You'll find more man-made amusements and attractions here, in fact, than anywhere else in the world.

Since the first moving picture was filmed in Hollywood in 1913, the world has been smitten with the processes as well as the products of this land of illusion. Movie and television studios let you peek behind the scenes, and some of them double as full-scale amusement parks. Celebrity-hunting is a big game, too, and many people come to the area hoping to rub elbows with the stars (we offer some tips on pages 20 and 21).

When Walt Disney created Disneyland in the 1950s in Anaheim, his first and foremost theme park set the standard for family fun. Then another Walter, Knott, expanded his nearby Berry Farm into 150 acres of amusements, and Orange County's reign as an entertainment capital began. To the south, one of the world's best zoos and renowned Sea World marine park are among San Diego's family-oriented attractions.

Southern California is also proud of its cultural complexes. Some of the world's finest museums, theaters, and music centers are here. "Under the stars" performances are popular, too, thanks to the balmy weather. In summer, the famed Los Angeles Philharmonic performs in the Hollywood Bowl, while across the Hollywood Hills top-name entertainers draw crowds for evening concerts at Griffith Park's Greek Theatre. San Diego's Balboa Park is the outdoor setting for summer musicals, and Santa Barbara offers song and dance spectacles in its Mission Bowl.

Land of diversity

The Indians were here first: the Diegueño and the Chumash along the southern coast and the Agua Caliente inland around the Coachella Valley's mineral springs. Traces of their cultures are still evident around San Diego, Palm Springs, and Lompoc.

The first Europeans arrived in 1542, when Portuguese navigator Juan

Continued on page 8

Fairs & Festivals

Mule races, Mexican fiestas, fiddling contests, an Arabian Nights pageant—Southern California offers a rich array of annual celebrations. Below are 15 of the most colorful events. For a complete calendar of festivities throughout the state, contact the California Office of Tourism (see page 4).

Tournament of Roses, January 1 in Pasadena. Elaborate floral floats, marching bands, and equestrian teams parade through the city before the Rose Bowl football game (free curbside or limited grandstand seating). Contact: (818) 449-4100 or (213) 681-3724.

National Date Festival, mid-February (beginning Presidents' Day weekend) in Indio. An elaborate outdoor Arabian Nights pageant (free) and daily camel and ostrich races highlight this 10-day festival marking the end of the date harvest. Contact: (619) 347-0676.

Hullabaloo Days, March or April (Palm Sunday weekend) in Calico. Mojave Desert ghost town celebrates its mining heritage with flapjack races, horseshoe pitching, pole climbing, and the world tobacco spitting championships. Contact: (619) 254-2122 or (714) 780-8810.

Cinco de Mayo, May 5 in Los Angeles and other cities with sizable Hispanic populations. Celebrate colorful Mexican holiday—commemorating an 1862 victory in the fight for independence from France—on Olvera Street in the Old Town section of Los Angeles. Contact: (213) 628-7833 or (213) 625-5045. San Diego celebrates on the weekend closest to May 5 at Old Town. Contact: (619) 237-6766.

Mule Days, May (Memorial Day weekend) in Bishop. Marking the start of the annual summer mule-packing season in the Sierra, this 4-day event demonstrates the versatility of mules in competitions ranging from steer roping to chariot racing. The wild packers' scramble is a highlight. Other events include a parade, country and western dances, barbecues, pancake breakfasts, and an arts and crafts show. Contact: (619) 873-8405.

Lompoc Valley Flower Festival, mid-June in Lompoc. With its flower fields at peak bloom, the "flower seed capital" celebrates with field tours, flower shows, a parade, an arts and crafts fair, food booths, and other events. Contact: (805) 735-8511.

Festival of Arts & Pageant of the Masters, July–August in Laguna Beach. Works by more than 150 top artisans go on display, a children's art workshop is held, and great works of art are created in pageant tableaux. Contact: (714) 494-1145. The simultaneous Sawdust Festival features local arts and crafts and continuous entertainment. Contact: (714) 494-3030.

Old Spanish Days, first week of August in Santa Barbara. The city's oldest and largest annual festival celebrates Santa Barbara's Spanish and Mexican heritage with 5 days of colorful activities—parades, two Mexican marketplaces, food and crafts booths, a rodeo, a carnival, and nightly shows. Contact: (805) 962-8101.

Nisei Week Japanese Festival, mid-August in Los Angeles. The city's "little Tokyo" offers a week of traditional sports competitions (aikido, karate, and kendo), arts displays (bonsai, calligraphy, and ceramics), and other special events (including a parade). Contact: (213) 687-7193.

Los Angeles County Fair, September (beginning after Labor Day) in Pomona. The world's largest county fair features acres of home arts, floral, and agricultural displays, plus livestock judging, wine competition, a circus, horse racing, carnival rides, and headliner entertainment. Contact: (714) 623-3111.

Danish Days, second or third weekend of September in Solvang. Along Copenhagen Street and in the city park, you can eat traditional Scandinavian fare, watch village dancers, listen to folk music, and see a parade on Saturday. Contact: (805) 688-0701.

Clam Festival, third weekend of October in Pismo Beach. Along with a parade, a fishing derby, a clam dig, sports and games, live entertainment, and crafts booths, there's plenty of clam chowder at this lively celebration. Contact: (805) 773-4382.

Annual 49ers Encampment, November (Veterans Day weekend) in Death Valley. This commemoration of the 1849 crossing of Death Valley features a liar's contest, a fiddling competition, a horseshoe tournament, art and lapidary shows, country and western music, and a barbecue. Contact: (619) 852-4524.

Trek to the Nation's Christmas Tree, second Sunday in December in Kings Canyon National Park. Participants leave Sanger (west of the park on State 180) at noon for the 50-mile bus caravan to the park's huge General Grant sequoia, site of a moving ceremony. Reserve bus seats by November 1. Contact: (209) 875-4575.

Christmas Boat Parades, December 17–23 in Newport Beach and mid-December in San Diego. Local yachts strung with lights parade on Newport Harbor for 7 successive nights. Contact: (714) 644-8211. In San Diego, fishing boats join with other vessels for a parade of lights from Harbor Island to Seaport Village. Contact: (619) 236-1212.

Stepping into a Spanish mission is like walking back in time. Beginning in 1769, Spain established a chain of 21 missions in California—institutions mandated not only to spread Christianity to the native Indian population but also to settle the frontier. These were California's first European communities, and today they constitute the oldest historic relics along the Pacific coast.

The mission chain is strung out along or near U.S. 101, which closely follows the original "royal road"—El Camino Real—started as a footpath linking the settlements. Eleven of the missions, plus two sub-missions, are in the area covered by this book. Five of these were begun by Father Junipero Serra, the Franciscan priest designated by Spain as the original father-president of the missions—and thus often considered the founder of California.

What you see today is a far cry from when the missions were miniature cities, teeming with activity. Thanks to restoration efforts, though, you can get some idea of what life must have been like in those early days. Missions welcome visitors daily on self-guided tours (some close on major holidays); most charge a small fee. Many still function as churches.

San Diego de Alcala. Father Serra founded California's first mission on July 16, 1769 atop Presidio Hill. It was moved to its present Mission Valley site in 1774. Taped tours include a small museum with Serra's records and relics.

Santa Ysabel. Inland Indians found it difficult to get to San Diego, so a branch mission was established 60 miles to the east in 1818. The present stucco chapel dates from 1924. Located on State 79 near Julian, the mission still serves area Indians.

San Luis Rey de Francia. Started in 1798 by Father Fermin Lasuen, Father Serra's successor, this impressive mission once included nearly 6 acres of buildings and had 3,000 Indian neophytes. Now well restored, the present 1815 church is framed with fine gardens. San Luis Rey is 5 miles east of Oceanside off State 76.

San Antonio de Pala. Established in 1815 as a sub-mission to San Luis Rey de Francia, this active church and school serves a Pauma Indian congregation. The chapel frescoes were painted by Indian artists. The gift shop and museum close Monday. Pala is on State 76 east of Interstate 15.

San Juan Capistrano. The picturesque ninth mission was founded in 1775, abandoned, and reestablished a year later by Father Serra. Its chapel is the only place standing where he is known to have said Mass. An 1812 earthquake destroyed much of the original mission and took many lives. Today, the mission is known for the swallows that still arrive from Argentina each year around St. Joseph's Day (March 19). Take Ortega Highway exit west from Interstate 5.

San Gabriel Arcangel. Founded in 1771 and moved to San Gabriel in 1774, the cathedral-style mission is presently closed because of earthquake damage. You can still tour the lovely grounds (534 Mission Drive), site of the state's oldest winery.

San Fernando Rey de España. Founded in 1797, this mission has been damaged several times by quakes, the last in 1971. A careful replica of the 1806 church now stands among manicured gardens 5 blocks east of Interstate 405 on San Fernando Boulevard.

San Buenaventura. Ventura's mission was the last one founded by Father Serra, in 1782. The expansive grounds are gone, but the red-trimmed church at 224 E. Main Street, reconstructed after the quake of 1812, looks much like its first incarnation. Among the museum relics are the original wooden bells.

Santa Barbara. The Queen of the Missions graces a hillsite above the city at Laguna and Los Olivos streets. Founded in 1786 and completed in 1820, the mission was enlarged by a second tower in 1831 (rebuilt in 1833).

Santa Ines. This well-restored mission in the heart of Solvang was founded in 1804 and served as temporary quarters for the state's first educational institution; the present building dates from 1817.

La Purisima Concepcion. Perhaps the most worthwhile stop along the route, this 1787 mission is now a completely restored 967-acre state historic park. Rooms are furnished as they would have been in the early 1800s; mission-era crafts are demonstrated in summer. Head west about 15 miles from U.S. 101 on State 246 toward Lompoc.

San Luis Obispo de Tolosa. Father Serra's fifth mission (in the heart of the city at Monterey and Chorro streets) was founded in 1772. The present building was finished in 1794. Once modernized with wooden siding, it has been restored to its original simple appearance.

San Miguel Arcangel. Nine miles north of Paso Robles off U.S. 101, Mission San Miguel was founded in 1797 by Father Lasuen. The present church was completed in 1818. Simple and severe on the outside, it glows inside with colorful murals.

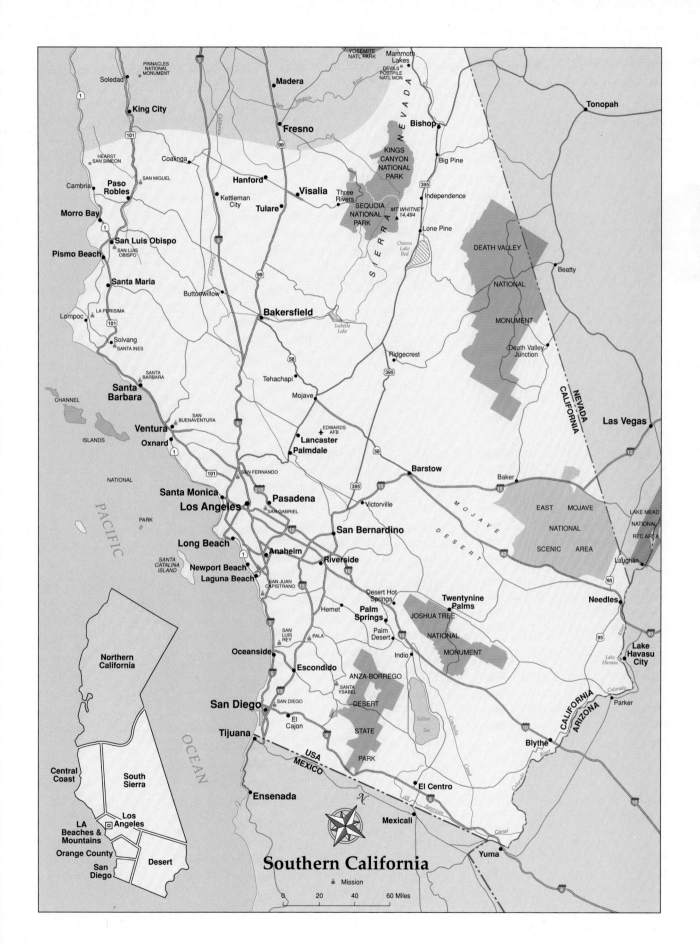

Southern California

...from page 4

Rodriguez Cabrillo landed at what is now San Diego. Colonization nonetheless didn't begin until the first Spanish mission was established in 1769. As a chain of missions extended northward (see page 6), Southern California's cities grew up around them. A walk through San Diego's Old Town, the Pueblo de Los Angeles, or the streets of Santa Barbara provides insight into the Spanish era.

The Hispanic influence remains strong, but more recently still more cultures have added to the area's rich diversity: Chinese, Japanese, Filipino, Korean, Vietnamese, and others. L.A.'s Chinatown, Japantown, and Koreatown showcase the lifestyles of these ethnic groups. But Southland diversity extends even beyond its great ethnic mix. From frontier days, this land has attracted and absorbed all sorts of lifestyles and life views, the mixture seeming to create an energy of its own.

About this book

Southern California is defined as much by personality as by geography. For the purposes of this book, we've chosen a generous interpretation, stretching north into the San Joaquin Valley and the Sierra Nevada and taking in both Inyo and Mono counties, major recreation targets for Southland residents though arguably "northern" in terms of geography. The book covers the Central Valley as far north as Visalia and the coast as far as Morro Bay and San Simeon, site of Hearst Castle.

The area north of this imaginary boundary is described in Sunset's companion *Northern California Travel Guide.*

This book begins with the sprawling West Coast anchor city of Los Angeles, starting point for the majority of Southland visits. Subsequent chapters cover L.A.'s coastal and mountain attractions, Orange County, San Diego, desert areas, the southern Sierra and surrounding region, and the central coast.

The map on page 7 shows how we've divided the state, chapter by chapter. Regional maps within each chapter, and detailed downtown maps of Los Angeles, San Diego, and Santa Barbara,

are offered as further aids in planning driving or walking tours.

A special guide at the back of the book breaks down the state by activity. Look here for specifics on camping in national parks and at state beaches plus directories of golf courses, theme parks, zoos, boat tours, whale-watching excursions, winery tours, health spas, bicycling routes, and ski resorts.

Some destinations may be covered in special features or in the activity guide as well as in the chapter describing that region; use the index at the back of the book to make sure you locate each entry.

A note on prices and hours: We've made every effort to be up to date. Admission fees and hours are constantly changing, however, so check locally to be sure.

When to visit

Southern California's biggest asset is its dry, subtropical climate. Very little rain, low humidity, little variation in temperature, and a lot of sun make it possible to enjoy outdoor activities the year around. Any time of the year is good somewhere in the sunny Southland.

Since this is a year-round destination, accommodations are usually not priced for a three-month "tourist season." The one exception is the desert, where room rates are on an inverse ratio with the temperature: the cooler the season, the higher the rates.

Southern California tourism does peak in the summer in terms of visitor numbers. Though the desert is *hot* (into the 100s) and you're likely to find smog around Los Angeles and its inland valleys, action picks up in the summertime along the coast and in the mountains.

What little rain there is falls mostly in winter, when resorts and wilderness parks in the desert are the goal of devoted sunseekers. Avid skiers can head north to Mammoth Mountain, one of the country's top ski areas.

Spring and autumn provide the Southland's mildest weather and the choice seasons for many of the largest fairs and festivals (see page 5). Wildflowers carpet desert floors and spread up into higher elevations beginning in

mid-February and extending through June. For some of the best flowering displays, turn to page 88.

How to get around

Southern California offers a choice of entry points—sprawling international airports, teeming freeways, busy ports, or rejuvenated railway terminals. No matter how you arrive, though, you'll need some form of transportation to explore the many attractions in and around the major cities.

If you're not driving your own car, rental cars are available in all large cities. If this is your first visit or you haven't been here recently, get a detailed map and plot your course before you take to the road.

Forget hair-raising tales you may have heard about freeway driving. This inter-connecting highway system is usually the fastest, most direct, and often only way to get around. If you avoid the freeways when people are going to and coming from work, learn where to get on and off easily, watch the traffic flow, and keep to your own lane, you should have few problems.

Southern California's Rapid Transit District operates a good bus and light rail system in and around L.A., including minibuses linking points of interest downtown, trolleys to Long Beach, and service to Disneyland. In Orange County, Palm Springs, and San Diego, shuttles are available to whisk passengers to major attractions. A trolley connects the latter city with Tijuana, just across the border in Mexico.

Don't overlook sightseeing tours as a means of getting around. They give good background information and spotlight the high points of an area. For details, check with your hotel desk or an area visitor center.

Where to stay

Accommodations are as varied as the region's topography, ranging from elegant self-contained resorts and high-rise city hotels to more modest hotels, motels, bed-and-breakfast inns, and RV parks. Advance reservations are almost always advisable, especially in summer and on weekends year-round.

This guide takes a look at landmark hotels in the Los Angeles area, historic hostelries in San Diego County, selected desert oases in and around Palm Springs, coastal B & Bs, and health spas. For more comprehensive suggestions in any area, write or call the contacts listed on the first page of each chapter.

Many of Southern California's national parks and state beaches offer campgrounds—see pages 120 and 121. For a listing of national forest campgrounds, contact the U.S. Forest Service, 830 Sansome St., Room 527, San Francisco, CA 94111; (415) 556-0122.

Information sources

Advance planning will help you make the most of your Southern California trip. For up-to-the-minute information on transportation, accommodations, dining options, and special events, contact visitor and convention bureaus and chambers of commerce listed in each chapter. For general information about the state, contact the California Office of Tourism (address on page 4). In addition, several agencies provide help for travelers with special needs.

Handicapped travelers. In the last few years California has made great strides in assisting disabled travelers. Special license plates and permits, available from the state's Department of Motor Vehicles, allow the physically impaired to park in convenient slots close to entryways. California also honors permits and plates issued by other states.

For additional information, contact the Department of Motor Vehicles, P.O. Box 942869, Sacramento, CA 94269-0001; (916) 732-7243. Many attractions provide free or rental wheelchairs. And most new and recently refurbished hotels have a few rooms equipped especially for the handicapped. For referrals, contact the California Travel Industry Association at 2500 Wilshire Blvd., Suite 603, Los Angeles, CA 90057; (213) 384-3178.

Senior citizens. Older travelers will receive hotel and transportation discounts, special dining rates, and reduced entrance fees at many places in Southern California. The age of eligibility varies widely, so ask about these special fares in advance.

Dining Delights

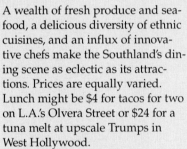

A wealth of fresh produce and seafood, a delicious diversity of ethnic cuisines, and an influx of innovative chefs make the Southland's dining scene as eclectic as its attractions. Prices are equally varied. Lunch might be $4 for tacos for two on L.A.'s Olvera Street or $24 for a tuna melt at upscale Trumps in West Hollywood.

Free dining guides preview restaurants in major cities around the area. The monthly *Los Angeles* magazine (available at newsstands) lists hundreds more throughout the region. We mention other notable dining spots throughout this book and take a look at some San Diego waterfront choices on page 63.

Trendy eateries in Beverly Hills, Los Angeles, and Santa Monica are frequent haunts of celebrities. Getaways around Santa Barbara and Palm Springs also attract the famous. If you're hoping to glimpse a well-known face, you'll usually need advance reservations (often difficult to get) and plenty of money. Even if you don't see a soul you recognize, you'll have eaten in some of the area's hottest spots.

Possible star-gazing is cheapest at Hampton's in Burbank, Hollywood's Cafe des Artistes, and Century City's Hamburger Hamlet.

Los Angeles. *Citrus*, 6703 Melrose Boulevard, (213) 857-0034, Franco-Continental cuisine; *Patina*, 5955 Melrose Avenue, (213) 467-1108, imaginative combinations, lunch and dinner; *Morton's*, 8800 Melrose Avenue, (310) 276-5205, forget about finding a table on weekends; *Spago*, 1114 Horn Avenue, (310) 652-4025, pizza supreme by chef Puck; *Tulipe*, 8630 Melrose Avenue, (213) 655-7400, light and modern French cuisine.

Beverly Hills. *The Bistro*, 246 N. Cañon Drive, (310) 273-5633, venerable dining spot with French cuisine; *Jimmy's*, 201 Moreno Drive, (310) 879-2394, French with a flourish.

Santa Monica. *Chinois on Main*, 2709 Main Street, (310) 392-9025, upscale Chinese at another Puck entry; *DC3*, 2800 Donald Douglas Loop North, (310) 399-2323, innovative concoctions,

expensive lunchtime favorite; *Louise's Trattoria*, 1008 Montana Avenue, (310) 394-8888, inexpensive and informal Italian; *72 Market Street Oyster Bar & Grill*, Venice (310) 392-8720, a Dudley Moore favorite; *The Ivy at the Shore*, 1541 Ocean Avenue, (310) 393-3113, casual tropical beach decor.

Santa Barbara. *Cold Spring Tavern*, 5995 Stagecoach Road, (805) 967-0066, out-of-the-way retreat; *El Encanto*, 1900 Lasuen Road, (805) 687-5000, secluded dining with a view; *Michael's Waterside*, 50 Los Patos Way, (805) 969-0307, classic cuisine and attention; *Ranch House*, S. Lomita Avenue, Ojai, (805) 646-2360, garden setting for garden-fresh food.

Palm Springs. *Bono*, 1700 N. Indian Avenue, (619) 322-6200, Sonny sans Cher; *Cunard's*, 78045 Calle Cadiz, La Quinta, (619) 564-4443, open for winter season; *Las Casuelas Nuevas*, 70-050 State 111, Rancho Mirage, (619) 328-8844, branch of popular Mexican eatery.

Los Angeles

*C*alifornia's largest city, in terms of both area and population, sprawls over 464 square miles, roughly the size of the entire state of Rhode Island. Almost 3½ million people call Los Angeles home (only New York City is bigger nationwide), and L.A. County is approaching 9 million residents. Some 50 million more people visit annually.

Why do they come? Despite L.A.'s very real problems of traffic and smog (generally at its worst in summer), its charms are many. A fine setting between mountains and sea is enhanced by year-round sunshine, and an innovative lifestyle has made the area a trendsetter in the fields of fitness, fashion, food, and film.

Entertaining is big business in Los Angeles, and the city boasts some of the country's premier hotels, shops, and restaurants, plus a wealth of elaborate—and unique—amusements. If you think museums, concerts, and theaters are the measure of a city, you'll find some fine ones here. But where else would you also discover cemeteries listed as tourist attractions, pizza elevated to an edible art form, and replicas of Ice Age creatures emerging from a tar pit?

Huge and constantly changing, L.A. is best approached by breaking it into small components. This chapter focuses on the attractions that draw most visitors, from the glamour of Hollywood and the movie studios to the upscale glitter of Beverly Hills or the cultural melange of the downtown area. Roundups of city museums, favorite diver-

Sleek skyscrapers define downtown L.A.'s business district. To the right rise the futuristic glass silos of the Westin Bonaventure Hotel.

sions for children, and a host of free attractions are evidence of the depth of the city's capacity to please visitors.

For a look beyond the city core to the beach and mountain playgrounds that frame Los Angeles, turn to the chapter beginning on page 30.

A pattern of growth

Los Angeles started as a Spanish village in 1781, when 44 settlers recruited by the California provincial governor, Felipe de Neve, reached the banks of the Los Angeles River after a seven-month colonizing expedition from Sonora, Mexico. They marked off the lots that gave birth to El Pueblo de Nuestra Señora la Reina de los Angeles—the town of Our City the Queen of Angels.

Eventually the city with the tongue-tangling name became Mexican (after independence from Spain in 1822), and then finally Yankee (after its surrender in 1847). Today, L.A. is a collection of communities where you can savor sights, sounds, foods, and goods from around the world. It has the nation's largest Hispanic population (more than 3½ million in the greater L.A. area), and only Honolulu boasts a greater Asian population.

The cattle ranches and citrus groves that gave Los Angeles its first claim to fame have long since given way to freeways, industrial growth, and dense residential sprawl. Instead, L.A. is now a world trade center and a leader in the financial, aerospace, and oil industries. One early enterprise does remain, however. Sunny weather allowing year-round filming of movies made the L.A. area an entertainment capital early in the century, and the city has yet to relinquish the title, thanks to the number of movies, television shows, and radio broadcasts produced here.

Planning a trip

Year-round sunshine helped make Los Angeles famous in the first place. The sun may be filtered through smog much of the time these days, but the benign climate still makes for a nearly seamless 12-month tourist season.

First-timers and even those who haven't been to L.A. for awhile may need help in finding their way around. Stop by one of the two offices of the Los Angeles Convention and Visitors Bureau (addresses below) for maps, visitor guides, discount coupons to at-

Contacts

These agencies offer information on attractions and accommodations. See additional contacts throughout this chapter.

Los Angeles Convention and Visitors Bureau

Downtown Visitor Information Center
685 S. Figueroa St.
Los Angeles, CA 90017
(213) 689-8822

Hollywood Visitor Information Center
The Janes House
6541 Hollywood Blvd.
Hollywood, CA 90028
(213) 461-4213

Beverly Hills Visitors Bureau
239 S. Beverly Dr.
Beverly Hills, CA 90212
(310) 271-8174

tractions, and free tickets to television shows. The downtown center is open 8 A.M. to 5 P.M. daily except Sunday; the Hollywood center opens at 9 A.M.

Getting there. Los Angeles International Airport (Century and Sepulveda boulevards) is the world's third largest in terms of passenger traffic. The free LAX "A" shuttle makes a circuit of the international and seven domestic terminals at the lower level. An information board in each terminal baggage claim area lists most ground transportation. Get information and tickets for many scheduled and on-call shuttles at sidewalk booths in front of the terminals. SuperShuttle, (213) 338-1111, is one of the least expensive (around $12 to downtown, less to the Westside). Hotel and rental car courtesy trams, taxis, and limos depart from marked islands on the lower level.

Four other major metropolitan airports—Burbank (14 miles northwest of the city center), Long Beach (22 miles south), Orange County (30 miles southeast), and Ontario (40 miles east)—provide supplemental service.

If you're arriving by train, Amtrak uses the handsome Union Station depot at 800 N. Alameda Street, close to El Pueblo and the Civic Center. Greyhound and Trailways share a bus terminal at 6th and Los Angeles streets.

Getting around. Driving L.A.'s maze of freeways can be a daunting experience for newcomers, but a car is almost a necessity for any ambitious sightseeing. Two suggestions: Avoid peak times—6:30 to 9:30 A.M. and 3:30 to 6:30 P.M.—and plan routes in advance. Good map sources are the Automobile Club of Southern California, 2601 S. Figueroa Street (AAA members only), and Thomas Brothers Maps and Travel Bookstore, 603 W. 7th Street.

Interstate 5, California's major north-south artery, slices through the heart of L.A., entering from the north as the Golden State Freeway and exiting as the Santa Ana Freeway. Interstate 405 (San Diego Freeway) offers access to the city's western and southern reaches. The direct route from the east is Interstate 10 (San Bernardino Freeway), which becomes the Santa Monica Freeway downtown at the Civic Center. Interstate 110 (Harbor Freeway) connects L.A. and the port at San Pedro.

The city's public transportation system (RTD) has route maps to local attractions at its downtown customer center, Level B Arco Plaza, 515 S. Flower Street (closed weekends); (213) 626-4455. Frequent daytime DASH (Downtown Area Short Hop) shuttles cover the city's heart. An extensive light-rail system is being built. The Blue Line to Long Beach is complete; call (213) 620-7245 for details.

Taxi service is available from the airports, train and bus terminals, and major hotels. Cabs do not cruise the streets looking for passengers.

Tours. Half-day and longer city sightseeing tours give a good orientation. Gray Line and several other companies offer scheduled tours year-round; check your hotel desk for schedules. Customized shopping, dining, and celebrity-seeking tours are also available. The Los Angeles Convention and Visitors Bureau has details (see page 11).

Free bus tours of downtown Los Angeles depart from the firehouse at Old Town Plaza (see page 16) on the first and third Wednesday of each month. Reservations are required for the 2-hour tours; call (213) 628-1274.

Los Angeles Conservancy conducts guided walking tours of historic downtown L.A. at 10 A.M. Saturday from the Olive Street entrance of the Biltmore Hotel (506 S. Grand Avenue). Tours last 2 hours and cost $5; call (213) 623-2489 for reservations.

Accommodations. For a detailed accommodation guide, contact the Los Angeles Convention and Visitors Bureau (page 11). Some top-of-the-line lodgings are listed on the facing page.

Rooms can also be booked through the Southern California Hotel Reservation Center; for rates and confirmations, call (800) 527-9997 in California, (800) 537-7666 outside the state.

Entertainment. Star-studded theatrical and musical performances are year-round attractions. Visitors' guides and the Sunday "Calendar" section of the *Los Angeles Times* list current events.

The theaters and concert halls of the downtown Music Center (135 N. Grand Avenue) play host to city ballet, opera, symphony, and theatrical companies. The Los Angeles Theatre Center, an intimate four-theater complex at 514 N. Spring Street, offers works from the Los Angeles Actors Theatre.

Plays and musical performances are also held at other large entertainment centers, like Century City's Shubert Theatre, Universal City's Amphitheatre, and Hollywood's Pantages Theatre. In summer, the Greek Theatre and the Hollywood Bowl are popular for outdoor plays and concerts.

Spectator sports. The L.A. area teems with sports activities. Suburban Inglewood (near LAX) is home to beautifully landscaped Hollywood Park race track and to the Great Western Forum, setting for Lakers pro basketball and Kings ice hockey games.

In Exposition Park southwest of downtown off Interstate 110, the Los Angeles Memorial Sports Arena hosts Clippers basketball games, the L.A. Memorial Coliseum features college and pro football (Raiders), and the Swimming Stadium is a venue for water sports competitions.

The Dodgers play pro baseball just north of the L.A. Civic Center at Dodger Stadium, and free polo practices are held Tuesday and Thursday evenings in Griffith Park's Equidome.

Shopping. From the chic and pricey boutiques of Rodeo Drive in Beverly Hills to Olvera Street's souvenir stands, L.A. is a browser's paradise. Of special interest are the downtown wholesale garment and jewelry districts (see page 14). Old Town, Little Tokyo, and Chinatown offer a wealth of gift shops.

For a riot of scents and colors, pay an early-morning visit to the Flower Mart around 6th and San Julian streets, or wander through the food stalls of Grand Central Public Market at 3rd and Hill streets or the Farmers Market at 3rd and Fairfax (see page 17).

Museum shops and art galleries offer other gift possibilities; the largest Westside gallery concentrations are along Melrose, La Brea, La Cienega, and Robertson avenues.

Noted for ambience, architecture, and location, some of L.A.'s classic hotels have become visitor attractions in themselves, worth a look even if you're not planning a stay. Most are old-timers that have undergone recent face-lifts; a couple are newer beauties.

Double rooms at the "budget" lodgings among the group start at $100 or so; rates are considerably steeper for most of these hotels. For detailed information on rates and amenities, call hotels directly or obtain a copy of the lodging guide published by the Los Angeles Convention and Visitors Bureau (address on page 11).

For more help, check with the Automobile Club of Southern California (AAA members only), a travel agent, or the Southern California Hotel Reservation Center, (800) 527-9997 in California, (800) 537-7666 nationwide.

Bel-Air Hotel, 701 Stone Canyon Rd., Los Angeles, CA 90077; (310) 472-1211. Constantly rated as one of the world's most romantic retreats, the tranquil Bel-Air Hotel is tucked into a wooded canyon above Sunset Boulevard. Private bungalows sprinkled throughout 12 acres of lush gardens look out to a waterfall and a swan-filled lake.

Beverly Hills Hotel, 9641 Sunset Blvd., Beverly Hills, CA 90210; (800) 792-7637. This sprawling Mission-revival hotel, built in 1912, has reopened after several years of extensive renovation. The property has long been popular with celebrities and movie moguls, who make deals over meals in the Polo Lounge.

Beverly Wilshire Hotel, 9500 Wilshire Blvd., Beverly Hills, CA; (800) 421-4354. The impressive hotel across from Rodeo Drive has

long been a haven for the rich and the royal. The Regent Group, its current owners, recently completed a handsome renovation of rooms, lobby, and restaurants.

Biltmore Hotel, 506 S. Grand Ave., Los Angeles, CA 90071; (800) 421-8000. A $40 million face-lift returned the glow of 1920s youth to one of the city's grande dames. New entry court, relocated lobby, additional dining rooms, impressive health club, and new and refurbished rooms are highlights.

Century Plaza Hotel, 2025 Avenue of the Stars, Los Angeles, CA 90067; (800) 228-3000. Designed by architect Minoru Yamasaki and built in the 1960s on land once owned by Twentieth Century Fox Studio, the soaring Century Plaza resembles a modernistic Rockefeller Center; the tower is a 1980s addition. The first astronauts to reach the moon were honored here at a Presidential State Dinner.

Checkers Hotel, 535 S. Grand Ave., Los Angeles, CA 90071; (800) 628-4900. Guests of the old Mayflower Hotel that once occupied the site would never recognize this renovated version. The chic boutique hostelry has 190 antique-furnished rooms and a top-rated restaurant.

Hollywood Roosevelt Hotel, 7000 Hollywood Blvd., Hollywood, CA 90028; (800) 950-7667. First home of the Academy Awards, this lovingly restored hotel in the heart of Hollywood has a jazz bar, a restaurant, a health club, and a mezzanine lined with "tinsel town" history.

Queen Mary Hotel, Pier J, Long Beach, CA 90801; (800) 437-2934. Once the largest and fastest luxury liner afloat, the venerable ship has 12 decks open for guided and self-guided tours (see page 40). State-

rooms and restaurants have been refurbished and shops added to round out the maritime experience.

Ritz-Carlton Huntington Hotel, 1401 S. Oak Knoll, Pasadena, CA 91109; (800) 241-333. The Huntington Hotel was Pasadena's social hub from the time of its opening in 1914 until the main building was razed in the late 1980s because it didn't meet earthquake standards. A new and larger replica now stands on the site, surrounded by nicely refurbished cottages and some of the original gardens.

St. James's Club, 8358 Sunset Blvd., Los Angeles, CA 90069; (800) 225-2637. Clark Gable and Marilyn Monroe were among the movie stars who had apartments in this art deco building with the grand view. Still a favorite with celebrities, it's now a private club with an elegant restaurant and spa. Membership privileges are extended to overnight guests.

Westin Bonaventure, 404 S. Figueroa St., Los Angeles, CA 90071; (800) 228-3000. Five mirror-glass silos make this futuristic hotel a latter-day landmark. Marble, brass, and glass gleam around its Flower Street entry and lobby area, part of a renovation to make the hotel and its shopping complex more "pedestrian-friendly."

Westwood Marquis Hotel, 930 Hilgard Ave., Los Angeles, CA 90024; (800) 421-2317. Once a girls' dormitory, later an apartment building, this is now an all-suites hotel with impressive pools, gardens, and restaurants (Garden Room's Sunday brunch is notable). The Westwood setting makes it a base for strolls to the village, U.C.L.A., and the Armand Hammer Museum.

Downtown L.A.

Fear of earthquakes forced Los Angeles to grow out, not up. But when height restrictions were removed in 1957, the city began to soar. High-rise office buildings, hotels, and "in-city" residences rose on the site of now-flattened Bunker Hill (once home to elegant Victorian mansions) and south along the Harbor Freeway. Newest and as-yet tallest of the skyscrapers is the 73-story world headquarters of the First Interstate Bank at Library Square, 5th and Hope streets.

Just east of the Harbor Freeway between 11th Street and Pico Boulevard sprawls the Los Angeles Convention Center, site of large business gatherings and trade shows. Across the freeway and a bit farther south, the University of Southern California (page 17) stands adjacent to Exposition Park, site of several notable museums (page 27) and the Los Angeles Memorial Coliseum (page 17). Just across from U.S.C., Jewish culture is highlighted at the Skirball Museum (3077 University Avenue, scheduled to move to 2701 N. Sepulveda Boulevard in 1992).

An overview

Finding your way around downtown is relatively easy. Traffic isn't bad except during weekday rush hours, and parking garages are plentiful if not cheap. In the evening and on weekends, the area is virtually deserted.

Transportation. DASH shuttles loop through the downtown area every few minutes from 6:30 A.M. to 6:30 P.M. weekdays and 10 A.M. to 5 P.M. Saturday. You'll need exact change (25 cents).

Hotel and dining scene. Downtown hotels make good choices for convention-goers or anyone planning to take in shows at the Music Center, Theatre Center, or Japanese American Cultural and Community Center; see page 13 for a listing of some of the choices.

Downtown has a handful of fine restaurants such as Engine Co. No. 28 (644 S. Figueroa), Original Sonora Cafe (445 S. Figueroa), Rex II Ristorante (617 S. Olive), and Stepps (330 S. Hope). Hotels like the Biltmore, Checkers, and Inter-Continental also have noted dining rooms.

Shopping. The central city's major shopping malls are Levels B and C of the subterranean Arco Plaza (5th and Flower streets), the Broadway Plaza (7th and Flower), the Seventh Market Place (7th and Figueroa), and the shops at the Westin Bonaventure Hotel.

Bargain hunters head east to the Jewelry District (Hill Street from 5th to 8th) and the Garment District (between Los Angeles and San Pedro streets from 7th to Pico). Though geared to the wholesale market, many shops are open to the public; the Cooper Building (860 S. Los Angeles Street) is a vertical discount center with 76 stores and several fast-food restaurants.

A city walk

Contrary to popular opinion, people do walk in L.A. It's the best way to get a close look at major attractions in the surprisingly compact downtown area. Our route takes a leisurely half-day.

The walk follows the general routes of DASH shuttles. You can board the B Line at the end of your walk to return to your starting point, or even make the entire tour by bus. (Transfer to the A Line to see Little Tokyo and the Temporary Contemporary Museum.)

Financial District. A cluster of high-rise bank buildings and corporate offices flanking the Harbor Freeway makes up the downtown business and financial heart. Above-street promenades connect many structures.

To get an overall view, start from the 35th-floor rooftop lounge of the futuristic Westin Bonaventure Hotel (5th and Flower). Then cross the footbridge over 5th Street to reach the landscaped garden atop the 52-story Arco Plaza Complex. Underneath its twin towers is one of the country's largest subterranean shopping centers.

Along both sides of Flower to the north of 4th Street hulk the World Trade Center and the Security Pacific headquarters building; note the latter's water-filled garden plaza. At 4th and Hope, walk through the glass-enclosed garden pavilion between the Wells Fargo Bank headquarters and the IBM towers to Grand Avenue. (A free history museum on the ground level of the bank is open from 9 A.M. to 4 P.M. weekdays—see page 29.)

Across Grand is the massive California Plaza shopping, office, hotel, and park complex. Its Watercourt frames outdoor stages; the sandstone building (250 S. Grand) houses the Museum of Contemporary Art (see page 27).

Music Center. Two blocks north, at 1st and Grand, L.A.'s Music Center is the city's cultural heart and home to the respected Los Angeles Philharmonic. A landscaped mall links the elegant Dorothy Chandler Pavilion, largest of the center's three halls, to the intimate Mark Taper Forum and the Ahmanson Theatre. The Frank Gehry-designed Walt Disney Concert Hall is scheduled to join this trio in the mid-1990s.

For more information on touring the center, see page 17. You might want to round out your visit with a stop at one of the three restaurants in the complex or at the performing arts–oriented gift shop.

Civic Center. L.A.'s Civic Center is one of the largest government complexes in the country. The building with the reflecting pool west of the Music Center houses the Department of Water and Power; the other municipal buildings lie to the east.

The 32-story, pyramid-shaped City Hall at 200 N. Spring Street—Southern California's tallest building when it was built in 1928—offers views as far as Mount Wilson, 15 miles away, on rare clear days. The observation deck on the 27th floor is open 10 A.M. to 4 P.M. weekdays. Near City Hall at 202 W. 1st Street is the Los Angeles Times Building (see page 17).

Many of the Civic Center's major buildings stand at the perimeter of

Beyond a pennant-adorned courtyard in the heart of the city stands the Dorothy Chandler Pavilion, largest of the Music Center halls and home to the Los Angeles Philharmonic and Joffrey Ballet companies as well as the annual Oscar ceremonies.

...Downtown L.A.

landscaped Los Angeles Mall, a sunken shopping center between Main and Los Angeles streets that includes the Los Angeles Children's Museum (see page 29).

Little Tokyo. This redeveloped Japanese neighborhood southeast of the Civic Center, roughly bounded by 1st, Alameda, 3rd, and Los Angeles streets, combines peaceful gardens with colorful collections of shops and restaurants. The garden atop the south wing of the New Otani Hotel (120 S. Los Angeles Street) and another at the Noguchi Plaza's Japanese American Cultural and Community Center south of San Pedro and 2nd streets (also the setting of the handsome Japan America Theatre) are particularly noteworthy.

From Noguchi Plaza, cross 2nd Street to reach the stores and eateries of Japanese Village Plaza. Across the plaza, at 1st and Central, stands the original Museum of Contemporary Art, now an annex known as the Temporary Contemporary (see page 27). The Japanese American National Museum is in a rehabilitated Buddhist temple at 369 E. 1st.

El Pueblo de Los Angeles. To reach L.A.'s Old Town, where the city began, head north on Main Street across the freeway. The 44-acre state historic monument is bounded by Alameda, Arcadia, Spring, and Macy streets.

To get the most out of a visit, join a free guided tour (Tuesday through Saturday at 10 and 11 A.M., noon, and 1 P.M.) from the Docent Center fronting on the plaza. Or pick up a self-guided walking tour map at the visitor center in the Sepulveda House (622 N. Main Street). A 20-minute film on the history of the park is shown daily except Sunday at 11 A.M. and 2 P.M. The center is open Monday through Friday from 10 A.M. to 3 P.M., Saturday until 4:30 P.M.

Park highlights include a display of antique firefighting equipment in the two-story Old Plaza Firehouse (134 Paseo de la Plaza), the Old Plaza Church on North Main (the city's oldest), and the restored Avila Adobe at 10 E. Olvera Street, which dates back to about 1818 (closed Monday). All are open to visitors at no charge.

Lively Olvera Street, a block-long Mexican marketplace, is the Pueblo's greatest magnet. Streetside shops and stalls sell handicrafts and such treats as sugary *churros* (Mexican-style donuts). Restaurants serve typical Mexican cuisine (El Paseo Inn is a local favorite). Shops are open daily from 10 A.M. to 8 P.M., later in summer. A museum dedicated to the history of Chinese Americans in the U.S. Southwest introduces the district north of the Pueblo.

Chinatown. Walk 3½ blocks north on Broadway to the main entrance to Chinatown, several blocks of shop-lined lanes with names like Gin Ling (a pedestrian mall), Sun Mun, and Lei Ling. Like Olvera Street, the area is touristy, although it's also a cultural center for Chinese Americans. Food markets stock intriguing wares, shops offer everything from Hong Kong reproductions to antiques, and restaurants specialize in moderately priced tank-fresh seafood.

The district's most authentic Chinese section is on North Spring Street, southeast of the tourist zone. You can buy a walking tour map of the area from the Chinese Historical Society of Southern California at 970 N. Broadway or 982 Gin Ling Way.

To return to the starting point of your downtown walk, catch the southbound B Line bus on Broadway.

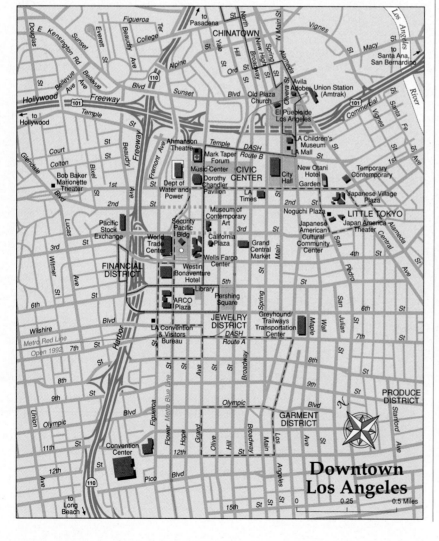

Downtown Los Angeles

The 12 tours listed below are examples of things you can do in Los Angeles without spending a cent. Other ideas for cash-free entertainment sprinkled throughout the chapter include television tapings, museum visits, strolls through the city's rich ethnic neighborhoods, and a trek to Mann's Chinese Theatre to view hand, foot, paw, and hoof prints of Hollywood stars.

For more suggestions, pick up a visitor guide listing events, tours, exhibits, sports, and musical happenings. It's available at visitor information centers (addresses on page 11).

Farmers Market, 3rd Street and Fairfax Avenue; (213) 933-9211. Pick up a map of this 20-acre market-restaurant-shopping complex at the office on the second floor above Gate 1. The market got its start in 1934, when 18 hard-pressed farmers decided to sell their produce directly to the people. Now boasting more than 160 stalls, shops, cafes, and dining plazas, it is expanding to include a theater and a hotel. Hours are 9 A.M. to 6 P.M. Monday through Saturday, 10 A.M. to 5 P.M. Sunday (an hour later in summer). Du-Par's Restaurant, noted for pancakes and pies, is open from 6 A.M. until midnight.

Forest Lawn, 1712 S. Glendale Avenue, Glendale; (213) 254-3131. Only in L.A. are cemeteries renowned for their art collections, museums, and theaters. The Forest Lawn visitor center displays gems and biblical coins and offers guides to artwork (10 A.M. to 4 P.M. daily). At another Forest Lawn cemetery (6300 Forest Lawn Drive, Hollywood Hills), you can see a film on the birth of liberty.

Hollywood Walk of Fame, Hollywood. View the memorial to the movie greats that made this city the world's most famous. Bronze stars line both sides of Hollywood Boulevard between Gower and Sycamore streets and Vine Street from Yucca Street to Sunset Boulevard.

Los Angeles Memorial Coliseum, 3911 S. Figueroa Street; (213) 747-7111. Tours of the site of the 1932 and 1984 Olympic Games are offered when no events are scheduled; call for information. While in Exposition Park, visit the world's largest rose garden; peak blooming periods are April and May, September and October.

Los Angeles Music Center, 1st Street and Grand Avenue; (213) 972-7483 for tour reservations. Hour-long tours of the center's three theaters let you view sets and props of current productions and an eclectic and impressive art collection. Tours begin every half-hour from 10 A.M. to noon Saturday year-round. From May to October, tours are also offered weekdays except Wednesday between 10 A.M. and 1:30 P.M. Winter weekday tour schedule is Monday through Thursday.

Los Angeles Times, 202 W. 1st Street; (213) 237-5757. The nation's largest standard-size daily newspaper offers hour-long tours weekdays, except holidays, at 11:15 A.M. and 3 P.M. (no children under 10).

Lummis Home, 200 E. Avenue 43 off the Pasadena Freeway; (213) 222-0546. Wander on your own through the stone "castle" that was home to Charles Fletcher Lummis, founder of the Southwest Museum (see page 27). Now headquarters of Southern California's Historical Society, the house is open 1 to 4 P.M. Wednesday through Sunday.

Mormon Temple, 10777 Santa Monica Boulevard; (213) 474-1549. Unless you're a Latter-Day Saint, your tour of this huge temple is on film in the visitor center, but anyone can walk through the beautiful gardens. The center is open daily from 9 A.M. to 9:30 P.M.

Pacific Coast Stock Exchange, 233 S. Beaudry (between 2nd and 3rd streets west of the Harbor Freeway); (213) 977-4500. A visitors' gallery on the 12th floor gives you a view of the trading floor. Exchange hours, 6:30 A.M. to 1:30 P.M. weekdays, coincide with those of the New York Stock Exchange.

Rancho La Brea Tar Pits, Wilshire Boulevard and Curson Avenue; (213) 936-2230. Ice Age fossils trapped in bubbly black pits some 40 centuries ago have been recreated in asphalt at the scene of their demise. You can see them from a viewing station west of the George C. Page Museum (see page 27). Guided tours depart the observation pit (open weekends 10 A.M. to 5 P.M.) Thursday through Sunday at 1 P.M., except on major holidays.

University of Southern California, Exposition Boulevard and S. Figueroa Street next to Exposition Park; (213) 743-2983. Make an appointment to take an hour-long walking tour of one of the West's oldest private universities (weekdays from 10 A.M. to 2 P.M.). For a tour through the 1890s museum (weekdays by appointment), phone (213) 743-5213. A free art gallery is open Tuesday through Saturday afternoons.

Watts Towers, 1765 E. 107th Street; (213) 569-8181. Simon Rodia, an immigrant Italian tilesetter, spent 33 years creating these three 99-foot towers from cement, steel rods, broken tile, bottles, and seashells. He completed the task in 1954. For a good view, stop at the adjacent art center.

"Where Music Meets the Stars" is the theme of the Hollywood Bowl's popular
summer concert series. Sellout crowds jam the outdoor amphitheater to enjoy
performances ranging from classical favorites to pops and jazz.

Hollywood

Hollywood Boulevard is a comparatively short street, but it may be the best known of all L.A.'s thoroughfares—and it's a major magnet for Southland visitors. At first glance this may look like any Main Street of any town, but its wealth of art deco architecture has elevated it to the status of a national historic district.

In its heyday, from the 1920s to the 1950s, Hollywood boasted some of L.A.'s largest movie palaces and most exclusive department stores. Studios such as Paramount and Metro Goldwyn Mayer ate up acres of real estate. And uphill, such cinema royalty as Gloria Swanson and Tyrone Power built hideaways.

When retail business moved to the suburbs and the movie industry expanded into other areas of the city, Hollywood lost its luster. But the faded star is staging a comeback. The Hollywood Roosevelt Hotel (7000 Hollywood Boulevard), where the first Academy Awards were presented, has been renovated, and an ambitious 2½-block redevelopment project around Sid Grauman's 1927 Chinese Theatre at 6925 Hollywood Boulevard—now called Mann's—offers state-of-the-art cinemas, specialty shops, and the Hollywood Exposition Museum, dedicated to the entertainment industry.

Exploring Tinsel Town

Hollywood is still a lot of fun. On a day's excursion, you might take a bus tour, visit a museum, and lunch at an old restaurant near a studio. Or take a look at the boulevard's architecture, search out the hillside Hollywood sign and Rudolph Valentino's crypt, and then catch a film in a resplendent movie house.

Guided tours. An excellent introduction to the boulevard is a walking tour led by actor-members of Hollywood Heritage, a preservation organization. The 2-hour Saturday and Sunday morning tours stop in movie palaces and turn down side streets. Cost is $6; to reserve a place, call (213) 465-5993.

For a wider overview, take a double-decker bus trip with Hollywood Fantasy Tours. The guides' patter includes the omnipresent movie trivia, but there's substantial history, too. You'll see landmarks like Capitol Records (1750 Vine Street), built in 1954 to resemble a record stack. The 2-hour excursions leave 1744 N. Highland Avenue at 10:30 A.M. and 1 P.M. daily; cost is $12 adults, $10 children. For reservations, call (213) 469-8184.

Grave Line Tours, Hollywood Boulevard and Orchard Avenue, takes you on a hearse-drawn tour of the city's more macabre side. Call (213) 876-0920 for information.

On your own. If you prefer to choose your own route, park in any of the lots or parking structures on or near Hollywood Boulevard.

You can't explore the boulevard without stepping on one of Hollywood's earliest attempts to spruce up. The Walk of Fame, begun in 1958, features some 2,500 celebrity-named stars inset along both sides of the street for the half-mile from Gower Street to Sycamore Avenue and along Vine Street from Sunset Boulevard to Yucca Street. To view them in order, start outside the Hollywood Roosevelt Hotel.

Eating spots. Golden-age restaurants still exist. The most famous is Musso & Frank Grill, 6667 Hollywood Boulevard, known since 1919 for no-nonsense American food. Dating from the same year, C.C. Brown's Ice Cream Parlour, 7007 Hollywood Boulevard, lays claim to having served the country's first hot fudge sundaes. (Both are closed Sunday.)

Patina (5955 Melrose Avenue), an understated culinary delight near Paramount Pictures serves Franco-California cuisine with Teutonic touches. And tiny Formosa Cafe (7156 Santa Monica Boulevard) is a favorite with people from Warner Hollywood Studios. Crammed with Elvis memorabilia, the cafe serves old-fashioned American-Chinese dishes (closed Sunday).

Movie magic

Three studios in the Hollywood area offer peeks into the world of filming. Paramount and KCET Television are still operating studios that you can tour (see page 20). The third pays homage to the industry's early days.

You can only drive by Charlie Chaplin's picturesque studio at 1416 N. La Brea Avenue. The storybook hamlet of tiny buildings from the early 1900s now houses A & M Records offices.

Hollywood Studio Museum. When Cecil B. DeMille came to Hollywood in 1913, he rented part of a barn to use as a studio. It sat on the Paramount lot for decades, playing bit parts in the TV series *Bonanza*, and then was moved to its present location at 2100 N. Highland Avenue (across from the Hollywood Bowl) and opened to show off movie memorabilia. The studio is open from 10 A.M. to 4 P.M. Tuesday through Sunday; admission is modest.

Around town

Two ways to put Hollywood into perspective are from the hills above the boulevard or at the quiet cemetery on its boundary.

Hillside views. For a brief foray into the hills in back of town, drive or climb up to Yamashiro (1999 N. Sycamore Avenue). Built in 1913 in the style of a 16th-century palace, the former mansion is now a Japanese restaurant.

To see how close you can come to the fabled Hollywood sign that overlooks the town, head up Beachwood Drive (off Franklin Avenue). The 50-foot-high letters were erected for this 1920s housing development, Hollywoodland; the "land" disappeared years ago.

Hollywood Memorial Cemetery. You can pick up a free map at this memorial park to find monuments to De Mille, Fairbanks, Valentino, and other Hollywood legends. The cemetery is just north of the Paramount studio at 6000 Santa Monica Boulevard.

The star-gazing game—hunting for celebrities—is avidly practiced around L.A. If your curiosity is piqued but your observation time limited, the best way to sight famous faces may be to drop by places where they work.

The following is a rundown of movie studios with back-lot tours and TV shows looking for audiences, along with "homes of the stars" tour possibilities. Even if you don't see your favorite celebrities in person, you can visit their stars on Hollywood's Walk of Fame (see page 19), measure your feet against their footprints in the forecourt of Mann's Chinese Theatre (6925 Hollywood Boulevard), or buy star-related memorabilia at movie and television studio shops.

Studio tours

Movie studios created L.A.'s aura of glamour in the heyday of the 1920s and 1930s, and film and TV studios still play a big role in attracting visitors to the area.

Universal Studios Hollywood, Lankershim Boulevard east of the Hollywood Freeway in Universal City; (818) 508-9600. The best-known studio in Southern California, Universal has evolved into a complete destination with theme park, movie theater complex, amphitheater, and hotels. Latest addition is CityWalk pedestrian-only village on a hill above the theme park. There's no charge to visit the shops, restaurants, and relocated Museum of Neon Art.

Plan to spend a full day for your behind-the-scenes look at filmmaking. A narrated tram ride takes you through famous sets on the 420-acre back lot and lets you see yourself on live action shows. Trams leave frequently, but you might be assigned a boarding time.

While you wait, you learn about special effects. You tour the entertainment center on your own. A Back to the Future ride is the current crowd-pleaser.

The Universal box office is open from 7:30 A.M. to 8 P.M. daily in summer, 8:30 A.M. to 4 P.M. the rest of the year (closed Thanksgiving and Christmas). Admission is $27 adults, $21 ages 3 to 11 and over 60.

Burbank Studios, 4000 Warner Boulevard, Burbank; (818) 954-1744. Less glitzy than Universal, bustling Burbank Studios houses both Warner Brothers (here since 1928) and Columbia Pictures. Guides lead 10 to 12 persons at a time through sound stages, a $20 million wardrobe inventory, and back lots such as Midwest Street, where Ronald Reagan starred in *King's Row*. Expect a lot of walking.

A prop room stores a chandelier from Errol Flynn's *Captain Blood* and lamps from *Casablanca*, two of the classics shot here. If you're lucky, you may pass by during a rehearsal or taping of a TV show.

The 2-hour tours leave at 10 A.M. and 2 P.M. weekdays, with additional tours at 9:30, 10:30, and 2:30 in summer (closed holidays). Call for reservations and directions at least a week in advance. Admission is $25; children under 10 are not admitted.

Paramount Pictures, 5555 Melrose Avenue, Hollywood; (213) 468-5575. Limited first-come tours at this studio right in the heart of Hollywood provide glimpses of movie and TV production. You may visit the room where technicians create and dub sounds not recorded with the actors' dialogue—everything from gunshots to footsteps.

Two-hour tours ($10) start at 11 A.M. and 2 P.M. weekdays; no children under 10 are admitted. Arrive early at the visitor center on the

Gower Street side. After the tour, you may want to stop at the studio store.

NBC Television Studio, 3000 W. Alameda Avenue, Burbank; (818) 840-3537. A 1¼-hour walking tour offers highlights of a television production studio: set construction, special effects, make-up, and wardrobe. You'll also get a look at yourself on camera. Don't expect to watch a show being taped—for that you need tickets. Some are available at the box office (see next page).

Studio tours are offered on the hour between 9 A.M. and 3 P.M. weekdays, 10 a.m. and 4 p.m. Saturday. The cost is $6 adults, $3.75 children.

KCET Television. The oldest continually operating studio—since 1912—lets you tour its complex at 4401 Sunset Boulevard most Tuesday and Thursday mornings with advance notice. Call (213) 667-9242 at least a week ahead for reservations for the free 90-minute behind-the-scenes look. Children under 6th-grade level are not allowed on the tour.

Now a major public television studio, it once housed silent film companies and then B-movie giant Monogram Studios, which made the Bowery Boys and Charlie Chan series.

Live filming

To get a free schedule of sites where movie and television crews are filming, check with the L.A. Convention and Visitors Bureau (see page 11). You can also buy more up-to-date schedules from the following companies. Luck and timing play a big role in what you may see.

Hollywood on Location. This company's filming lists and maps ($29) even mention what stars are expected to be on hand. The lists are published weekdays only, at 9:30 A.M. Pick them up from offices at 8644

Wilshire Boulevard (west of La Cienega), Beverly Hills. To reserve a copy, call (213) 659-9165.

Motion Picture Coordination Office. For a minimal charge, this industry office gives you a copy of the daily location list for shooting around L.A. (Don't expect the details available from Hollywood on Location.) Call (213) 485-5324 for information, or stop by the office at 6922 Hollywood Boulevard.

TV shows

Most television sitcoms, game shows, and talk shows are taped live in the L.A. area, and you can be part of the studio audience. You'll learn what goes into producing your favorite show, how the sets look, and how sequences are pieced together.

Most studios restrict audiences to 16 years and up, though some drop the age to 12. No cameras or food are allowed.

Winter is the peak production period for most shows. Crowds shrink as summer tourists return home, increasing your chances of getting a ticket. Most shows tape in early afternoon and early evening, sitcoms generally on Tuesday, Wednesday, and Friday and game shows all week long. Some shoot for only 45 minutes, others for up to 3 hours at a time.

Tickets are free (on a first-come basis) but don't guarantee admittance. Lining up early is the key. To play it safe, arrive a good 2 hours in advance, considerably earlier for the most popular shows. (In summer some audience hopefuls wait as long as 7 hours.)

ABC, NBC, CBS, and Paramount offer tickets at on-site offices and by mail. Some independent studios offer seats through agencies. A few tickets (usually to new or less popular shows) are available daily outside Mann's Chinese Theatre in Holly-

wood. For additional information, check with visitor information centers (addresses on page 11).

Most tickets are available a week ahead; for popular shows, they may be gone in 2 hours. To find which ones are available, and how many you can get (most programs have limits), call the studio or the audience service directly.

The best way to have a ticket in hand is to order it by mail at least 3 weeks in advance of your visit. Send a stamped, self-addressed envelope; include the name of the show and preferred date.

Ticket agencies. Audiences Unlimited is good for game shows. Offices are in Hollywood at Fox Television Center (5746 Sunset Boulevard; open 8:30 A.M. to 6 P.M. weekdays) and in Panorama City at Panorama Mall (corner of Van Nuys and Roscoe boulevards; open 10 A.M. to 9 P.M. weekdays, 10 A.M. to 7 P.M. Saturday, 11 A.M. to 6 P.M. Sunday). Tickets are available starting Wednesday the week before shooting. Call (818) 506-0067, or write to Audiences Unlimited, 100 Universal City Plaza, Building 153, Universal City, CA 91608.

Audience Associates, (213) 467-4697, offers guaranteed reserved seating a day or two ahead and bus rides to the studios. Audiences Inc., (714) 527-0246, has some success with same-day requests, including *Arsenio Hall Show* tickets.

ABC. The office at 1776 Talmadge Street in Los Angeles is open 9 A.M. to 5 P.M. weekdays; for details, call (213) 557-4396. To order by mail, write to ABC Show Tickets, 4151 Prospect Ave., Los Angeles, CA 90027.

CBS. Ticket office and mail-order address is 7800 Beverly Blvd., Los Angeles, CA 90036. Hours are 9 A.M. to 5 P.M. daily. For information, call (213) 852-2458.

NBC. Most tickets are available on the day of the program only. Office and mail-order address is 3000 W. Alameda Ave. (corner of Olive Avenue), Burbank, CA 91523. Hours are 8:30 A.M. to 5 P.M. weekdays, 9:30 A.M. to 4 P.M. weekends. From 9 A.M. to 5 P.M., you can call (818) 840-3537 for information.

Paramount Television. The ticket office is at 780 N. Gower Street, Hollywood (no mail orders). Hours are 8 A.M. to 4 P.M. weekdays. For details, call (213) 468-5575.

Homes of the stars

Most of L.A.'s celebrities hide out in the hills above Hollywood, in the canyons of Bel Air, around the crest of the Santa Monica Mountains in Beverly Hills, or farther west near Pacific Palisades and Malibu. You can drive around on your own or join a bus or van tour. Several leave from Mann's Chinese Theatre.

Bus tours. Gray Line offers daily narrated tours of the Hollywood and Beverly Hills area; call (213) 481-2121 for details. Hollywood Fantasy Tours, (213) 469-8184, often uses double-decker buses with open-air seating topside. Starline Sightseeing Tours offers general area tours as well as a rib-tickling tour past stars' homes; call (213) 463-3131.

Tour lengths and prices vary according to destination; most operators provide pickup at area hotels. You may need reservations.

Touring on your own. To drive past some stars' former abodes, buy a map from one of the hawkers along Sunset Boulevard. Maps may not be accurate, but they provide a pleasant way to spend a couple of hours.

Westside

Many of L.A.'s most exclusive shops, restaurants, art galleries, and entertainment centers are west of downtown in the fashionable communities of Beverly Hills, Century City, Westwood, and Bel Air.

To visit this area, get off the freeways and drive some of the city's famed boulevards: Wilshire, Sunset, and Santa Monica. Almost every attraction in the western sector of L.A. is on or near these thoroughfares.

Wilshire Boulevard. Stretching 16 miles from the center of L.A. to the Pacific Ocean, Wilshire is one of the city's prestige streets, often compared to New York's Fifth Avenue. Launched in the 1920s with the opening of the Miracle Mile (the area between La Brea and La Cienega avenues, now known as Mid-Wilshire), the thoroughfare was soon lined with upscale stores, prominent business firms, smart apartment houses, plush restaurants, and well-known hotels.

From the Harbor Freeway northwest to Lafayette Park, Wilshire cuts through a melting pot of Hispanic and Asiatic cultures. A few blocks to the west, Koreatown's colorful shops, markets, and restaurants turn the section south of Wilshire between Vermont and Western avenues into a tourist attraction. An interesting stop is the Korean Shopping Center (3300 W. 8th Street), a small arcade with several boutiques.

Mid-Wilshire draws visitors to the Hancock Park area, site of the La Brea Tar Pits, the George C. Page Museum, and Los Angeles County Museum of Art (page 27).

Sunset Boulevard. Gloria Swanson immortalized this street on film; she even lived on the famous thoroughfare, across from the Beverly Hills Hotel. Her home is gone, but other celebrities live nearby.

Even if you're not a star-gazer, Sunset is a worthwhile drive. Beginning at El Pueblo downtown (see page 16), it proceeds through Hollywood, wanders past estates (and the exclusive Beverly Hills Hotel) at the base of the Santa Monica Mountains, and finally intersects with the Pacific Coast Highway 25 miles away in Malibu.

There's still plenty of activity in West Hollywood's 20-block swath of neon and nightclubs known as the Sunset Strip, though its character has changed. Where fans once gathered to watch the movie colony of the 1930s and 40s enter Trocadero, Mocambo, and Ciro's nightclubs, the young and trendy now stroll in and out of loud, gaudy lounges and glorified hamburger stands. The street costumes and billboard art seem to catch people's eyes these days more than the view, but the garden of Butterfield's Restaurant (8426 Sunset Boulevard), once Lionel Barrymore's home, offers a good vantage for looking out over the city.

Santa Monica Boulevard. Originating in the Silver Lake district east of Hollywood, Santa Monica parallels Sunset for a stretch, then turns south, cutting through Beverly Hills and across Wilshire on its way to the ocean. Though not as glamorous a thoroughfare as Wilshire and Sunset, it offers an entrée to Century City. And if you take Wilshire to Beverly Hills, Santa Monica is a good alternate route back to Los Angeles and Hollywood.

Other notable streets. The trendy section of Melrose Avenue stretches from artsy West Hollywood (center of L.A.'s gay community) west to Beverly Hills. Weekends are lively, with crowds thronging to avant-garde shops and restaurants between La Brea and San Vicente. The Pacific Design Center at Melrose and San Vicente (known familiarly as the Blue Whale) is the center for interior design (not open to the general public). Nearby at Beverly and La Cienega, the dramatic Beverly Center (L.A.'s largest retail building) contains an eclectic collection of stores, restaurants, and theaters.

Fairfax Avenue (between Beverly Boulevard and Melrose) is the heart of L.A.'s largest Jewish neighborhood; this is the place to look for Jewish delicatessens, bakeries, bookstores, and newsstands. Farmers Market at 3rd and Fairfax bustles with food stands, produce stalls, and shops (see page 17). Cafe Largo (432 N. Fairfax) hosts evening poetry readings and offbeat entertainers that attract the younger celebrity set.

Beverly Hills

One of Southern California's most eagerly sought addresses, Beverly Hills is home to many well-known personalities of stage and screen and, consequently, a mecca for visitors who come to mix and mingle in the affluent city where stars live, dine, and shop.

Flags mark the Academy of Motion Picture Arts & Sciences (8949 Wilshire Boulevard), home of the Oscars. Exhibits related to motion pictures are open to the public weekdays from 9 A.M. to 5 P.M. The academy's library collection, at 333 S. La Cienega Boulevard, is also open to the public.

Though completely surrounded by Los Angeles, Beverly Hills is a fiercely independent municipality. At the busy intersection of Olympic Boulevard and Beverly Drive, a monument honors celebrities who helped preserve the community when annexation seemed likely.

Beverly Hills' boundaries extend roughly from San Vicente Boulevard on the east to Century City and Benedict Canyon Boulevard on the west, and from Olympic Boulevard on the south to the hills above Sunset Boulevard on the north. But most visitors are mainly interested in the shopping area, a triangle of streets bounded by Wilshire Boulevard, Cañon Drive, and Little Santa Monica Boulevard (separated from Santa Monica Boulevard by railroad tracks).

Getting around. Two-hour-free parking structures in the heart of town are well marked. A motorized trolley ($1) shuttles passengers around the main shopping area Tuesday through Saturday. For details, call the Beverly Hills Trolley at (310) 271-8174.

*You don't need a Rolls Royce to shop on Rodeo Drive in Beverly Hills, but you do
need an appointment to look at the exclusive fashions in bijan.*

...Westside

For maps, shopping and restaurant guides, and touring information, stop by the Beverly Hills Visitors Bureau, 239 S. Beverly (south of Wilshire in the center of the city's latest dining row).

Rodeo Drive. Several major department stores have luxurious branches along Wilshire Boulevard, but *the* shopping street is Rodeo Drive, north of the Beverly Wilshire Hotel. Strolling the 3-block stretch past Giorgio, Hermes, Gucci, Tiffany, and other sites of conspicuous consumption has become a spectator sport. When browsing palls, patio and sidewalk cafes guarantee good views of the passing scene.

Gardens. Two Beverly Hills estates open their gates for garden touring. Greystone Park, 905 Loma Vista Drive (in the hills above Sunset Boulevard at Doheny Drive), offers superb views from 18½ acres of formal gardens, woods, and lakes. The free gardens are open daily from 10 A.M. to 5 P.M.; the mansion is closed to the public.

You'll need advance reservations to visit the lush patio gardens of the city's oldest residence, the Virginia Robinson estate at 1008 Elden Way. Built in 1911, the home is open from 10 A.M. to 1 P.M. Tuesday through Friday; call (213) 276-5367. A small admission is charged to tour the grounds.

Century City

The somewhat sterile-looking contemporary enclave southwest of Beverly Hills was once the back lot of Twentieth Century Fox. Though filming continues, the studio (10201 Pico Boulevard) is not open for public tours. But you can glimpse the facades of the *Hello, Dolly!* set through the gates.

The entrance to the Avenue of the Stars, Century City's main thoroughfare, is from Santa Monica Boulevard just south of Wilshire. No cars park along the broad street; all lots are underground. The Century City Marketplace at 10250 Santa Monica has a variety of eating spots and specialty stores.

The ABC Entertainment Center, across from the fan-shaped Century Plaza Hotel at 2025 Avenue of the Stars (see page 13), features the large Shubert Theatre (setting for Broadway productions), two first-run cinemascopic theaters, shops, restaurants, and clubs.

Westwood Village

Known primarily as home to the University of California at Los Angeles (U.C.L.A.), Westwood is also L.A.'s movie theater capital (most of the new films preview here) and the location of the prestigious Armand Hammer Museum of Art and Cultural Center (see page 27). Marilyn Monroe and Natalie Wood are among celebrities buried in

the cemetery at Lindbrook and Glendon avenues.

The intersection of Wilshire and Westwood boulevards is one of the area's busiest, and all of the main shopping streets are clogged with daytime browsers and nighttime diners, strollers, and theater-goers.

To avoid the weekend gridlock, take the DASH bus that operates Friday evening (7 P.M. to 2 A.M.) and Saturday (from 11 A.M.) from the Federal Building at Wilshire and Veteran boulevards. The bus stops at all theaters; a ride costs 25 cents.

Village streets. Dining outlets of all types, trendy clothiers, bookstores, video shops—Westwood appeals to the upscale collegiate. Movie-goers make the pedestrian crossing in the 900 block of Broxton Avenue, between the landmark Village and Bruin movie palaces, the city's liveliest.

Contempo-Westwood Center (10886 LeConte Avenue), once a Masonic temple, is now entrenched as a shopping, dining, and art center. The 500-seat Westwood Playhouse here presents plays, musicals, and revues.

U.C.L.A. This mammoth educational center enrolls more than 34,000 students and has more than 85 buildings on its 411-acre campus south of Sunset Boulevard. Free tours familiarize visitors with the university's facilities, architecture, and history, or you can wander around on your own.

On 1½-hour walks, guides point out landmarks like Royce Hall (one of the original buildings, a concert center), Wight Art Gallery, an outstanding 20th-century sculpture garden, botanic gardens, and sports complexes. Tours depart the visitor center in the Ueberroth Building, 10945 Le Conte Avenue, at 10:30 A.M. and 1:30 P.M. weekdays. Call (213) 206-8147 for information on weekend walks and other special tours.

The visitor center is open weekdays from 8 A.M. to 6 P.M. On-campus parking next to the center costs $3. A shuttle between Westwood Village and the campus stops at the visitor center; the bus operates every 5 to 10 minutes weekdays from 7:15 A.M. to 6 P.M.

City Mountains

L.A. has a mountain range right in its midst, an east-west chain that extends 47 miles west from the Los Angeles River into Ventura County. The Santa Monicas embrace 150,000 acres of rugged heights and steep canyons; almost half is parkland. At their eastern end lies Griffith Park; their western peaks wade right into the ocean.

Roads from Malibu and Agoura (in the San Fernando Valley) reach interior parks like former Para-

mount and Twentieth Century Fox filming sites. You get good views from Mulholland Drive, which stretches from the Pacific Coast Highway to the Hollywood Freeway (unpaved for 10 miles between Topanga Canyon and San Diego Freeway).

For information on outdoor activities, contact the Santa Monica Mountains National Recreation Area, 22900 Ventura Blvd., Woodland Hills, CA 91364; (818) 888-3770.

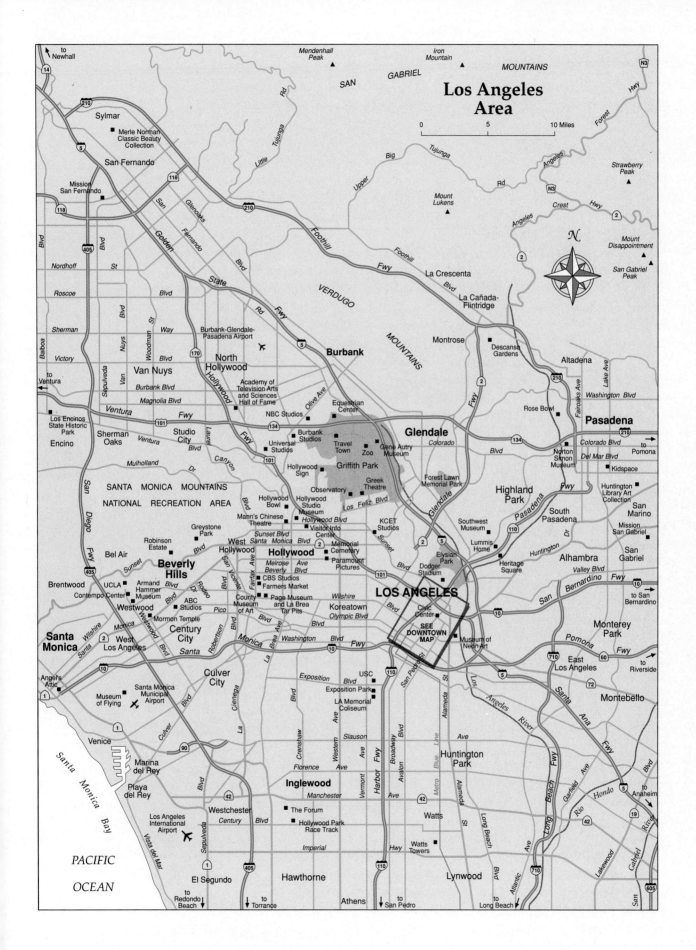

Los Angeles
Area

One of the city's most striking architectural works, the Museum of Contemporary Art building in downtown Los Angeles hints by virtue of its bold exterior at the dramatic collection displayed inside.

L.A.'s Grand Museums

It's been said cities wear museums the way admirals proudly display a chest of gleaming medals. If so, L.A.'s acclaimed awards range from Ice Age fossils to contemporary art. The museums profiled below—along with Malibu's J. Paul Getty Museum, San Marino's Huntington Museum, and Pasadena's Norton Simon, all discussed in the following chapter—contain the area's major collections of art, history, and science.

Armand Hammer Museum of Art and Cultural Center. Located at 10889 Wilshire Boulevard in Westwood, this innovative new museum houses Hammer's personal collection of Western European art. Exhibits include 10,000 Daumier works and the only Leonardo Codex in the western hemisphere. The museum has a below-level garage. Admission is $4.50 adults, $2.50 children; hours of operation are 11 A.M. to 7 P.M. (closed Tuesday). Contact: (213) 443-6471.

California Afro-American Museum. This free museum in Exposition Park (600 State Drive) offers an excellent introduction to Afro-American life and culture. Exhibits range from books clandestinely published by blacks in the antebellum South to contemporary sculpture. Hours are 10 A.M. to 5 P.M. daily. Contact: (213) 744-7432.

California Museum of Science and Industry. There's always something new at the West's most popular science center, crammed with hands-on exhibits. Open daily from 10 A.M. to 5 P.M., the museum is in Exposition Park at 700 State Drive. Admission is free; IMAX Theater programs are $5 for adults, $3.50 for children and seniors. Recorded show information: (213) 744-2014 or 2015.

George C. Page Museum. Skeletons and re-creations of mastodons, dire wolves, imperial mammoths, and other prehistoric animals trapped in the Rancho La Brea Tar Pits during the Ice Age are displayed in this museum at 5801 Wilshire Boulevard, almost directly above their engulfing ooze. More than a million plant and animal fossils have been recovered from the site over the years. A 15-minute film depicts life in the Pleistocene era and shows how the remains were uncovered.

At an observation building in the northwest corner of the park, you can see the bubbling asphalt-laden water. The free observatory is open weekends from 10 A.M. to 5 P.M. The museum is open Tuesday through Sunday from 10 A.M. to 5 P.M.

Museum admission is $3 for adults, $1.50 for students and seniors, and 75 cents for children 6 to 12 (free for everyone the second Tuesday of each month). Contact: (213) 936-2230.

Los Angeles County Museum of Art. From pre-Columbian art to 20th-century sculpture, this encyclopedic collection at 5905 Wilshire Boulevard takes several hours to view. The museum's size was doubled when the Anderson building (a wedge of limestone and glass with a heroic entry portal), a central courtyard, and the Pavilion for Japanese Art (home for the internationally renowned Shin'enkan paintings) were added to the original Ahmanson, Hammer, and Bing pavilions in the late 1980s.

Admission is $5 adults, $3.50 students and seniors, $1 children ages 6 to 12 (free for everyone the second Tuesday of each month). The museum is open 10 A.M. to 5 P.M. weekdays, 10 A.M. to 6 P.M. weekends (closed Monday and major holidays). There's a parking lot southeast of the museum at Wilshire Boulevard and Spaulding Avenue (fee). A plaza cafe is open for lunch. Contact: (213) 857-6111.

Museum of Contemporary Art. The bold architecture of the museum building makes a fitting showcase for the important collection it houses. Art from the 1940s through abstract expressionism is displayed, including works by Pollock, Rauschenberg, Nevelson, and Diebenkorn.

The downtown museum is at 250 S. Grand Avenue. An auxiliary facility at 152 N. Central Avenue, dubbed the Temporary Contemporary, was the museum's original home.

Both museums are open Tuesday through Sunday from 11 A.M. to 6 P.M. (Thursday until 8 P.M.). Admission is $4 for adults, $2 for seniors and students, free for children under 12 and for all visitors after 5 P.M. Thursday. Contact: (213) 621-2766.

Natural History Museum. Egyptian mummies, reconstructed dinosaurs, glittering gems, dioramas of animals in natural settings, Hollywood memorabilia—this museum is almost overwhelming in its diversity. A Discovery Center for children is packed with hands-on exhibits.

The museum (900 Exposition Boulevard) also operates a Burbank satellite (3rd and Cypress streets) and the Petersen Automotive Museum (Wilshire Boulevard and Fairfax Avenue). Hours at all locations are 10 A.M. to 5 P.M. Tuesday through Sunday. Admission at any location is $6 adults, $3.50 juniors and seniors, $2 children 5 to 12. Contact: (213) 744-3466.

Southwest Museum. This hillside museum west of the Pasadena Freeway at 234 Museum Drive contains one of the country's best displays of Native American art and artifacts, from prehistoric times to the present.

There's hillside parking above the building, but it's more interesting to park below and enter through a diorama-lined tunnel. An elevator whisks you up to the gallery. Admission to the museum (open Tuesday through Sunday, 11 A.M. to 5 P.M.; closed holidays) is $3 for adults, $1.50 for seniors and students, $1 for children 7 to 18. Contact: (213) 221-2163.

Most of the Hispanic collection is housed in nearby Casa de Adobe (4605 N. Figueroa Street), once part of a Mexican/Californian rancho. This free museum operates on the same schedule as the Southwest Museum.

San Fernando Valley

Bounded by the Santa Monica, Santa Susana, Verdugo, and San Gabriel mountains, lies the 250-square-mile San Fernando Valley. If it were a single city, it would rank among the country's top ten. Today, thanks to the 1994 Northridge earthquake, it's best known as the site of this century's costliest U.S. natural disaster.

Though the sometimes smoggy basin gets little respect from residents in other parts of L.A., its middle-class lifestyle has spawned more swimming pools per square mile than anyplace outside of Palm Springs, and "valley girl talk," first overheard at Sherman Oaks Galleria mall, added words to our vocabulary.

Most of the visitor interest centers on Universal, Burbank, and NBC studios (see pages 20–21) and on North Hollywood's new Academy of Television Arts and Sciences Hall of Fame (Lankershim and Magnolia boulevards). But a few historic remnants, including the San Fernando Mission (see page 6) also draw visitors "over the hill."

Getting around. The Hollywood Freeway (U.S. 101) and the San Diego Freeway (Interstate 405) enter the valley from Los Angeles. Most visitors from the north arrive on the Golden State Freeway (Interstate 5) or the Ventura Freeway (U.S. 101).

The valley is laid out in a grid pattern, with major thoroughfares running in a straight line for 20 miles. Ventura Boulevard, the main artery, extends east-west through the valley for 21 miles.

Los Encinos State Historic Park. The valley's recorded history began more than 200 years ago when the Portola party camped here. Old olive trees, the 1849 Osa adobe, and some turn-of-the-century sheep ranch buildings stand on the site at 16756 Moorpark Street in Encino. There's a small charge to visit the park, open Wednesday through Sunday from 10 A.M. to 5 P.M.

William S. Hart Park. Once the home of a Western star of the silent screen, the ranch house at the bottom of the hill contains mementos of his career; the Spanish-style mansion atop the hill houses vintage weapons, Native American artifacts, and fine Western art. A herd of bison roams the range.

The ranch (Newhall Avenue and San Fernando Road, Newhall) is open from 10 A.M. to dusk daily; free mansion tours operate every hour from 10 A.M. to 5 P.M. weekends, 10 A.M. to 3 P.M. Wednesday through Friday. There's free shuttle service from the park entrance.

Placerita Canyon Park. A small deposit of gold was discovered here in 1842, six years before the strike at Sutter's Mill began Northern California's gold rush. A pleasant place to picnic or hike, the small park lies about 5 miles east of Newhall off U.S. 14.

Ronald Reagan Presidential Library. A museum in Simi Valley showcases the 40th president's life and accomplishments. The library, at 40 Presidential Drive, is open 10 A.M. to 5 P.M. Monday through Saturday, from noon Sunday. Those over 15 pay a small admission fee.

L.A.'s Playground

Sprawling Griffith Park is the site of the city's zoo, an observatory and planetarium, an outdoor theater, a bird sanctuary, an equestrian center, and an antique vehicular museum. And that's not all: its 4,107 acres contain golf courses, tennis courts, cycling paths, polo grounds, a swimming pool, and a cricket field.

Griffith Park straddles the eastern end of the Santa Monica Mountains in the northern part of the city. More than half of its rugged terrain is a sort of domesticated wilderness laced with miles of horseback and hiking trails. But its flat perimeter is easily accessible from the Ventura, Golden State, and Hollywood freeways. Both Western and Vermont avenues lead into the park from the south.

For free maps and information on Griffith Park's attractions and activities, stop by the visitor center (open daily, 10 A.M. to 5 P.M.) at 4730 Crystal Springs Drive, off Riverside Drive south of the zoo. A 1926 carousel operates opposite the center. See page 29 for information about the zoo and Travel Town transportation museum.

Greek Theatre. Nestled among the foothills near the park's southern edge, this 6,000-seat natural amphitheater is a popular setting for summer concerts; call (213) 410-1062.

Griffith Observatory. From its perch on the slopes of Mount Hollywood in the southern part of the park, the observatory commands a spectacular view of the city at night. A 600-seat planetarium theater replicates eclipses, northern lights, and other celestial phenomena. Another show pulses with laser light and sound.

Admission to the observatory and its science exhibits is free. The observatory is open Tuesday through Sunday from 7 to 10 P.M. The science hall is open Sunday through Friday from 12:30 to 10 P.M. (from 2 P.M. weekdays in winter), Saturday from 11:30 A.M. to 10 P.M.

L.A. for Children

Where do you take the younger set after they've toured Universal Studios, seen the footprints in Mann's Chinese Theatre, and (with luck) watched a filming somewhere in the city? The answer might be to a puppet show, on a train or stagecoach ride, to the zoo, or to a children's museum. Even without kids in tow, adults are likely to enjoy many of the following diversions.

This is only a sampling of what's available in the greater L.A. area. Among other good choices are Santa Monica's Angel's Attic and Pasadena's Kidspace (page 41) and the Long Beach Children's Museum (page 40). The whole family will enjoy fossils at Rancho La Brea Tar Pits (page 17), "please touch" displays at both the Museum of Science and Industry and the Discovery Center in the Natural History Museum (page 27), and planetarium and laserium shows at Griffith Park (page 28).

The only place young children are *not* encouraged is in the audience of a television filming. Because of the fear of disruption, kids usually must be 16 to get a ticket.

Los Angeles Children's Museum. The museum in the mall at Civic Center (310 N. Main Street) is just for kids, although adults may tag along to watch youngsters make a recording, take part in a videotape filming, paint their faces, or build with giant foam blocks. Exhibits show ages 2 to 12 how to learn by doing.

In summer, the museum is open weekends 10 A.M. to 5 P.M., weekdays from 11:30 A.M. to 5 P.M. Hours the rest of the year are 2 to 4 P.M. Wednesday and Thursday, 10 A.M. to 5 P.M. weekends. Admission is $5 (adults free weekday afternoons during the school year).

Wells Fargo History Museum. The Old West lives downtown at 333 S. Grand Avenue, where the whole family learns about the rigors and adventures of early-day travel by climbing aboard a stagecoach for a simulated ride. Among the historic highlights: an 1880s ore cart, a fist-size gold nugget, and photos of notorious bandit Black Bart. The free museum is open 9 A.M. to 4 P.M. weekdays.

Bob Baker Marionette Theater. Dancing skeletons, toy soldiers, and skate-boarding clowns are among the whimsical characters that make this puppet theater the most endearing—and enduring—in the country. Performances take place daily at 10:30 A.M. weekdays and 2:30 P.M. weekends. The $7 admission fee includes the show, a backstage tour, and refreshments.

The theater is located west of the Harbor Freeway at 1345 W. 1st Street. Reservations are a must; phone (213) 250-9995.

Gene Autry Western Heritage Museum. Walt Disney Imagineering created the exhibits and sound tracks in seven galleries tracing America's Western heritage. You're introduced to soldiers and Indians, trappers and sodbusters, outlaws and good guys in white hats—and some of the actors who played them. Of special appeal to kids of all ages is The Spirit of Imagination gallery (film clips and other Hollywood cowboy artifacts).

To reach the museum (4700 Zoo Drive at the edge of Griffith Park), take the Golden State Freeway (Interstate 5) north from downtown to the Zoo Drive exit. Museum hours are 10 A.M. to 5 P.M. Tuesday through Sunday. Admission is $6 for adults, $4.50 for students and seniors, $2.50 for children 2 through 12. A museum shop and restaurant round out the amenities.

Los Angeles Zoo. More than 2,000 mammals, birds, and reptiles live on this fine zoo's 113 hillside acres. Key exhibits include a large Koala House and a walk-in aviary. Adventure Island, a special children's section of the zoo, has five major Southwest environments: sea lions cavort along the Shoreline, bats inhabit the Cave, mountain lions roam around the Mountain, prairie dogs poke their heads above the Meadow, and roadrunners dash about the Desert. Other zoo child-pleasers are the nursery orphans and the domestic array at the Spanish Hacienda.

The Los Angeles Zoo is on Zoo Drive in the northern part of Griffith Park, at the intersection of the Ventura and Golden State freeways (State 134 and Interstate 5). Hours are 10 A.M. to 5 P.M. daily (to 6 P.M. in summer), except Christmas. Admission is $6 for adults, $5 seniors, and $2.75 for children 2 to 12, including various animal shows presented throughout the day (check the schedule when you arrive). Camel and elephant rides cost extra.

Travel Town. More than 30 steam locomotives and railroad cars, fire trucks, a horse-drawn milk wagon, and an 1849 circus wagon are part of the allure of this indoor/outdoor transportation museum in Griffith Park. Children of all ages love riding the miniature train that circles the park.

The museum opens daily at 10 A.M. and closes sometime between 4 P.M. and 6 P.M., depending on the day of the week and the season. There's no fee to visit, though donations are encouraged. Train rides cost $1.75 for adults, $1.25 for children under 14, and $1 for seniors. Travel Town is on Zoo Drive in the northern part of Griffith Park.

L.A.'s Beaches & Mountains

L.A.'s sandy front door and back-yard mountains add impressive dimensions to any Southern California visit. Residents and tourists alike flock to the string of beaches around the city; more than 50 million hit the sands annually. And the nearby mountains swarm with local hikers and campers, or sledders and skiers, depending on

the season. But the attractions don't stop with splendid scenery and outdoor recreation; along the shore and in mountain valleys are fine museums, historic sites, and gardens to tour.

Beach playgrounds

Stretching some 75 miles from Malibu on the west to Long Beach on the south, L.A.'s western and southern shores are used as a summer coolant by the city's huge population. It's usually about 10° cooler at beach communities than it is inland, and water temperatures are around 67° from July on into autumn.

But the beaches are more than just hot-weather destinations. They're a key part of the L.A. lifestyle, inviting every aquatic pleasure from boating and fishing to surfing, snorkeling, and scuba diving.

Mountain retreats

The San Gabriel and San Bernardino mountain ranges rise abruptly to peaks over 10,000 feet, separating Los Angeles from desert lands to the north and forming an imposing backdrop for the teeming city.

Lower elevations of the frontal slopes are closed in summer because of fire danger, but alpine lakes and pine-clad slopes higher up offer quick relief from the inland area's heat and smog. In winter, locals head for the hills to belly-thump down slopes on improvised sleds or ski at such resorts as Lake Gregory–Crestline and Big Bear.

The Santa Monicas, the state's only east-west mountain range, march right into the Pacific Ocean west of the city, their rocky tops forming the offshore Channel Islands. Mountains and beaches meet at Point Mugu, where this chapter begins.

Planning a visit

Many visitors to L.A. establish cool summer bases in beach towns like Santa Monica (a short distance from Westside attractions), Marina del Rey (close to the L.A. airport), or Long Beach (near Orange County).

Cabins, bed-and-breakfasts, motels, and a few large hotels welcome mountain-goers. Lake Arrowhead and Big Bear have the best accommodations.

Getting there. Long Beach Municipal Airport is a convenient alternative to LAX or Orange County traffic. More than 40 daily flights offer service from 27 cities across the country. For mountain destinations, the closest large airport is at Ontario; a few air charters also serve larger resorts.

Though there is shuttle service from Los Angeles and Long Beach airports to a few beach hotels, light-rail service between L.A. and Long Beach (see page 40), and spotty city bus transportation, a car makes it easier to explore both coastline and mountains.

State 1, the Pacific Coast Highway, ties the beach communities together. Inland, Interstate 405 provides coastal access from the north and south, and Interstate 10 reaches the beach from the east at Santa Monica. Access roads to the San Gabriels and the San Bernardinos are easily reached from Interstate 210 and Interstate 215.

At Marina del Rey's harbor, Fisherman's Village imparts a turn-of-the-century, Cape Cod ambience for shopping and dining. Tour boats offer cruises of the man-made marina, the West Coast's largest.

Contacts

These agencies offer information on attractions and accommodations. See additional contacts throughout this chapter.

Santa Monica Convention & Visitors Bureau
P.O. Box 5278
Santa Monica, CA 90405
(310) 393-7593

Long Beach Area Convention and Visitors Council
One World Trade Center, Suite 300
Long Beach, CA 90831-0300
(800) 262-7838

Pasadena Convention & Visitors Bureau
171 S. Los Robles Ave.
Pasadena, CA 91101
(818) 795-9311

Inland Empire Tourism Council
800 N. Haven, Suite 100
Ontario, CA 91764
(714) 941-7877
For mountains, inland valleys

The Beaches

The county's long stretches of sand and water, from Santa Monica Bay southwest to Long Beach Harbor, are dotted with fishing piers, marinas, museums, and shopping complexes. Carefully tony and innocently shabby, purveying cracked crab and caramel corn, these beach communities are where Southern California's sandcastle vision of health and happiness is made real.

Days start early at the shore, especially the crescents along Santa Monica Bay. By 7 A.M. anglers are in position on piers and fleets of beach-cleaning machines are raking the sand. They're soon joined by joggers and—if radio prognostications are favorable—by surfers.

State beaches provide a variety of facilities; the map on the facing page shows their locations. For state beach camping, see page 121.

Beach parking can be a problem. Bring plenty of quarters to feed meters at city and county parks.

Point Mugu to Point Dume

The south slope of the Santa Monica Mountains drops abruptly into the sea in the westernmost section of a Los Angeles area beach tour, forming rocky headlands and intimate pocket beaches. Farther to the east you'll find good swimming beaches.

Point Mugu to Malibu has the cleanest ocean along the metropolitan coast, with clear water, healthy kelp beds, the best shore and offshore fishing and diving, and some very good surfing.

Zuma Beach. Just west of Point Dume off State 1, L.A.'s largest county-owned beach offers excellent swimming, except for occasional summer riptides. Big parking lots, tots' playgrounds, volleyball courts, and food stalls make it a popular place.

Point Dume Whale Watch. A stairway from Westward Beach Road at Point Dume leads up to a good spot from which to watch the annual winter whale migration (see page 124).

Malibu & east

Surfing movies in the 1950s and 60s helped popularize L.A.'s beaches. *Gidget* and *Beach Blanket Bingo* were just two of a whole genre of beach films set in Malibu. But this community has long been home for celebrities who brave winter surf and mud slides for summer fun. David Letterman, Larry Hagman, Rob Lowe, and Goldie Hawn are but a few of the prominent citizens who might be glimpsed around town.

Maybe that's why there's such a high concentration of oceanview restaurants along State 1, including Geoffrey's, Alice's, Don the Beachcomber, Malibu Sea Lion, Moonshadows, Charthouse, and Gladstones 4 Fish. Some are expensive; others have surprisingly down-to-earth tabs. Zonker Davis Accessway (named after a "Doonesbury" comic strip character) is one of several public-access footpaths that thread between the beachhouses to the sand.

At Malibu's pier, you'll find sportfishing boats and a restaurant. You can fish from the pier with a license, and buy bait and tackle.

History and birds. A showcase of Spanish-Moorish architecture, the Adamson House at 23200 Pacific Coast Highway was built in 1929 on what was then the last undivided Spanish land grant in California. Now it is part of the Malibu Lagoon Museum. After touring the house and 13 acres of gardens, visit the former garage to see exhibits on Malibu from Chumash Indian days to the present. The museum is open from 11 A.M. to 3 P.M. Wednesday through Saturday; for details, call (310) 456-8432. Admission and parking fees are charged.

East of the house, at Malibu Lagoon State Beach, restoration gave new life to a 5-acre coastal wetlands visited by more than 250 species of birds. Kiosks explain bird and plant life. The beach fronting the lagoon is a surfer's haven.

J. Paul Getty Museum. One of America's richest art museums stands on a bluff at 17985 W. Pacific Coast Highway, between Sunset and Topanga Canyon boulevards.

A wealthy American industrialist who began collecting art in the 1930s, Getty left the bulk of his estate to the museum when he died in 1976. His interests centered on Greek and Roman antiquities, Renaissance and Baroque paintings, and European decorative arts. Though greatly expanded now (recent acquisitions include Van Gogh's *Irises*), the museum's collections still reflect Getty's imprint. Hands-on displays in a second-floor gallery help explain exhibits.

The building itself is a replica of the Villa dei Papiri, an ancient Roman country house at Herculaneum destroyed by the eruption of Vesuvius in 79 A.D. Its gardens include trees, flowers, shrubs, and herbs similar to those that might have been growing two thousand years ago at the villa.

The museum is open Tuesday through Sunday from 10 A.M. to 5 P.M. year-round except on major holidays. Admission is free, but you'll need a parking reservation. No walk-in traffic is permitted. Call (310) 458-2003 at least a week in advance of your visit; the office is open daily from 9 A.M. to 5 P.M.

Plan on spending about 3 hours to thoroughly explore the museum, perhaps taking lunch in the Garden Tea Room and visiting the bookstore.

By the mid-1990s, a new J. Paul Getty Center off Interstate 405 and Mulholland Drive will showcase the paintings, drawings, manuscripts, and decorative arts now on display in the Malibu museum, plus others previously in storage. The Greek and Roman collections will remain at the present Malibu site.

Inland forays

From Malibu, Sunset Boulevard winds along the base of the Santa Monicas en route to downtown L.A. Just a mile or so inland from the coast highway lie two peaceful parks worth a detour.

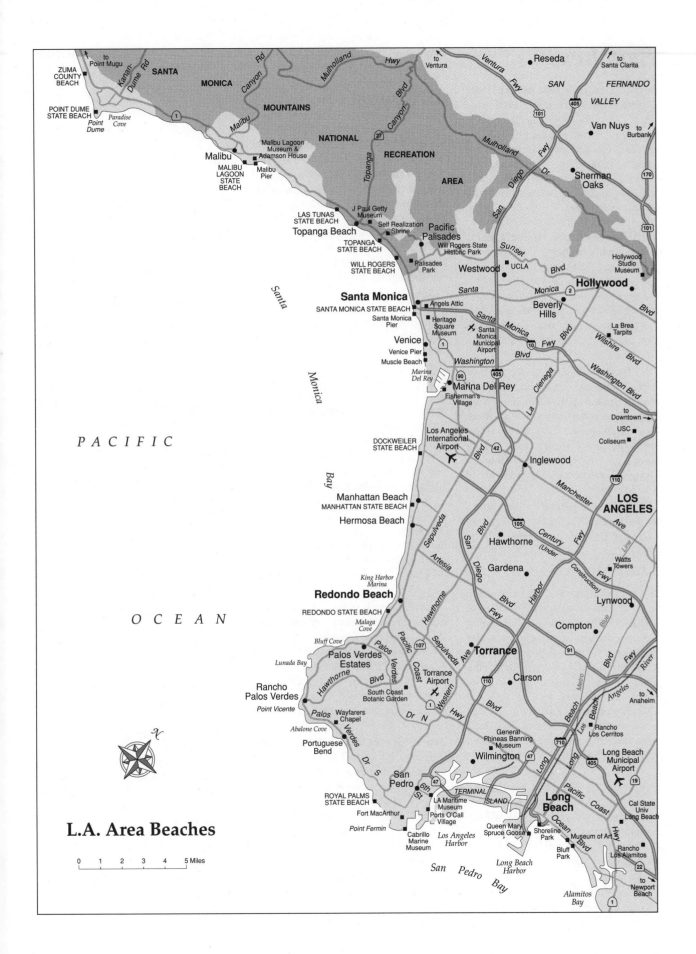

L.A. Area Beaches

ZUMA COUNTY BEACH

to Point Mugu

POINT DUME STATE BEACH

Point Dume

Paradise Cove

Kanan-Dume Rd

SANTA

MONICA

MOUNTAINS

Malibu Canyon

Mulholland Hwy

Topanga Canyon Blvd

NATIONAL

RECREATION

AREA

to Ventura

Ventura Fwy

Reseda

SAN FERNANDO VALLEY

to Santa Clarita

Van Nuys

to Burbank

Sherman Oaks

Mulholland Dr

San Diego Fwy

Hollywood Studio Museum

Malibu

MALIBU LAGOON STATE BEACH

Malibu Lagoon Museum & Adamson House

Malibu Pier

LAS TUNAS STATE BEACH

Topanga Beach

J Paul Getty Museum

Self Realization Shrine

TOPANGA STATE BEACH

Pacific Palisades

Will Rogers State Historic Park

WILL ROGERS STATE BEACH

Palisades Park

Westwood

UCLA

Sunset Blvd

Monica Blvd

Hollywood

La Brea Tarpits

Wilshire Blvd

Santa Monica

SANTA MONICA STATE BEACH

Santa Monica Pier

Angels Attic

Heritage Square Museum

Beverly Hills

Santa Monica Blvd

Santa Monica Municipal Airport

Venice

Venice Pier

Muscle Beach

Washington Blvd

Marina Del Rey

Fisherman's Village

Marina Del Rey

Washington Blvd

to Downtown

USC

Coliseum

DOCKWEILER STATE BEACH

Los Angeles International Airport

Inglewood

Manchester

LOS ANGELES

PACIFIC

Manhattan Beach

MANHATTAN STATE BEACH

Hermosa Beach

Sepulveda Blvd

Artesia Blvd

San Diego Fwy

Century Blvd

Hawthorne

Gardena

Watts Towers

Lynwood

Compton

OCEAN

King Harbor Marina

Redondo Beach

REDONDO STATE BEACH

Malaga Cove

Bluff Cove

Lunada Bay

Palos Verdes Estates

Point Vicente

Abalone Cove

Portuguese Bend

Rancho Palos Verdes

Hawthorne Blvd

Pacific Coast Hwy

Sepulveda Ave

Torrance

Torrance Airport

South Coast Botanic Garden

Wayfarers Chapel

Palos Verdes Dr S

San Pedro

ROYAL PALMS STATE BEACH

Fort MacArthur

Point Fermin

Cabrillo Marine Museum

6th St

LA Maritime Museum

Ports O'Call Village

TERMINAL ISLAND

Los Angeles Harbor

Carson

Harbor Blvd

Western Ave

Wilmington

General Phineas Banning Museum

Long Beach Blvd

Queen Mary Spruce Goose

Shoreline Park

Bluff Park

Museum of Art

Long Beach Harbor

San Pedro Bay

Alamitos Bay

Rancho Los Cerritos

Long Beach Municipal Airport

Long Beach

Ocean Blvd

Pacific Coast Hwy

Cal State Univ Long Beach

Rancho Los Alamitos

to Newport Beach

to Anaheim

Los Angeles River

0 1 2 3 4 5 Miles

...Beaches

Self-Realization Fellowship Lake Shrine. A quiet retreat at 17190 Sunset Boulevard, this 10-acre hillside meditation garden contains a spring-fed lake, shrines, gazebos, a waterfall, and a windmill chapel. You can visit between 9 A.M. and 4:45 P.M. except on Mondays, holidays, and occasional Saturdays (no admission charge).

Will Rogers State Historic Park. Cowboy philosopher Will Rogers lived in the large (31 rooms) but unassuming house on this 186-acre Pacific Palisades ranch from 1928 until his death in 1935. On tours you'll see the Western paintings, rugs, lariats, and saddles that played such an important part in his life.

Stables, polo fields (matches are held most weekends), and riding and hiking trails make up the rest of the spread. The entrance road to the hillside park overlooking the Pacific is at 14253 Sunset Boulevard. The park is open daily from 8 A.M. to 7 P.M. (per-car admission charge); house tours take place from 10 A.M. to 5 P.M.

A state beach named for the humorist lies beneath Pacific Palisades, south of Sunset Boulevard on State 1.

Santa Monica

At Santa Monica the shore turns south for a splendid sweep of 20 miles of almost wholly accessible, broad, sandy beach encompassing eight public beaches, five fishing piers, and two small craft harbors. Then it rounds the Palos Verdes Peninsula for 15 rocky miles before losing itself among the channels of two big harbors, Los Angeles and Long Beach. A bike path stretches 19 miles south from Santa Monica to the bluffs at Palos Verdes.

Exploring the city. Over the last few years, Santa Monica has been transformed from a slightly stodgy seaside community that did little to encourage visitors into a dynamic city noted for its upscale art galleries, restaurants, and shops as well as its famed beach.

Make your first stop the Santa Monica Visitor Center at the south end of beautiful Palisades Park (1400 Ocean Avenue, between Santa Monica Boulevard and Broadway).

New hotels like Loews, Park Hyatt, and Guest Quarters Suites have joined such longtime favorites as the Miramar-Sheraton, Pacific Shore, Shangri-la, and two Holiday Inns. More than 400 restaurants, cafes, and pubs are crowded into the city's 8 square miles, including the elegant Michael's, Wolfgang Puck's Chinois on Main, and Ivy at the Shore. Patrick's Roadhouse (106 Entrada Drive at Pacific Coast Highway) is so popular that you need reservations for breakfast on weekends; call (310) 459-4544.

Boutiques, chic stores, and art galleries line Montana Avenue from 7th to 17th streets and fill Santa Monica Place mall (between 2nd and 4th streets, Broadway and Colorado Avenue). Renovated Main Street and the Third Street Promenade hold other one-of-a-kind shops. A remodeled, turn-of-the-century egg warehouse (2437 Main Street) is now the city's downtown art museum.

For a look at local history, visit the free Heritage Square Museum at 2612 Main Street. Period furnishings and old photographs decorate the rooms of this 1894 house (open Thursday through Saturday from 11 A.M. to 4 P.M. and Sunday from noon). Children love the antique toys and dolls displayed at Angel's Attic, 516 Colorado Avenue (see page 41).

Airplane buffs will enjoy the exhibition of antique aircraft—from World War I biplanes to Spitfires and P51s—at the Museum of Flying (Santa Monica Airport, 2772 Donald Douglas Loop North near Ocean Park Boulevard). Next door is the trendy DC3 Restaurant, a huge hangar-style eatery.

Santa Monica Pier. Hard-hit and truncated by a 1983 storm, the West Coast's oldest pleasure pier has been restored once more. A gathering place for generations of residents, the pier at the foot of Colorado Avenue in the midst of Santa Monica State Beach is the perfect place from which to view the action on the esplanade below and the cliffside park above.

Arcades, amusement rides, restaurants, shops, and a Victorian-era merry-go-round vie for attention. A roller coaster and 11-story ferris wheel are being added. Some activities are free—fishing from the pier (no license required) or watching nearby surfers, volleyball players, and acrobats.

Venice

Venice of America was the formal name for the watery resort of isthmuses and canals built by Abbot Kinney in 1904 as a mecca of art and enlightenment. Grand hotels lined Windward Avenue, symphony orchestras performed at the Summer Assembly, and gondoliers plied their fleet along the waterways. Later Kinney added plunges, bathhouses, amusement piers, and a midway where thrill rides whirled within screaming distance of the ocean's breakers.

Venice thrived as a West Coast Coney Island well into the 1920s. Then misfortunes—flood, fire, the imposition of L.A.'s blue laws—spun the town into decline. By 1929, even the famous canals had been largely filled in and paved.

Today's version, though, remarkably resembles Kinney's original dream. Part souk, part circus, it harbors artists, writers, restaurateurs, remnant hippies, and retirees. Other beach towns are relaxing. Venice is not.

Ocean Front Walk. Any stroll, bike ride, or roller skate along Ocean Front Walk, with its array of outdoor cafes, shops, vendors, and street artists, is entertaining. Walkers take the sidewalk nearest the buildings; cyclists and roller skaters ride a few yards nearer to the ocean. (You can rent bikes or skates anywhere along the walk.)

You might start your tour near the Venice Pavilion at the foot of Windward Avenue about a mile seaward of Lincoln Boulevard (State 1). Muscle Beach lies south of Windward; to the north are several good cafes (among them Sidewalk and Figtree's) with ringside views of fire-eaters and fortune-tellers.

Venice Pier. The fishing pier at the foot of Washington Street is organized for round-the-clock angling (no license needed). Bays at short intervals expand its perimeter to about 400 yards.

Bright umbrellas line the beach along one of Santa Monica's broad stretches of sand.
Excellent swimming, diving, surfing, and fishing make the area a favorite destination
for both vacationers and L.A. area residents.

...Beaches

Canals. To take a look at the few remaining canals, turn inland on South Venice Boulevard and then south onto Dell Avenue. You can stroll the bridges and the canal banks, even though sidewalks are sometimes missing. At Sherman Canal and Dell Avenue, a restoration project uses concrete blocks and native pickleweed to stablize the canal banks.

Marina del Rey

When you see the forest of masts at Marina del Rey, it's easy to believe that this man-made recreational boat harbor is the world's largest. To reach the visitor center from State 1, head seaward on Mindanao Way to 4701 Admiralty. Here, you can pick up maps and information on parking, restaurants, entertainment, and hotels, including the glamorous new Ritz-Carlton entry.

Touring the harbor. Narrated harbor tours depart Fisherman's Village docks on Fiji Way on the hour from 11 A.M. to 4 P.M. daily (see page 124). Buy tickets ($5) at the blue boathouse near the lighthouse in Fisherman's Village (13755 Fiji Way).

Rent-a-Sail, at Fisherman's Village, rents sailboats, motorboats, catamarans, and canoes.

Fisherman's Village. Though touristy and usually crowded on weekends, this New England–style shopping and dining complex is worth a look. Some 40 shops feature everything from seashell statues to fine jewelry. You'll hear live jazz from 2 to 5 P.M. many Sundays. After shopping, take a stroll along the esplanade to view incoming boats.

Manhattan, Hermosa & Redondo Beach

There's little visible glamour in this trio of older seaside cities, but you'll find more youthful beach aficionados per square yard than almost anywhere else along the coast.

Both Manhattan and Hermosa Beach have public fishing piers, each with bait and tackle shops, rest rooms, and snack shops. Redondo State Beach adjoins a marina complex (King Harbor) of restaurants, motels, yacht clubs, and boat facilities. Next door, shops and restaurants line two piers that give a good view of the 1½-mile beach.

Two oceanside boulevards, the Esplanade in Redondo Beach and the Strand in Hermosa Beach and Manhattan Beach, offer plenty of people-watching action.

Palos Verdes Peninsula

Following scenic Palos Verdes Drive south around the peninsula is a pleasant alternative to State 1. Beginning in plush Palos Verdes Estates and ending at San Pedro's Point Fermin Park, it follows the rugged clifftop for a 15-mile stretch, passing several noteworthy attractions and a number of ocean overlooks en route to the busy ports of Los Angeles and Long Beach.

Three coves below the cliffs are accessible to the public. Malaga Cove lies next to Torrance County Beach on Paseo de la Playa; Bluff Cove and Lunada Bay are reached by following Paseo del Mar west to trailheads.

South Coast Botanic Garden. This 87-acre oasis, once a mine and later a landfill project, makes a pleasant detour off Palos Verdes Drive at 26300 Crenshaw Boulevard. The garden (open 9 A.M. to 5 P.M. daily) has native plants, ground covers, and flowering trees. There's a small fee to tour.

Point Vicente Interpretive Center. Adjacent to the lighthouse at 31501 Palos Verdes Drive W., the center has exhibits on area history and geology and on the California gray whale. An observation area on the second floor provides panoramic views. The center is open daily, 10 A.M. to dusk; there's a token admission charge.

Wayfarers Chapel. On a hill at Portuguese Bend sits a striking glass chapel designed by Lloyd Wright, son of the famed architect, for the Swedenborgian church. A 50-foot white stone campanile surmounts the chapel. The grounds are landscaped with plants mentioned in the Bible. The chapel (5755 Palos Verdes Drive S.) is open daily from 9 A.M. to 5 P.M. for free self-guided tours.

Point Fermin Park. Near the Old Point Fermin Lighthouse, this 37-acre blufftop facility is a good place from which to explore tidepools, watch for whales, and observe the windsurfing activities at Cabrillo Beach. The restored lighthouse, built in 1874 of lumber brought around Cape Horn, is not open to the public.

Los Angeles Harbor

The ports of Los Angeles and Long Beach share the world's second largest man-made harbor (Rotterdam is first). Shielded by a 9-mile breakwater, its maze of channels, inlets, and islands covers 50 miles of developed waterfront.

The port (which includes San Pedro, Terminal Island, and Wilmington) is a leader in total tonnage processed and in modern handling techniques. It's also the center of the country's seafood canning industry and home to more than 100 commercial fishing vessels.

Soaring 185 feet above the harbor's main channel, Vincent Thomas Bridge (50-cent toll) connects San Pedro with Terminal Island and Long Beach. Under the bridge's western end lies the Catalina Terminal, departure site for ferries and seaplanes to Santa Catalina Island (see facing page).

Concrete bunkers and a small museum in Fort MacArthur, above Angel's Gate Park near the harbor entrance, testify to the protection planned for the harbor during World War II.

Now noted as the West Coast's premier cruise center, San Pedro has been busily changing its image from industrial to recreational. It's added a marina, the World Cruise Center, several upscale hotels, trendy restaurants, and new shopping complexes along 6th Street in the revitalized downtown.

Cabrillo Marine Museum. Southern California's largest collection of marine life is found in the free museum at 3720 Stephen White Drive, down the hill from Fort MacArthur and adjacent to Cabrillo Beach. Aquariums contain an assortment of creatures from anchovies

Santa Catalina Island

California's only offshore resort has lured local pleasure-seekers since the 1890s, but it took chewing gum magnate William Wrigley, Jr. to thrust the 76-square-mile isle into the national limelight.

First he built a mountaintop summer mansion (now the elegant Inn at Mount Ada). Then he brought his Chicago Cubs baseball team over for spring training, and then, in 1929, he built the huge, circular Casino Building. It's not actually a casino, but it *is* a signature landmark in the little town of Avalon at the island's south end. Broadcasts from its ballroom brought the nation the big-band sounds of the 1930s and 40s.

No longer do you arrive by steamer. But you can still cross the 22 miles from the mainland by sea, bands still perform occasionally in the Avalon Ballroom, and your hotel—though somewhat modernized—may date back to the early 1900s.

Transportation. Getting to Catalina is part of the fun—by boat, plane, or helicopter. Flights from Los Angeles and Orange counties take about 15 minutes, from San Diego 30 minutes.

Ferries from Long Beach and San Pedro shuttle passengers to and from Avalon on almost an hourly basis (more limited service is available from Newport Beach and San Diego). Crossings take from 1½ to 2 hours. In the L.A. area, call Catalina Express, (310) 519-1212; or Catalina Cruises, (213) 253-9800.

Touring. Since Avalon is only 1 square mile, it's best explored on foot. You can board a shuttle or rent a bicycle or golf cart to view its attractive shops and restaurants, but cars are off-limits to visitors. To get the lay of the land, walk along Crescent Avenue to the Chamber of Commerce office at the 1909 Green Pleasure Pier (center for boat tours and rentals, fishing trips and gear, diving rentals) or the Island Company's Visitor's Information Center at 423 Crescent.

Daily guided tours of the Casino show off its well-preserved art deco movie palace and ballroom. A free museum (open daily from 10:30 A.M. to 4 P.M.) contains historical mementos.

Half-day bus tours transport visitors to the island's rugged interior for a look at scenery and wildlife, including a free-roaming herd of 400 bison descended from a few left after Zane Grey's 1925 filming of *The Vanishing American*. One tour stops at an Arabian horse ranch.

Glass-bottom boat trips explore the colorful undersea marine life and vegetation of the island's legendary clear waters. From May through September, several coastal and sunset dinner cruises are added. A nighttime Flying Fish Boat Tour lets you watch winged fish perform acrobatics 25 feet above the water.

Some 50 miles of trails and a handful of campgrounds welcome hikers. Contact the Los Angeles County Department of Parks and Recreation, 213 Catalina Street, (310) 510-0688, for free hiking permits and campsite information.

Lodging. Avalon offers more than 40 hotels, motels, and inns, ranging from moderate to luxurious. A 2-night stay is usually required on summer weekends.

For information, write to the Catalina Island Chamber of Commerce & Visitor's Bureau (Box 217, Avalon, CA 90704) or call the Island Company's Visitor's Information Center, (800) 428-2566.

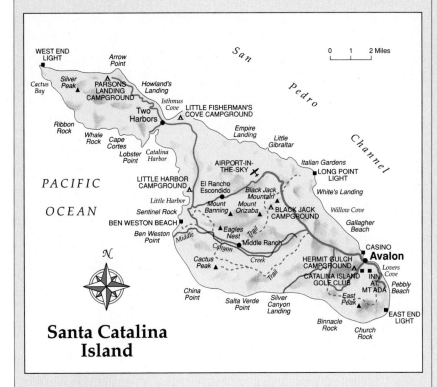

Santa Catalina Island

Once the pride of the British fleet, the elegant Queen Mary now rides serenely at anchor in the Long Beach Harbor. Explore the regal liner, both a hotel and a floating museum, on guided tour or roam on your own. Nearby lies the seaport's collection of shops and kiddie rides.

...Beaches

to sharks. The museum is open from noon to 5 P.M. Tuesday through Friday and from 10 A.M. to 5 P.M. weekends. There's a $5.50 charge to park in the beach lot.

Ports O' Call Village. An extensive shopping and dining complex faces the harbor's main channel at Berth 77 on Harbor Boulevard. Ever-changing and constantly expanding, the colorful center (open 11 A.M. to 9 P.M. daily) currently contains 75 shops and 15 restaurants on 15 acres.

Several companies offer hour-long narrated harbor cruises from the village. Most operate on weekends and summer weekdays. Whale-watching cruises take place from December through March. For details on cruises, see page 124 or contact the San Pedro Chamber of Commerce, (310) 832-7272.

Los Angeles Maritime Museum. On San Pedro's waterfront at Berth 84 (foot of 6th Street), this museum houses a wealth of nautical displays, from 19th-century steam sloops to World War II battleships. Included are an 18-foot model of the *Titanic* and a 21-foot scale model of the *Queen Mary*. The mu-

seum is open 10 A.M. to 5 P.M. Tuesday through Sunday except on major holidays; donations are encouraged.

General Phineas Banning Museum. The man who founded the town of Wilmington north of L.A.'s harbor built a 30-room colonial showcase in 1864 and landscaped it with acres of beautiful gardens. Now completely restored, the mansion at 401 E. M Street (2 blocks east of Avalon Boulevard off the Pacific Coast Highway) is a museum filled with 19th-century antiques. Hourly tours take place Tuesday through Thursday and weekends from 12:30 to 3:30 P.M. A donation is suggested.

Top Spots Underwater

A mask, fins, a snorkel, and a bathing suit are all you need to get an intimate look at colorful undersea life in summer. Add a wet suit for the rest of the year.

For greatest visibility and safety, you'll have the best luck in coves and other protected waters on calm days. Avoid heavy surf; it kicks up sand and clouds the water. Conditions change rapidly, so check with lifeguards on arrival.

The following are some of Southern California's best snorkeling spots, listed from north to south.

Malibu. Paradise Cove to the south of Point Dume has some good rocky spots close to shore just west of the pier. Unless it's calm, visibility is less than 10 feet. Nearby kelp beds are great for scuba, but inexperienced snorkelers should avoid them.

Palos Verdes Peninsula. Abalone Cove, a county beach below Wayfarers Chapel (page 36), has some of the finest snorkeling within easy reach of Los Angeles. Swim close to rocky outcroppings in the warm, shallow underwater reserve.

Santa Catalina Island. You'll find clear, sparkling water at Avalon's Lover's Cove, just southeast of the passenger boat dock. Children can swim close to shore in shallow water. You can rent equipment at island dive shops.

Newport Beach area. "Big" and "Little" Corona, just east of Newport Harbor's entrance jetty, shelter good snorkeling beneath their cliffs. Flat, sandy bottoms and rocky reefs grace both areas, and swim lines and kelp beds protect snorkelers from boat traffic. To get there from Pacific Coast Highway in Corona del Mar, turn southwest onto Marguerite Avenue. Drive right on Ocean Boulevard to Big Corona, then left to Little Corona.

Farther south at Reef Point, part of Crystal Cove State Park, you can expect to see perch, brilliant orange garibaldi, lobster, and octopus among the reefs. Access is from the parking lot just down from Crystal Cove.

Laguna Beach. Northwest of Laguna's main beach, three fine snorkeling areas are tucked under cliffs in a protected ecological reserve. Best parking for Rock Pile (also popular with surf-

ers), Picnic Beach, and Divers Cove is on Cliff Drive beside Heisler Park.

About a mile southeast of the main beach, Woods Cove offers a large rock and reef a short swim offshore. Enter from Diamond Street. Moss Point (good diving) can be reached from Moss Street, two blocks from Diamond. Laguna's surf conditions differ daily, so check first at the main guard tower.

La Jolla. La Jolla Cove, best-known part of an underwater park, has a great variety of undersea activity. On a calm day, strong swimmers can explore beyond the cove; check with the lifeguard first.

Casa Cove (also known as "The Children's Pool") lies just to the southwest. Though protected by a breakwater, it can still be rough, and only outside the breakwater does it have the underwater range of La Jolla Cove.

Patchy reefs and a sandy bottom (6 to 10 feet deep) make Marine Street Beach (foot of Marine Street) and Windansea Beach (foot of Bonair Street) good choices.

...Beaches

Long Beach

An important naval base, port, and manufacturing center, Long Beach has resurfaced as a resort and recreational center as well. Thanks to thoughtful planning, the state's fifth-largest city (second in L.A. County) is no longer the "Coney Island of the West." Indeed, the former Pike amusement area is to become a high-rise complex with hotels, shops, offices, and residences.

Today, downtown Long Beach features sleek high-rises, a sophisticated city transit system, and an attractive pedestrian promenade stretching from the shore to Long Beach Plaza mall between Pine Avenue and Long Beach Boulevard, 3rd and 6th streets. (Long Beach Children's Museum at the mall has imaginative play paraphernalia for tots to preteens; moderate admission fee.) Even the oil drilling rigs that dot the harbor have been cleverly concealed on palm-studded, man-made islands.

Getting around. The city is linked to Los Angeles, 22 miles to the north, by the Long Beach Freeway (Interstate 710) and connected to other coastal towns by Pacific Coast Highway (State 1) and the San Diego Freeway (Interstate 405).

The Metro Blue Line light-rail system, operated on the same route used by the famed Big Red Cars from 1902 to 1964, makes its 22-mile run to downtown L.A. in 50 minutes. Trains depart from the Willow Street Station (at Long Beach Boulevard) every 10 to 15 minutes during the day, every 20 minutes in the evening until midnight.

Make your first stop the Long Beach Visitor Center (3387 Long Beach Boulevard, at the corner of Wardlow). The center provides maps and information on attractions, events, accommodations, and dining choices.

Ocean Boulevard. Several attractions lie along Ocean Boulevard, which parallels the bayshore. The Long Beach Convention & Entertainment Center at Pine and Ocean is the location of the Terrace Theater (home to symphony, civic light opera, ballet, and opera companies), the more intimate Center The-

ater, and the Arena (for sporting events). Note the Arena's marine mural. Painted by acclaimed environmental marine life artist, Wyland, it's the world's largest—10 stories high and 1,180 feet in diameter.

The Children's Museum (445 Long Beach Boulevard) welcomes tots to a land of kid-sized fun. The center (small fee) is open Thursday through Saturday 11 A.M. to 4 P.M. and Sunday from noon. Children must be accompanied by an adult.

About 1½ miles east, the Long Beach Museum of Art (2300 E. Ocean Boulevard) is an avant-garde museum of modern culture housed in a charming early-1900s house. The museum and adjoining bookstore and gift shop are open Wednesday through Sunday from noon to 5 P.M. (small donation is suggested).

Farther southeast on Ocean, the Bluff Park Historic District encompasses several blocks of carefully preserved residences built early this century.

At the south end of Ocean in Alamitos Bay is Naples, a tiny group of islands threaded by canals and linked by walkways. Best way to get a look at the delightful maze of homes is from the water. Gondola Getaway at 5437 E. Ocean Boulevard, (310) 433-9595, offers hour-long cruises departing Alamitos Bay from sunrise to midnight. You can also rent kayaks and small boats at Alamitos Bay.

Waterfront. Parks, marinas, tourist-oriented shopping complexes, and hotels line the harborside. Harbor cruises and Catalina trips (see page 37) are offered from several locations.

Shoreline Park, at the foot of Pine Avenue, is a 100-acre aquatic playground with fishing platforms, picnic sites, and an RV park. Next door, Shoreline Village is fashioned after an early 1900s seaside hamlet. Specialty shops and restaurants cover 7 acres along the water. A ride on one of the hand-carved Looff carousel animals (vintage 1906) is sufficient reason to make the trip.

Every April, Shoreline Drive becomes a raceway during the Toyota Grand Prix. This nerve-jingling, ear-popping event attracts some 200,000 visitors from all over the world.

Queen Mary. Across Queensway Bay at Pier J looms the regal *Queen Mary*, a retired Cunard liner that sailed under the British flag from 1939 to 1967. Long Beach's most famous resident, the 1,000-foot-long liner, now a 365-room hotel and floating museum, is open daily for tours, dining, and shopping. There is a small boarding fee, which can be redeemed later for tours, rides, and food. Pier parking is $5 for cars, $7 for larger vehicles.

To explore the ship, join a guided tour (small fee) or amble around on your own with a self-guiding brochure that covers the bridge, engine room, officers' quarters, and upper decks.

Howard Hughes' gigantic wooden "flying boat", the *Spruce Goose*, was housed inside the huge aluminum dome near the ship until its 1993 departure to Oregon. The dome is now a convention site. Alongside lies the Queen's Playground, with kiddie-sized rides, shops, and other attractions.

To reach the site, exit Interstate 710 at Harbor Scenic Drive and follow the signs; or cross the channel on Queensway Bridge from Shoreline Drive.

Spanish ranchos. There's no charge to visit two charming remnants of former cattle-ranching days, both owned by the city.

Rancho Los Cerritos (4600 Virginia Road) once served as headquarters for a 27,000-acre cattle ranch. Built in 1844 and remodeled in 1930, the two-story house is open Wednesday through Sunday from 1 to 5 P.M. (weekend guided tours on the hour from 1 to 4 P.M.). From Interstate 405, exit north on Long Beach Boulevard; turn left at San Antonio Drive, then right onto Virginia.

Rancho Los Alamitos (6400 Bixby Hill Road) is one of the area's finest restored adobes. The 1806 adobe and 4-acre garden were part of a working cattle ranch until 1953. Once owned by Jose Figueroa, an early California governor, the adobe is filled with original furnishings.

One-hour guided tours of the house and barns are offered Wednesday through Sunday from 1 to 5 P.M.; you walk through the gardens on your own. From Interstate 405, take Palo Verde Avenue south to the rancho gate.

"Only in L.A." might be an appropriate comment after visiting some of the intriguing and lesser-known museums around the area. From the world's oldest rock to laser art. Here's a small sampling of lively collections.

American Heritage Park, 1918 N. Rosemead Boulevard, El Monte; (818) 442-1776. Tanks, trucks, jeeps, and an assortment of large artillery make this private military museum look like the staging ground for an invasion. Open noon to 4:30 P.M. weekends, weekdays by appointment. Fee: $2 adults, $1 ages 10 to 16, and 50 cents ages 5 to 10.

Angels Attic, 516 Colorado Avenue, Santa Monica; (310) 394-8331. Antique dolls and dollhouses, vintage toy soldiers, model trains, and other century-old toys crowd the rooms of a lovingly restored Victorian. Open 12:30 to 4:30 p.m. Thursday through Sunday. Admission: $4 adults, $3 seniors, $2 children 12 and under.

Barnsdall Art Park, 4804 Hollywood Boulevard, Hollywood; (213) 485-4581. A Frank Lloyd Wright–designed house, L.A.'s Municipal Art Gallery, and a junior art center crown Olive Hill at the eastern end of the boulevard. The gallery is open to visitors from 12:30 to 5 P.M. daily except Monday. Admission: $1 ages 14 and above. For recorded information on Hollyhock House guided tours, call (213) 662-7272. Admission: $1.50 ages 12 and up.

Cabrillo Marine Museum, 3720 Stephen White Drive, San Pedro; (310) 548-7562. Southern California's largest display of marine life includes aquariums, a tidepool, and a collection of whale bones you can touch. Open noon to 5 P.M. Tuesday through Friday, 10 A.M. to 5 P.M. weekends. Free admission.

California Museum of Photography, 3824 Main Street, Riverside; (714) 787-4787. Here you'll see the state's grandest display of photographic masterpieces. A history of photo technology includes three-dimensional stereographs. Open 10 A.M. to 5 P.M Tuesday through Saturday (to 9 P.M. Wednesday), noon to 5 P.M. Sunday. Admission: $2 adults, $1 seniors, free for children under 12.

Frederick's of Hollywood Museum, 6608 Hollywood Boulevard, Hollywood; (213) 466-5151. This homage to intimate apparel includes garments worn by celebrities for films and videos, such as Lana Turner's black slip from *The Merry Widow* and some of Madonna's concert attire. Open 10 A.M. to 8 P.M. Monday through Thursday, 10 A.M. to 9 P.M. Friday, 10 A.M. to 6 P.M. Saturday, and noon to 5 P.M. Sunday. Free admission.

Heritage Square, 3800 Homer Street, Los Angeles, (Avenue 43 exit off Interstate 110); (818) 449-0193. A village of eight eclectic structures built between 1865 and 1914 showcases the area's early architecture. Among the vintage buildings are Victorian houses, a small church, and a railroad station. Open noon to 4 p.m. weekends. Admission: $4.50 adults, $3 seniors and ages 12 to 17, free under 12.

Kidspace, 390 S. El Molino Avenue, Pasadena; (818) 449-9143. A mechanical robot greets children at the door to this hands-on museum. Two- to 12-year-olds enjoy a variety of learning equipment, from face paints to fire engines. Open 2 to 5 P.M. Wednesday, 12:30 to 5 p.m. weekends. Admission: $5 ages 3 to 12, adults $4.

Long Beach Firefighters Museum, 1445 Peterson Avenue, Long Beach; (310) 597-0351. Actual pumping takes place from 10 A.M. to 3 P.M. the second Saturday of each month. But drop by any Wednesday to chat with firemen.

Notable items include a 1923 aerial-ladder truck and a 1922 Ahrens Fox pumper.

Merle Norman Classic Beauty Collection, 15180 Bledsoe Street, Sylmar; (818) 367-2251. Not makeup, but more than 200 classic and antique cars compose this award-winning collection; thirty are on display. A fourth-floor gallery displays musical instruments, including a Wurlitzer theater organ. Two-hour tours by appointment only; call for reservations.

Beit Hashoah-Museum of Tolerance, 9760 W. Pico Boulevard, West L.A.; (310) 553-9036. Inside a striking building the haunting story of Nazi persecution of Jews is told through films, documents, and personal memorabilia. The tolerance section also looks at civil rights. Open weekdays from 9:30 A.M., Sunday 11 A.M. to 4 P.M. Free admission.

Museum of Neon Art, 1000 Universal Drive, Universal City. This futuristic museum moved from downtown Los Angeles to Universal Studio's free CityWalk pedestrian-only village. Visitors get a colorful—and electrifying—look at artworks of bubbling gas and glass. Some two dozen vintage museum pieces also adorn nearby shop facades.

Raymond M. Alf Museum, Webb School, 1175 W. Baseline Road, Claremont; (714) 624-2798. Tracing life from the beginning of time, this paleontological museum displays fossilized plants, insects, and mammals. Oldest of the exhibits is a rock that dates back 3.8 billion years; among the most interesting is a footprint of a prehistoric man. Open 1 to 4 P.M. Monday through Thursday during the school year. Donations are encouraged.

Mountains & Valleys

Southern Californians really can ski and surf the same day—given favorable traffic. Ski season in the San Gabriel and San Bernardino mountains, a couple of hours north and east of L.A., often extends well into spring. While the runs may not appeal to experts, beginning and intermediate skiers flock to the slopes shortly after the first good snowfall (see page 126).

These recreationally rich mountain ranges also offer a wealth of summer activities: boating, camping, cycling, hiking, picnicking, parasailing, and waterskiing. Sightseers attend weekend arts festivals and explore village craft shops.

Mountain communities have accommodations for all tastes, from rustic to resort, and a variety of restaurants from fast food to continental cuisine. En route to the mountains, valley towns hold their own discoveries: gardens, historic landmarks, and some outstanding museums.

Pasadena

The San Gabriel Valley's grande dame, this attractive residential community at the base of the San Gabriel Mountains is best known for the colorful New Year's Day Tournament of Roses Parade and annual Rose Bowl football game. A revitalized Old Town shopping and dining area (roughly bounded by Arroyo Parkway, Pasadena Avenue, Union Street, and Green Street), fine museums, noted gardens, and a full calendar of performing arts are other reasons to visit.

You can pick up visitor guides and self-guided auto tour maps from the Pasadena Convention & Visitors Bureau (see page 30).

Gamble House. One-hour guided tours through one of the best works of renowned architects Charles and Henry Greene are offered Thursday through Sunday from noon to 3 P.M. Admission to the house, located at 4 Westmoreland Place, is $4 for adults, $3 for college students (children free).

Tournament House & Wrigley Gardens. A 4½-acre site at 391 S. Orange Grove Boulevard contains the ornate mansion once owned by chewing gum magnate William Wrigley, Jr. Free guided tours of the mansion, now headquarters for the Tournament of Roses Association, take place from 2 to 4 P.M. Wednesday, February through August. The formal rose gardens are open year-round except December 31 and January 1.

Pasadena Historical Society. Guided tours of the 18-room mansion at 470 W. Walnut offer glimpses of an earlier, more elegant lifestyle. Open from 1 to 4 P.M. on Tuesday, Thursday, and Sunday (closed in August), the museum includes historical displays and the Finnish Folk Art Museum. Admission is $4.

Norton Simon Museum of Art. The cornerless, tile-clad museum at 411 W. Colorado Boulevard baffles design critics, but most admire its classic setting. Its well-regarded collection of artwork spans the globe, from Indian and Southeast Asian sculpture to European old masters, American impressionist and modern paintings, and medieval tapestries. Galleries and gardens display sculpture. The museum is open Thursday through Sunday from noon to 6 P.M. Admission is $4 for adults, $1.50 for seniors and students.

Pacific Asia Museum. Appropriately housed in an old building that looks like the Chinese Imperial Palace, Southern California's only Asian arts museum is built around a peaceful courtyard with a koi-filled brook. Located at 46 N. Los Robles Avenue, the center is open Wednesday through Sunday from noon to 5 P.M., with guided tours on Sunday (modest admission charge).

Brookside Park. With the Rose Bowl in its center, this park in Arroyo Seco Canyon covers more than 500 acres. Here, too, are a four-pool aquatic center, municipal golf course, playgrounds, picnic areas, and hiking trails. On the second Sunday each month, the Rose Bowl hosts a gigantic swap meet and flea market; take Rosemont Avenue to the stadium entrance.

Around the San Gabriel Valley

Of the three large valleys around Los Angeles, the San Gabriel is certainly the most lush, in terms of greenery, and the most plush, in terms of wealth and architecture. It contains one of Southern California's finest museums, and a trio of impressive parks (one a race track) are worthy detours off Interstate 210 (Foothill Boulevard). The fourth in the chain of California missions is here as well—Mission San Gabriel Arcangel (see page 6).

Huntington Library, Art Collections, and Botanical Gardens. Don't miss a visit to this magnificent museum in San Marino. Pacific Electric tycoon H.E. Huntington willed his entire estate to the public, so there's no charge to visit, though $2 donations are encouraged.

The mansion contains one of the best collections of British and French 18th-century art in America, including Thomas Gainsborough's well-loved *Blue Boy* and Thomas Lawrence's *Pinkie*. An American art gallery displays paintings and furnishings from the 1730s to the 1930s.

The separate library boasts a rich assortment of British and American history and literature as well as many rare books and manuscripts, among them a Gutenberg Bible, Chaucer's *Canterbury Tales*, and Benjamin Franklin's hand-written autobiography.

Highlights of the 150 acres of gardens include desert plantings, a palm garden, Japanese-style oases, the region's first commercial avocado grove, and a Shakespearean-inspired retreat. A garden restaurant serves lunch from 1 to 4 P.M.

The museum is at 1151 Oxford Road north of Huntington Drive. Gates are open Tuesday through Sunday from 1

Cabins dot the wooded shores of Big Bear Lake in the San Bernardino Mountains,
about two hours by car from Los Angeles. This all-year resort is among a number of
cool, high-country retreats to the north and east of the L.A. basin.

...Mountains & Valleys

to 4:30 P.M.; tours are offered weekdays at 1 P.M. L.A. County residents need reservations to visit on Sunday; call (818) 405-2141.

Descanso Gardens. Once a private estate, this 165-acre garden in La Cañada Flintridge becomes a riot of color from October through March, when more than 100,000 camellias blossom. Peak blooming season for the multitude of old roses is May to early June, while the 4-acre All-American Rose Selection specimens blossom from May until December. Lilacs and orchids peak in April.

Descanso (1418 Descanso Boulevard) is open 9 A.M. to 4:30 P.M. daily except Christmas. There's a modest admission charge, and the gardens are free the third Tuesday of each month. You can take a guided tram tour ($1.50) from 1 to 3 P.M. Tuesday through Friday, 11 A.M. to 4 P.M. weekends. A teahouse in a serene Japanese garden operates Tuesday through Sunday from 11 A.M. to 4 P.M.

Los Angeles State and County Arboretum. Plantings from around the world are featured in this 127-acre arboretum (301 N. Baldwin Avenue, Arcadia).

Peacocks roam the grounds amid historic buildings that date from the time the property was Rancho Santa Anita. On a self-guided tour, you see a tropical jungle, demonstration home gardens, gardens using unthirsty plantings, and several greenhouses.

The arboretum is open daily from 9 A.M. to 5 P.M. except on Christmas. Guided walking tours are offered at 11 A.M. Wednesday. The modest admission charge is waived on the third Tuesday of each month. Guided tram tours ($1.50) take place weekdays from 12:15 to 3 P.M., weekends from 10:30 A.M. to 4 P.M.

Santa Anita Park. One of the country's most famous thoroughbred tracks lies near the arboretum (285 W. Huntington Drive, Arcadia). During racing season (October to November and late December to late April) fans throng to the 500-acre park. If you don't want to see a race, you can watch morning workouts (7:30 to 9:30 A.M.) and admire the well-landscaped grounds for free. There's a charge to park.

San Gabriel Mountains

The San Gabriels have been called L.A.'s mountain playground because they're easily accessible to hikers, riders, campers, picnickers, and skiers. In spring, scenic waterfalls are only a short stroll from canyon roads. The high-country wilderness areas can only be reached by trail.

The Angeles Crest Highway (State 2), access road to Mount Wilson Observatory, ascends the mid-range from La Cañada Flintridge (19 miles to the observatory). Open daily from 10 A.M. to 4 P.M. except on major holidays and in bad weather, the observatory offers views of the whole L.A. basin on the occasional clear day. There's a visitors' gallery for the 100-inch telescope (you can't actually look through the lens). To check on weather conditions, call (818) 449-4163.

State 39 from Azusa stretches up past San Gabriel Reservoir to Crystal Lake, and San Antonio Canyon Road curls up to Mount Baldy's ski slopes.

For area information and maps, write to Angeles National Forest Supervisor, 701 N. Santa Anita Avenue, Arcadia, CA 91006, or phone (818) 574-5200.

Pomona-Walnut Valley

The valley midway along the base of the San Gabriels and San Bernardinos is usually designated as Pomona-Walnut. Though smoggy and hot in summer, it's an area rich in culture, history, and entertainment.

Ontario's international airport is the region's gateway. You can pick up a guide to area attractions, including winery tastings, from the Greater Ontario Visitors & Convention Bureau at 421 N. Euclid, (714) 984-2450 (open weekdays). Ontario also offers samples of another agricultural product, olives. Stop in at the century-old Graber Olive House (315 E. 4th Street) for a walking tour of the processing plant; it's in full operation from October to December during the fall harvest, but you can visit anytime (open daily).

Pomona. Best known as the site of the huge Los Angeles County Fair every September, Pomona is also noted for horses and antiques. Some 400 antique dealers line a two-block mall downtown on E. Second Street between Garey Avenue and Gibbs Street.

At 2 P.M. on the first Sunday of the month (except in summer), the W. K. Kellogg Arabian Horse Center presents a 1-hour show with a flashy cast of 15 to 20 specially trained mounts. After the show, visitors can wander around the stables until 5 P.M. The modest ticket price includes a film on the ranch.

To reach the center (now part of California State Polytechnic University),

Ramona Pageant

Often called California's greatest outdoor spectacle, the dramatization of *Ramona* has been performed in a natural outdoor amphitheater outside Hemet every spring since 1923. More than 350 residents of this small town (southeast of Riverside) take part in the elaborate production of Helen Hunt Jackson's 1884 novel of early California Indian history.

Reservations are a must for the popular play, which is held on three successive weekends starting in late April. To get a ticket application form, send a stamped self-addressed envelope with your request to Ramona Pageant Association, 27400 Ramona Bowl Road, Hemet, California 92344. For information on dates, prices, and transportation, phone (714) 658-3111.

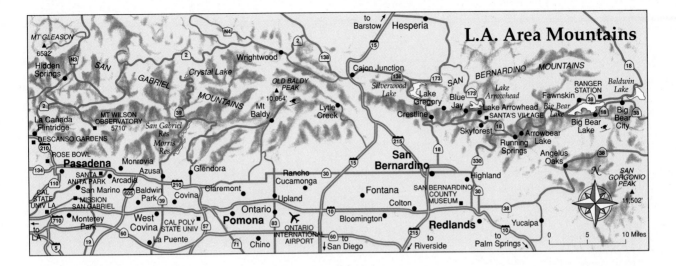

exit Kellogg Drive from Interstate 10, go about half a mile southwest and turn left on Citrus Lane, then turn right on Eucalyptus Lane. For more information, call (714) 869-2224.

Claremont. Home to such prestigious colleges as Claremont McKenna, Pomona, Scripps, Harvey Mudd, and Pitzer, the city of Claremont is also the setting for Rancho Santa Ana Botanic Gardens, an 85-acre collection of native plantings. The free garden (open daily except major holidays) is at its most colorful from February to June, when the poppies bloom. Enter from College Avenue north of Foothill Boulevard.

Chino. This city is devoted to flight. Head for the airport (7000 Merrill Avenue) to see the Planes of Fame Air Museum, a respected collection of vessels from 1896 through World War II. The museum (about $5 for adults, $2 for children 5 to 10) is open daily except Christmas. An annual air show is held the third weekend in May.

Riverside. It's ironic that the city that gave birth to California's navel orange industry is now often smothered by crop-damaging smog. To glimpse its more romantic past, stop by the Riverside Municipal Museum at 3720 Orange Street or tour the nicely restored Heritage House, a few blocks away at 8193 Magnolia Avenue.

The free museum is open 9 A.M. to 5 P.M. Tuesday through Friday and 1 to 5 P.M. on weekends. Free mansion tours

take place from noon to 2:30 P.M. Tuesday and Thursday, noon to 3:30 P.M. Sunday.

Nearby, the landmark Mission Inn (bounded by 6th, 7th, Main, and Orange streets) is being renovated.

Redlands. A wealth of beautifully restored Victorians can be seen on a drive-by tour. Purchase a guidebook from the Chamber of Commerce, 1 E. Redlands Boulevard.

Edwards Mansion, a Victorian at 2064 Orange Tree Lane (California Street exit off Interstate 10), is now a restaurant. Next door, the free San Bernardino County Museum (open 9 A.M. to 5 P.M. Tuesday through Saturday and Sunday afternoon) has a not-to-be-believed collection encompassing anthropology, archaeology, ornithology, history, and fine arts.

San Bernardino Mountains

Pine forests, hidden lakes, fabulous vistas, and crisp, cool air lure vacationers year-round to the San Bernardino range. Peaks here commonly top 10,000 feet, and Mount San Gorgonio reaches 11,502 feet. Yet this alpine land is only an hour's drive from San Bernardino via State 18 (also known as the Rim of the World Drive) or snaky State 330 (shortest route to Big Bear Lake). Many campgrounds lie along State 38, a longer back-door approach to Big Bear.

To get maps of the 660,000-acre San Bernardino National Forest's suggested

walking and driving tours, contact the U.S. Forest Service at 1824 Commercenter Circle, San Bernardino, CA 92408-3430; (714) 383-5588. Maps cost $2 each.

Lake Arrowhead. This man-made lake in its picturesque resort setting offers a variety of water sports and beautiful scenery. Stop at the marina to find out about waterskiing instruction, lake cruises, boat rentals, and swimming and fishing areas. In the village, some 60 shops and restaurants attract browsers. Upscale resorts, motels, cabins, and campgrounds dot the shoreline.

On your way up to the lake, short side roads lead past lookouts and to smaller resorts such as Strawberry Peak, Crestline, Lake Gregory (an old Mormon settlement), and Blue Jay (outdoor ice rink). Children love the shops, rides, and petting zoo at Santa's Village in Skyforest, open daily from 10 A.M. to 5 P.M. in summer and from mid-November through December. Admission is $8.50.

Big Bear Lake. One of the Southland's largest all-year recreation spots, Big Bear is popular with summer boaters, jetskiers, parasailers, anglers, horseback riders, hikers, and campers. A Bavarian-style festival in October draws large crowds, and slippers and sliders crowd the three ski resorts in winter. Small souvenir stores jostle up against craft shops, restaurants, inns, and motels along the lake's southern shore.

Orange County

*O*nce little more than a sleepy agricultural region scented by orange blossoms, Orange County was transformed by the magic wand of Walt Disney in the 1950s into the state's largest tourist mecca. Today it resembles a spread-out, continuous world's fair with enough diversions to earn the nickname Vacationland USA.

The link along the Pacific between Los Angeles and San Diego counties, Orange County reaches inland into the wilderness of the Santa Ana Mountains. Its towns, one after another, are part of the urban continuum of the Los Angeles metropolitan area, with here and there only a hint of the county's rural past.

Lure of the land

In addition to renowned Disneyland, a sampling of Orange County's man-made attractions includes ever-expanding Knott's Berry Farm, celebrity-studded Movieland Wax Museum, the jousting hall of Medieval Times, and Wild Rivers' refreshing plunges.

Thanks to the prestigious homes and marinas along its 42 miles of shoreline, the county's Pacific rim is dubbed Gold Coast. It extends from north of Huntington Beach (self-proclaimed surfing capital of the world) through the seaside communities of Newport Beach, Balboa, Corona del Mar, Laguna Beach, and Dana Point south to San Clemente.

Inland towns lie on land that once nourished bean fields and orchards.

For an upside-down and backward view of the world, take a heart-stopping ride on Montezooma's Revenge at Knott's Berry Farm in Buena Park. This family-oriented theme park started as a roadside fruit stand.

The University of California at Irvine and Saddleback Valley's foothill parks and recreational retreats sprawl over part of what was once a vast Spanish rancho. Remnants of mission days remain at San Juan Capistrano.

Planning a trip

More than 35 million people a year vacation in Orange County. The climate helps: with an annual rainfall of only 15 inches and an average temperature of 70°, this is a year-round playground. When summer days are hot and smoggy in the interior, residents head for the beach.

Getting there. Alaska, America West, American, Continental, Delta, Midway, Northwest, TWA, United, and a number of commuter airlines fly directly into John Wayne/Orange County Airport in Santa Ana. Rental cars, taxis, and limousines are available at the airport.

Two scheduled ground shuttles, Airport Coach and Airport Cruiser, and a number of on-call airport vans make nearby Los Angeles, Long Beach, and Ontario airports satisfactory alternates. One-way fares from Los Angeles (35 miles from Anaheim) run around $12.

Interstates 5 (Santa Ana Freeway) and 405 (San Diego Freeway) are the major ties to Los Angeles. Easiest route from the east is Interstate 10 (San Bernardino Freeway) to State 91 (Riverside Freeway). State 1 (Pacific Coast Highway) skirts the ocean.

Amtrak trains between Los Angeles and San Diego stop at Fullerton, Anaheim Stadium, Santa Ana, San Juan Capistrano, and San Clemente. Trains make 8 daily trips in each direction.

Greyhound buses connect Orange County with other parts of the country. The Southern California Rapid Transit District also offers bus service from its main Los Angeles terminal (6th and Los Angeles streets) to Disneyland, Knott's, and Movieland Wax Museum.

Getting around. The area has one of the best county-wide transit systems in Southern California. Bus maps and schedules are widely distributed; check with your hotel, or pick one up at the visitors bureau in the Convention Center (on Katella Avenue across from Disneyland).

Contacts

These agencies offer information on attractions and accommodations. See additional contacts throughout this chapter.

Anaheim Area Visitor & Convention Bureau
P.O. Box 4270
Anaheim, CA 92803
(714) 999-8999

Buena Park Convention & Visitors Office
6280 Manchester Blvd., Suite 103
Buena Park, CA 90621
(714) 994-1511

Newport Beach Conference & Visitors Bureau
366 San Miguel, Suite 200
Newport Beach, CA 92660
(800) 942-6278

Laguna Beach Chamber of Commerce
357 Glenneyre (P.O. Box 396)
Laguna Beach, CA 92652
(714) 494-1018

Many hotels and motels offer free shuttle service to Disneyland, Knott's, and other major attractions and shopping areas. For a moderate fee, you can ride Pacific Coast Sightseeing buses to major destinations around Orange County and Los Angeles. Buses stop at most large hotels and motels; check at the front desk or phone (714) 978-8855.

Lodging. The largest clusters of motels and hotels are around Disneyland in Anaheim and in Buena Park, home to Knott's. Business travelers find chain hotels around the airport and at Newport Center in Newport Beach.

For lodging suggestions around Disneyland or elsewhere in the county, contact the Anaheim Area Visitor & Convention Bureau (see address on page 47) or the Southern California Hotel Reservation Center, (800) 527-9997 in California, (800) 537-7666 outside the state.

Campers and RV owners have a choice of several private parks in Anaheim and the surrounding area. State and county beaches offer limited camping (see page 121).

Entertainment. The three-theater complex at the striking Orange County Performing Arts Center (600 Town Center Drive, Costa Mesa) presents musical theater, symphony, opera, and dance. Across the way, the intimate South Coast Repertory Theatre hosts classic and contemporary productions. For information on these and other events, contact the Anaheim Area Visitor & Convention Bureau (page 47).

Activities. No matter the sport, it's available in Orange County, from tennis, jogging, and cycling to wind surfing, sailing, and snorkeling. Golfers will need reservations for busy public courses (see page 123). Hikers and horseback riders head for mountain canyons or coastal trails. Surfers find the best wave action at Huntington Beach and Newport Beach.

Spectator sports abound. The California Angels baseball team and Los Angeles Rams football team share the 70,000-seat Anaheim Stadium (2 miles east of Disneyland at Katella Avenue and State College Boulevard). Los Alamitos Race Course (4961 Katella Av-

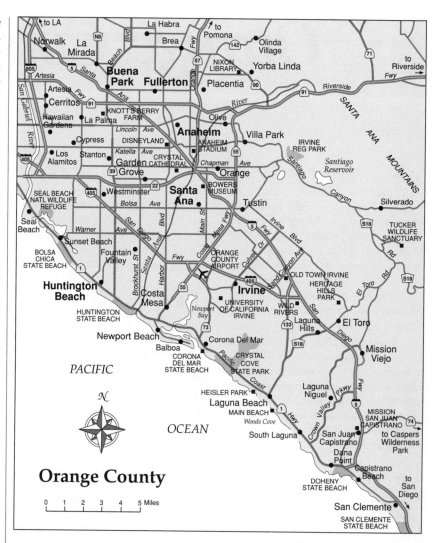

Orange County

0 1 2 3 4 5 Miles

enue) hosts year-round horse racing Tuesday through Saturday at 7:30 P.M.

Shopping. The range and variety of chic shopping in Orange County makes it an attraction in itself. Upscale malls and trendy boutiques, galleries, and specialty stores are scattered all around the region.

Laguna Beach may be better known for its art galleries, but it boasts more goldsmiths and jewelers per square foot than anywhere else in the country. In the market for antiques? San Juan Capistrano has numerous antique shops; they look right at home in the historic setting. Newport Beach's most posh outlets are tucked away in converted cannery buildings on the Balboa Peninsula.

For the Southland's busiest and largest shopping showplace, head for ele-

gant South Coast Plaza in Costa Mesa (Bristol Street exit off Interstate 405). When you arrive, pick up a map of the acres of department stores, specialty shops, and restaurants in the mall's Carousel, Jewel, and Crystal Court sections. (The Crystal Court is in a separate complex across Bear Street.)

Across Sunflower Street to the north, South Coast Plaza Village adds even more shopping and dining choices, including Antonello Ristorante, one of Orange County's finest.

Glamorous Fashion Island (Newport Center Drive off Pacific Coast Highway) contains all of the large upscale emporiums like Neiman-Marcus, Bullock's Wilshire, and Robinson's. Unique boutiques are found at the center's Atrium Court area. Lunch from food stalls around the lower-level Farmers Market is a treat.

World of Fun

The possibilities for entertainment in Orange County are endless. You might raft along a waterfall, cheer for a jousting knight, eat a slice of boysenberry pie while strolling the streets of a ghost town, watch a lagoonside water and light show, climb aboard a stomach-jerking roller coaster, or join Dorothy and her friends on the "yellow brick road."

And that doesn't even include Disneyland, the best-known park of all; to help plan a trip to the Magic Kingdom, see page 50.

Where to look. Three major attractions are clustered around Buena Park, 20 miles southeast of downtown Los Angeles and just a tempting 5 miles from Disneyland in Anaheim. Wild Rivers Waterpark is in Laguna Hills, about 15 minutes southeast by freeway. Other parks, amusement centers, special-interest museums, and theaters are sprinkled around Orange County.

You'll never see them all in one day, or even several. Tour companies offer limited-time visits to major attractions. If you prefer a less hurried pace, go on your own, with a good street map to help you get around.

Disneyland Hotel. Right across the street from Disneyland, this hotel is almost a destination in itself. It's connected to the park by fast monorail from Tomorrowland.

The 60-acre resort complex has 11 theme restaurants and lounges and 35 specialty shops. Activity revolves around the large marina, with its lush tropical gardens and waterfalls, koi ponds, and palm-studded beach.

Twice nightly, a pulsating Dancing Waters and Lights Fantastic Show is presented (no charge). In summer, a free Polynesian show is added. The hotel is also a good spot from which to get a free look at Disneyland's nightly fireworks.

You have to be a guest to swim in one of three pools or to get a preferred court at nearby Tennisland, but the other attractions are open to the public.

Knott's Berry Farm

Walter and Cordelia Knott came to Orange County to start a berry farm in 1920. When the Depression hit, Mrs. Knott began selling her homemade berry preserves at a fruit stand along the highway. Later she added chicken dinners. From those humble beginnings came the 150 acres of rides and attractions that make Knott's the country's third most popular theme park (after Disneyland and Florida's Disney World).

To reach Knott's (8039 Beach Boulevard, Buena Park), exit Interstate 5 at Beach and drive south about 2 miles. Pacific Coast Sightseeing Knott's Express bus connects the park with Disneyland and major hotels.

One entrance fee includes unlimited use of all rides and attractions ($26 adults, $18 seniors, $16 children under 54 inches). Winter hours are 10 A.M. to 6 P.M. weekdays, later on weekends; in summer, the park stays open to midnight Sunday through Friday, to 1 A.M. Saturday. Strollers and wheelchairs are available for use. For more information, call (714) 827-1776.

What you see. Five major theme areas offer adventure from Wild West to white water. More than 160 rides, shows, and attractions are concentrated on the west side of Buena Park's Beach Boulevard. Some spill across the street, like the full-scale reproduction of Independence Hall.

Everything is designed for family enjoyment, from the vaudeville show in the Calico Saloon (where the strongest drinks are sarsaparilla and boysenberry punch) to the Good Time Theatre, a 2,150-seat showcase for daytime ice shows and evening musical entertainment (some headliner concerts cost extra).

Dinner lines can be long at the popular chicken and steak restaurants, located near the gift shops and boutiques in the park's California Marketplace section along Beach Boulevard. It's a good idea to put your name in early.

Theme areas. When Walter Knott decided to provide guests with amusement while they waited for dinner, a Western-style Ghost Town was born. Start here for a sense of what Knott's was like in the early days. Visitors can ride shotgun on the stagecoach, pan for gold, tour a mine, or drop down a water flume. Passengers aboard the smoke-belching Denver & Rio Grande narrow gauge will be suitably affrighted by bandits.

Camp Snoopy, a more recent addition, is designed especially for children 3 to 7. Snoopy and other members of the "Peanuts" gang greet young guests. Thirty tot-sized attractions include a petting zoo, balloon ride, roller coaster, and pony-driven carousel; adults aren't even allowed on most of the rides. There's even a restaurant with scaled-down burgers.

Mexican food stalls and artisans and an authentic Denzel carousel enliven Fiesta Village, also home to a few stomach-gripping rides, like Montezooma's Revenge (360° loop coming and going), Tampico Tumbler, and Slingshot. But most of the park's thrill rides (20-story Parachute Sky Jump, XK-1 aircraft, Boomerang roller coaster, and others) lie in the Roaring 20s section. Here, too, are bumper cars, soap box derbies, game arcades, a dolphin and sea lion show, and the Kingdom of Dinosaurs ride through a landscape inhabited by huge animated creatures.

The Wild Water Wilderness area features Bigfoot Rapids, a white-water rafting experience (be prepared to get wet). Find out about Bigfoot from the on-duty naturalist or watch a show in the Wilderness Dance Hall.

Movieland Wax Museum

Just north of Knott's, at 7711 Beach Boulevard, is the biggest gathering of celebrities in the world. Featured at Movieland are more than 250 wax likenesses of film and television stars. You'll find more glitter and glamour here than in Hollywood and encounter more stars than on the busiest day at

Continued on page 52

More than 12 million visitors a year pour through the gates of Disneyland, making it the nation's most popular amusement park. To keep visitors coming back, the 76-acre Anaheim park is constantly adding more attractions, and future plans call for creation of another entire theme park nearby.

Children and adults alike find themselves enchanted by the Magic Kingdom's illusion and entertainment. The clean and well-landscaped park offers thrill and fantasy rides, musical performances, animated peeks at the past and the future, colorful parades, theme restaurants, shops, a sky full of fireworks at night—and, of course, Mickey Mouse.

Planning a visit. Disneyland is about an hour's drive east of downtown Los Angeles via Interstate 5. Freeway signs indicate the exit to the park (1313 Harbor Boulevard, Anaheim). Trams take visitors from parking lot to entrance. Shuttle services operate from many hotels.

Don't expect to whiz through all of Disneyland in a day. Eight themed areas offer hundreds of rides, arcades, and other adventures. First-timers might consider a 2½-hour tour of major attractions, about $10 over the regular admission. Circle rides on the Disneyland Railroad (at the entrance) or Tomorrowland's monorail also give good overviews.

The park is open 10 A.M. to 6 P.M. weekdays and 9 A.M. to midnight on weekends, with extended hours for summer and some holidays.

Lines for rides are shortest when the park first opens, a half-hour before it closes, and during parades. Many families get there early, leave around lunchtime, and return in the early evening. (Have your hand and parking pass stamped for re-entry.)

Know what your "must-see" attractions are before you arrive, then get right in line for the most popular ones—like Splash Mountain, Captain EO, Star Tours, Space Mountain, and Pirates of the Caribbean. Also note show and parade times.

Wheelchairs and strollers are available, and a "baby station" off Main Street offers a place—and supplies—to feed, change, and rock the youngest visitors. Kennels at the main gate accommodate pets for a small fee.

For additional information, call (714) 999-4565, or contact the Anaheim Area Visitor & Convention Bureau .

Cost. An Unlimited Passport admission covers all rides and attractions, excluding arcades, shops, and restaurants. One-day passports are $28.75 for adults, $23 for children 3 to 11. Two- and three-day passports reduce per-day rates slightly. Parking is $5.

Attractions. Walkways lead into the themed areas from a central plaza at the end of Main Street 1890, your point of entry.

Adventureland offers a jungle boat ride, the treehouse of the Swiss Family Robinson, and the "enchanted" Tiki Room. New Orleans Square has a Mississippi steamwheeler, the Pirates of the Caribbean ride, and the Haunted Mansion.

In Frontierland, you can career down Thunder Mountain on a runaway train or raft to Tom Sawyer's island. Critter Country is home to Splash Mountain flume ride and Country Bear Playhouse.

Fantasyland begins when you cross the moat of Sleeping Beauty's Castle. Tomorrowland keeps pace with science with Space Mountain, Star Tours, and Captain EO.

The park's first new "land" is Toontown. Children can visit the homes of Mickey, Minnie, Goofy, and Chip 'n' Dale, take zany rides, and interact with the cartoon characters. A second theme park with a WESTCOT Center is in the planning stage.

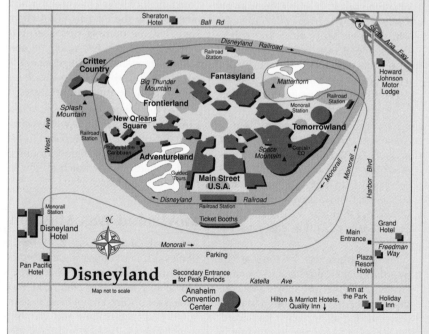

Going nose to nose with Pinocchio, one of Disneyland's popular resident characters, requires a boost from mom. Orange County's Magic Kingdom is the nation's most popular theme park.

...World of Fun

any studio lot. One caution: The sets seem so realistic that you may be tempted to touch the figures; if you do, you trigger an alarm.

Movieland is open daily 9 A.M. to 8 P.M. May through Labor Day, 9 A.M. to 7 P.M. the rest of the year. Tickets are $12.95 for adults, $10.55 seniors, $6.95 for children 4 to 11.

Movieland also operates Ripley's Believe It or Not collection of oddities at 7850 Beach Boulevard (separate admission).

Medieval Times

Across the street from Movieland, at 7662 Beach Boulevard in Buena Park, Medieval Times offers 11th-century entertainment in a castlelike setting. Guests watch tournament games, jousting matches, and sword fights while they feast in Middle Age fashion—with their fingers.

Performances take place nightly, with matinees on Sunday. Free tours are offered 9 A.M. to 3 P.M. except Sunday. Dinner prices (includes beverages and show) are $28 to $34 adults, $24 to $33 seniors, and $19 to $22 children. For required reservations, call (714) 521-4740 or, toll-free, (800) 899-6600.

Wild Rivers Waterpark

Forty wet rides, slides, and attractions make Wild Rivers a refreshing summer stop. Float around on an inner tube, go white-water rafting, peer through a waterfall, or just work on your tan. Facilities include changing rooms, showers, and lockers; gift shops can provide suntan lotion, towels, and even swimsuits.

Wild Rivers is just west of the junction of Interstates 5 and 405 in Laguna Hills (8800 Irvine Center Drive); head south from Interstate 405 at the Irvine Center Drive exit, or take Lake Forest Drive west from Interstate 5 and then turn right onto Irvine Center. The park is open mid-May through September; call (714) 768-WILD for times. Entrance is $15.95 ages 10 and over, $12.95 children 3 to 9, $8.95 over 55 or anyone after 4 P.M. in summer.

Specialty sightseeing

Small and specialized museums and an "only in California" glass cathedral offer new dimensions when you need a break from thrill rides.

Children's Museum. Kids are welcome to touch the exhibits at this learning center a few miles north of Disneyland (301 S. Euclid Street, La Habra). Set in and around an old railroad depot, the museum has model trains, a theater, a science gallery, and a nature walk (small admission). The museum is open 10 A.M. to 4 P.M. Monday through Saturday (closed major holidays).

Richard Nixon Library & Birthplace. Opened in 1990, this 9-acre site northeast of Anaheim in Yorba Linda includes the house where the former president was born, a 52,000-square-foot library highlighting historical events of his life, and a garden. Attractions are open from 8:30 A.M. to 5 P.M. daily ($3.95 adults, $2 seniors, free 11 and under).

The library is at 18001 Yorba Linda Boulevard; from State 57, exit east at Yorba Linda Boulevard.

Museum of World Wars and Military History. Close to Knott's (7884 E. La Palma Avenue, Buena Park), this intriguing collection belies its rather dull name. Military and historical relics from 1776 to 1945 create realistic battle settings; more than 200 uniformed figures stand among them.

The museum (modest admission) is open Monday through Saturday from 10 A.M. to 6 P.M., Sunday from noon to 6 P.M. (closed major holidays).

Hobby City Doll and Toy Museum. Antique dolls, teddy bears, and toy soldiers reside at this museum (1238 S. Beach Boulevard, Anaheim). More than 3,000 dolls and toys are housed in a half-scale model of the White House. The museum is open from 10 A.M. to 6 P.M. except on major holidays.

Crystal Cathedral. The enormous glass and steel edifice at Chapman and Lewis streets in Garden Grove is the Crystal Cathedral, home of television evange-

list Robert Schuller's Reformed Church in America. Hour-long tours include a look at one of the world's largest pipe organs (Monday through Saturday from 9 A.M. to 3:30 P.M., Sunday from 1:30 to 3:30 P.M.). Donations are encouraged.

Charles W. Bowers Museum. Newly expanded, Santa Ana's fine cultural arts museum at 2002 N. Main Street specializes in art from the Americas and Pacific Rim countries. A fascinating potpourri of African artifacts is also on display. Galleries are devoted to Southwest and Northwest Indian art.

The recently renovated museum is open Tuesday through Saturday, 10 A.M. to 5 P.M., and Sunday afternoon; donations are appreciated. Take the Main Street exit off Interstate 5.

Countryside retreats

In the countryside, several locations provide a pleasant contrast to the acres of homes found elsewhere.

Caspers Wilderness Park. A bit of old California, this 5,500-acre county park lies 7 miles inland from San Juan Capistrano via State 74 (Ortega Highway). You can picnic free beside the highway; there's a fee for picnicking in meadows within the park and for overnight camping. A hiker's and horseback rider's domain, the park has almost no facilities; bring your own water.

Tucker Wildlife Sanctuary. In the Santa Ana Mountains just past the charming old town of Modjeska, this beautiful oasis of trees, flowers, foliage, and wildlife is operated by California State University at Fullerton. The sanctuary is open from 9 A.M. to 4 P.M. daily, except Monday (small donation). To reach it from Interstate 5, take El Toro Road inland.

Irvine Regional Park. Created in 1897, this oasis of native sycamore trees and 500-year-old oaks is a good place to picnic, hike, and ride ponies or paddleboats. A small zoo is a good introduction to native Southwest creatures. To get to the park, take Chapman Avenue east from Interstate 55 in Orange.

Orange Coast

Orange County's coast presents two faces—wide, flat stretches of sand from the town of Seal Beach south to the Balboa Peninsula and more picturesque bluff-backed coves southward from Corona del Mar to San Clemente. Watch your driving all along this coast. Cars park wherever there's an inch of space, and it's not uncommon to see a horizontal surfboard with legs attached dashing across the highway.

Seal Beach & south

Seal Beach residents work hard to keep a low profile for their pleasant little town, not boasting about the fishing pier at the end of Main Street and the nice stretch of swimming and surfing beach that fronts the quiet community. Most visitors pass it by, only noticing the oil pumps, refineries, and storage tanks that line the inland side of State 1 as far south as Huntington Beach.

Sunset Beach. Boaters head for neighboring Sunset Beach's marina, aquatic park, and launching and trailer-parking facilities. The broad sandy stretches at Sunset and adjoining Surfside beaches are popular with residents.

Bolsa Chica State Beach. This day-use beach (fire rings, rest rooms, and lifeguards) to the south is 6 miles long, but only its northern end, a 3-mile strip of sand between the ocean and highway, is lined with sun-lovers. Steep cliffs between the road and beach make access difficult at the southern end. Some trails and a stairway near 16th Street penetrate the bluffs, and a cycling path and walkway extends its length. Clamming, diving, and fishing are popular here; grunion runs occur between March and August.

On the landward side of the highway across from the beach, Bolsa Chica Ecological Reserve's salt marshes provide a landing site for birds on the Pacific Flyway. A mile-long loop trail winds through part of the reserve's 530 acres.

Huntington Beach

Named Pacific City when it was first settled in 1902, this community was meant to rival Atlantic City. But unlike its East Coast counterpart, Huntington Beach rose to fame on the strength of wave action. The annual OP Surfing Championships take place Labor Day weekend, but you can watch surfers "hang ten" any day.

Most of the early-morning and late-day action takes place around the main pier at the foot of Main Street, which had to be rebuilt due to storm damage. The state beach that stretches 2 miles south of the pier is spectacular on summer nights when its 500 fire rings are ablaze with bonfires.

The renovated pier area at Huntington Street and Pacific Coast Highway includes a hotel, shops, and cafes. They were the beginnings of an ambitious redevelopment program—new and refurbished shopping centers, condominium complexes, and other lodging—scheduled to keep the city under construction for several years.

Huntington Harbor, west of downtown, consists of eight man-made islands top-heavy with luxury homes, waterside shops, and restaurants among a maze of marinas. A tour boat from Peter's Landing complex gives a look at the project.

Newport Beach–Balboa

In 1902, an ad for Newport Beach–Balboa claimed: "The best fishing on the Pacific coast, surf that's foamy and playful, a bay studded with islands around which you may row, fish, yacht, picnic, and stroll." It's still true if you know where to look.

Peeks at the Past

The bean fields, orange groves, and cattle ranches that once covered so much of Orange County's inland area have almost vanished. A few faint traces of the past have been preserved in two historic parks.

Old Town Irvine. Little is left of the famous Irvine Ranch that once sprawled over one-fifth of Orange County. The planned community of Irvine already occupies more than half its 108,000 acres. But you can get a look at some of the original ranch buildings when you pay a visit to Old Town Irvine, a renovation of the vintage town that once was the ranch's shipping center.

Onetime warehouses, granaries, and other outbuildings now house shops, galleries, offices, a restaurant, and a hotel. (Half of La Quinta Inn's guest rooms were converted from lima bean silos.) Other businesses occupy a former blacksmith shop, foreman's house, and general store.

Free walking tours take place from 10 A.M. to noon on the first Saturday of the month, but you can visit anytime. From Interstate 5, take Sand Canyon Avenue west, turn left at Burt Road, then turn right into the parking lot.

Heritage Hills Park. This peaceful preserve in the Laguna Hills area is the county's first historic park. To see an original adobe and three restored turn-of-the-century structures, exit Interstate 5 on Lake Forest Drive; head east for 2 miles, and turn north on Serrano Road.

The park is open daily from 8 A.M. to 5 P.M.; house tours take place at 11 A.M., 2 and 3 P.M. Just down the road is Serrano Creek Park, a pleasant place for a picnic or a jog.

To Southland surfers, the day is measured out in waves to ride into shore. These shimboarders catch the crest of a frothy breaker at Laguna.

...Orange Coast

The Balboa Peninsula, with its two piers, and Balboa Island offer the most visitor attractions, set against a backdrop of yacht clubs and ultra-expensive homes. Upper Newport Bay lures campers, bird-watchers, and water-lovers.

Newport Center, to the south, is the area's vast professional and financial complex, site of sleek hotels and Fashion Island (see page 48). Close by lies Newport Harbor Art Museum (850 San Clemente Drive), open Tuesday through Sunday; patio lunch is offered on weekdays.

To reach the Newport Beach–Balboa area, take State 1 (Pacific Coast Highway), State 55, or Jamboree Road from Interstate 405. Newport Beach Conference and Visitors Bureau, at the north end of Balboa Peninsula (address on page 47), has maps and brochures.

Balboa Peninsula. Access to this long, skinny sandspit is via Newport Boulevard. A good first stop is the free Newport Harbor Nautical Museum, 1714 W. Balboa Boulevard, where exhibits highlight the area's boating background and fishing history; hours are 10 A.M. to 3 P.M. Wednesday through Sunday.

If you turn southeast on Via Lido at the north end of the peninsula, crossing over a humpbacked bridge leads to Lido Isle, a posh residential area dredged up from the harbor's bottom. Boats tie up right at the back doors of these waterfront homes. Investigate the charming little labyrinth of shops and restaurants along the street before you reach the bridge.

Farther south along Newport Boulevard, browse around Cannery Village, an intriguing conglomeration of boutiques, galleries, restaurants, boat yards, and antique shops housed in former fish canneries. One converted warehouse, The Factory, has more than 30 tiny shops under one roof.

Newport Pier (west of the intersection of Newport and Balboa boulevards) sits over the deep marine canyon where the McFaddens built the county's first commercial wharf in 1888. Look for the dory fishing fleet, last on the Pacific Coast; its catch has been sold at market here since 1891. Baldy's Tackle at the pier's head, in business since 1922, rents bikes and beach gear. There's a seafood restaurant at the end of the pier.

To entice folks beyond the bustling Newport Pier area, developers built Balboa Pier and Pavilion in 1905. Drive southeast on Balboa Boulevard to pier parking at Palm Avenue. It's a 4-minute walk to the end of the pier where Ruby's 1940s-style diner serves hamburgers, floats, and shakes.

The ground-floor restaurant in Balboa Pavilion (now a center for deep-sea fishing, parasailing, and whale-watching trips) has photos from Victorian through big-band eras. To the left of the pavilion, the Fun Zone offers rides, ticket booths and docks for harbor tours, boat rentals, and waterside restaurants. The little ferry to Balboa Island leaves from here.

Expert body surfers challenge the waves at the Wedge, the area between the jetty and the beach at the tip of the peninsula.

Balboa Island. Built from a sandbar in 1906 as a subdivision of tiny lots, the island's homes sit cheek by jowl. Shops are crunched into about 3 short blocks along Marine Avenue. While you browse, try a local favorite: a Balboa Bar (vanilla ice cream hand-dipped in chocolate) or a chocolate-dipped frozen banana. A bayfront boardwalk circles the island, offering fine harbor views.

Upper Newport Bay. Newport Dunes Aquatic Park offers access to a 15-acre lagoon on the upper arm of Newport Bay. This private park (fees for day use and overnight camping) has picnic tables, dressing rooms, showers, wading pool, fire rings, and launching ramp. Paddleboards, kayaks, sea cycles, and sailboats can be rented for use on the quiet, warm waters.

A vast estuary on the east shore of the upper bay is a wildlife preserve. In fall, it swarms with ducks, geese, and other birds on the Pacific Flyway. Tours take place Saturdays in winter.

To reach the park and the preserve, turn west on Backbay Drive from Jamboree Boulevard just north of its intersection with State 1.

Around Corona del Mar

Most tourists only see the attractive shops and restaurants lining the Coast Highway in Corona del Mar. To get beyond them to the popular palm-lined state beach, turn west on any of the flower-named streets between Orchid and Iris.

Sherman Gardens. Photographers and horticulturists will enjoy a stop at Sherman Library and Gardens, 2647 E. Coast Highway. Early California architecture serves as a backdrop for annual plantings and tropical greenery. The gardens are open daily from 10:30 A.M. to 4 P.M.; there's a small charge.

Crystal Cove State Park. One of the Southland's newest state beach parks stretches 3¼ miles along the coast between Corona del Mar and Laguna and inland toward Irvine. Three coves offer swimming, surfing, snorkeling, and tidepooling; the offshore area is designated an underwater park for divers. Access to Crystal Cove is through a small colony of beach cottages, happily ramshackle remnants of an earlier era.

Laguna Beach

In a county that has changed dramatically over the last decades, Laguna Beach fights hard to keep its tone of tasteful Bohemianism. Hillside cottage studios, erected by artists who settled the town around the turn of the century, still stand next to more pretentious residences. Art galleries are prominent throughout town, and two annual art events—the summer Festival of Arts and Pageant of the Masters and the Winter Festival in February—draw large crowds.

To get to Laguna from Newport Beach, follow State 1 southeast 10 miles; from Interstate 405, take Laguna Canyon Road (State 133) 8 miles south. Traffic on the Coast Highway through town is a problem, particularly on summer weekends, and parking is a nuisance; 2-hour meters are the stroller's bane.

Art heritage. An art lover's first stop should be the Laguna Art Museum, Cliff Drive and North Coast Highway. The permanent collection in this hot

...Orange Coast

pink gallery (open 11 A.M. to 5 P.M. Tuesday through Sunday; small admission) stars California painters.

Many of the galleries on Forest Avenue, Laguna's eucalyptus-shaded artist's row, specialize in traditional works; you'll find more contemporary pieces along the Coast Highway. Several times a month the Chamber of Commerce hosts gallery tours; call (714) 494-1018 for information.

Town sights. Ocean views from Heisler Park (near the art museum) found their way onto many an early-century canvas; painters still daub here. Paths wind among bird of paradise plants; steps descend to the tidepools of the Glenn E. Vedder Marine Ecological Reserve. Stroll northwest past the lawn bowling grounds, in use most days.

You can picnic in the park or try a restaurant near the museum. Las Brisas, 361 Cliff Drive, offers Mexican brunches and dinners and the postcard-perfect setting you expect at Laguna. The Cottage Restaurant, 308 N. Coast Highway, is another local favorite (breakfast, brunch, and dinner).

From Las Brisas restaurant, take the path down to Main Beach and the country's most scenic basketball court. Pick-up games are hotly competitive—as is the beach volleyball. Shoppers will want to cross over at the Forest Avenue intersection to reach Lumber Yard Village shopping center; others might walk along the highway to white-towered Hotel Laguna, a landmark from 1930. Its handsomely restored lobby holds historic photos of Laguna; the restaurant has a gull's-eye ocean view. Rooms are tidily old-fashioned.

Dana Point & south

This resort area was named for Richard Henry Dana, Jr., author of *Two Years Before the Mast*, who was aboard the brig *Pilgrim* when it pulled into the cove to pick up cowhides in the 1830s. His statue stands not far from a full-size replica of the ship at the harbor (open Sundays March to Thanksgiving from 11 A.M. to 2:30 P.M.; admission fee).

Laguna Niguel. Atop a bluff in this newly annexed northern section of town sits the Ritz-Carlton at Laguna Niguel, one of the state's few oceanfront resorts built in recent times. The chic 393-room hostelry, opened in 1984, offers all amenities—golf, tennis, swimming, and glamorous restaurants.

You can sip a drink at the hotel and watch the surfers on the beach below catch the day's last ride. Or enjoy Salt Creek Beach, a bluff-backed county facility, with plenty of comfortable terrain for sunbathing and reading. The entrance is about half a mile south of Crown Valley Parkway.

Harbor. Dana Point Harbor Drive leads down from the Coast Highway to the 2,500-slip marina, numerous casual restaurants, three nautically inclined shopping centers, and a motel. Spread out on the bluff above, Dana Point Resort overlooks the entire area.

Visitors can rent boats, go parasailing and deep-sea fishing, or reserve a spot on December-to-March whale-watching trips. On Dana Island, inside the breakwater, grassy strip parks offer places to rest or look for crabs and starfish along the rocky shore.

The Orange County Marine Institute (open daily except Sunday, free admission), at the northwest end of the harbor, contains aquariums, marine exhibits, information on the area's tidepools, and a gift shop. The tall ship *Californian*, primarily a training vessel for young people, is moored nearby several months a year.

The lighthouse on Del Prado Avenue, north of Dana Point Resort, houses a free Nautical Heritage Museum, full of ship models, antiques, and memorabilia (open 10 A.M. to 4 P.M. Monday through Friday).

Doheny State Beach. Though the harbor is short of sand, there's plenty of it at this wide state beach to the east. Doheny offers camping combined with good surfing and safe waters. The lagoon at the northwest end is a wild bird habitat.

South to San Clemente. The pretty little town of San Clemente is best known as a retreat of former President Richard Nixon. Take Avenida del Mar from Interstate 5 to get to the beach and pier. There's no scenic coast drive, but marked accesses lead down from the bluffs to small coves.

Just south of San Clemente and over the county line, San Onofre Nuclear Power Plant is a startling contrast to the beach scene. There's an information center off the highway.

San Juan Capistrano

Once a sleepy little town that sprang up around the mission founded by Father Junipero Serra in 1776, San Juan is now a photogenic suburban community with Spanish-style homes and shops. From State 1, drive inland a couple of miles on Camino Capistrano. The turn-off from Interstate 5 also leads right to the center of town (Camino Capistrano and Ortega Highway), site of the mission and the Amtrak depot.

Mission. The mission and its grounds (small admission fee) are well worth a visit. An extensive renovation was necessary after the 1987 Whittier earthquake severely weakened the mission buildings. If you arrive between March and October, you may see some of the famous swallows that summer here, although they're far outnumbered by pigeons these days.

The mission chapel is one of only two remaining churches where Father Serra is known to have said Mass. Only ruins remain of the larger mission church, destroyed in an 1812 earthquake.

Around town. Good restaurants, art galleries, craft shops, and antique stores crowd the downtown area. The city's historical society conducts guided tours ($1) at 1 P.M. most Sundays. Meet the guide at El Peon, across from the mission entrance, or call (714) 493-8444 for further information. To look at historic adobes on your own, pick up a walking-tour map at the O'Neill Museum (31831 Los Rios Street).

Capistrano's recently renovated depot has been operating as a train station since 1895. Refurbished vintage cars line its tracks. The indoor-outdoor Rio Grande Bar & Grill restaurant is a favorite setting for Sunday brunch and an afternoon of Dixieland jazz.

B&Bs along the Coast

Breakfasts in flower-filled courtyards, wine on oceanfront terraces, take-along picnic lunches for cycling tours—these are only some of the touches offered by coastside inns. A few bed and breakfasts lie just a stone's throw from a beach, some are tucked into neighborhoods noted for historic architecture, and others survey hills and valleys a few miles inland.

Part of the charm of B & Bs is the chance they offer visitors to learn about the area from their host and other guests. It's a good way to exchange ideas on activities, restaurants, and "must sees." Inns seem to attract a compatible crowd.

The following is but a sampling of the small hostelries available in the Southland. Those described here are all situated in coastal towns, listed from south (San Diego) to north (Cambria). For a free guide to the hundreds of bed and breakfast inns throughout the state, write to the California Office of Tourism, Box 9278, Van Nuys, CA 91409, or phone (800) TO-CALIF.

Make reservations well in advance; inns book months ahead for summer weekends. All of the inns listed below serve breakfast. Most prohibit children, pets, and smoking. Facilities for handicapped are indicated, where available. Rates include breakfast for two: I= below $80, M=$80–$125, E=above $125.

Balboa Park Inn, 3402 Park Blvd., San Diego, CA 92103; (619) 298-0823. A Spanish-style complex built for 1915 exposition; 25 suites with antiques and fireplaces; some with kitchens; gardens; near zoo and museums; large continental breakfast. M-E

Heritage Park, 2470 Heritage Park Row, San Diego, CA 92110; (619) 299-6832. An 1889 charmer moved to Old Town; 8 rooms; 1 handicapped room; antiques; breakfast in bed or garden; dinner by arrangement; vintage movies. M-E

Bed & Breakfast Inn at La Jolla, 7753 Draper Ave., La Jolla, CA 92037; (619) 456-2066. Fifteen rooms with private baths; 1 wheelchair access; some ocean views; walk to village shops and restaurants. M–very E

Rock Haus, 410 15th St., Del Mar, CA 92104; (619) 481-3764. California bungalow overlooking the ocean; 10 rooms, some with private baths; wine and canapes. I–E

Carriage House, 1322 Catalina St., Laguna Beach, CA 92651; (714) 494-8945. Imaginatively furnished New Orleans–style colonial; 6 spacious suites with kitchens; breakfast in dining room off courtyard. M–E

Eiler's Inn, 741 S. Coast Highway, Laguna Beach, CA 92651; (714) 494-3004. Turning its back to busy highway, inn offers 12 simple rooms around lush courtyard; buffet breakfast; afternoon tea; sun deck. M–E

Doryman's Inn, 2102 W. Ocean Front, Newport Beach, CA 92663; (714) 675-7300. Overlooking beach and dory fleet, 10 luxurious rooms with fireplaces and sunken tubs; restaurant below; breakfast on balcony or in room. M–very E

Seal Beach Inn, 212 5th St., Seal Beach, CA 90740; (310) 493-2416. Garden entrance sets tone for French Mediterranean ambience; 23 rooms; breakfast room; swimming pool; 1 block from ocean. M–E

Lord Mayor's Inn, 435 Cedar Ave., Long Beach, CA 90802; (310) 436-0324. Restored home of first mayor; 5 rooms with antiques; gardens; full breakfast. I–M

Venice Beach House, 15 30th Ave., Venice, CA 90291; (310) 823-1966. Bungalow in eclectic beach town; 9 rooms, 4 with private bath; bicycles; picnic lunches. I–E

La Mer, P.O. Box 23318, Ventura, CA 93001; (805) 643-3600. An 1890 Cape Cod with European flavor; 5 rooms; fireplaces; antiques; gardens; picnic baskets. M–E

Bayberry Inn, 111 W. Valerio St., Santa Barbara, CA 93101; (805) 682-3199. Lovely Colonial-Federal building; 8 rooms; croquet; bicycles; large breakfast. M–E

Old Yacht Club Inn, 431 Corona del Mar Dr., Santa Barbara, CA 93103; (805) 962-1277. City's first inn in two buildings near beach; 9 rooms; beach chairs and towels; bicycles; picnic baskets; Saturday dinner. I–E

Ballard Inn, 2436 Baseline, Ballard, CA 93463; (805) 688-7770. Santa Ynez Valley retreat for wine touring, Solvang shopping; 15 rooms, some with fireplaces; 1 handicapped. E

Rose Victorian Inn, 789 Valley Rd., Arroyo Grande, CA 93420; (805) 481-5566. Lawn with arbor and gazebo surrounds former pioneer rancher's home; 11 rooms on 3 stories; restaurant; antiques; hearty breakfast and dinner. E

Beach House, 6360 Moonstone Beach Dr., Cambria, CA 93428; (805) 927-3136. Three-story beach house; 7 rooms with baths; gardens; bicycles. M–E

J. Patrick House, 2990 Burton Dr., Cambria, CA 93428; (805) 927-3812. Contemporary American-style log house; 8 rooms; handicapped access; gardens; picnic baskets. M

San Diego

San Diego has been charming visitors since the 1500s. At first glance, the city's modern facade belies its age. But California's oldest European settlement is ever mindful of its rich Spanish-Mexican heritage. Monuments report it and buildings preserve it. A legacy of Spanish place names and graceful architecture reflect the city's pride in its past.

California's history began here when Juan Rodriguez Cabrillo landed at Point Loma in 1542. Sixty years later Sebastian Vizcaino also reached the grand bay he named San Diego. But the West Coast's first settlement was not established until 1769, when Father Junipero Serra, a member of Gaspar de Portola's expedition, founded Mission San Diego de Alcala.

The village that grew up around the mission became the anchor for Spanish domain in California. Today the once-sleepy seaside community is the West Coast's second largest city.

Lay of the land

Seventeen-mile-long San Diego Bay is in many ways the heart of this water-oriented city. Vast, natural, and almost landlocked, the great harbor is one of the world's best deep-water anchorages. Host to ships from all ports, it's also home for most of the Navy's Pacific fleet as well as the world's largest sportfishing fleet.

Inland lie the modern city, Old Town (where the city began), and a world-famous park and zoo. East of the downtown, along Interstate 8, is Mission Valley, site of major shopping centers, hotel row, San Diego's mission, and Jack Murphy Stadium (venue for pro football and baseball).

Up the coast lie seaside towns, noted spas, colorful flower fields, and wide beaches. The interior holds a wealth of surprises, from impressive Wild Animal Park to the old mountain mining village of Julian. To the south, Mexico's colorful bargains are an easy 16-mile drive—or trolley ride—from downtown San Diego.

Planning a visit

A splendid natural setting, an equable climate (average temperature of 70° with low humidity), and a wealth of attractions and events make San Diego a favorite year-round vacation site.

Getting there. San Diego's international airport, Lindbergh Field, is only 3 miles northwest of downtown along the bay. Rental cars, taxis, and limos are available from the airport.

Greyhound provides bus service to San Diego. Amtrak passenger trains offer several daily round-trips between Los Angeles and San Diego, with stops at San Juan Capistrano, Oceanside, and Del Mar.

Interstate 5, en route south from Los Angeles to the border, skirts Mission Bay and Old Town before entering the heart of the city. Interstate 15 connects San Diego with the San Bernardino Mountains to the north, and Interstate 8 is the major east-west route.

Getting around. A network of freeways can get you anywhere within minutes. Except during rush hours, it takes only about 20 minutes to cross into Mexico or to drive up the coast to Del Mar.

Motorists can follow a 59-mile scenic drive all around town and into the surrounding area. Start at the Broadway Pier (foot of Broadway) or anywhere you see road signs bearing a white sea gull symbol.

The refurbished Santa Fe Depot downtown (Broadway and Kettner Boulevard), the Amtrak station, is also

A graceful belltower and a simple adobe facade characterize Mission San Diego de Alcala, founded in 1769 as the first link in California's 21-mission chain.

the departure point for the San Diego Trolley, the city's light-rail transit system. Bright red cars run through the city to the border in about 40 minutes, including frequent stops for loading passengers; a $1.50 ticket takes you the whole distance. An extension connects bayside hotels and attractions. Trolley cars operate daily between 5 A.M. and 1 A.M. For schedules, call (619) 233-3004.

For an overview of city attractions, ride the trackless Old Town Trolley. You can get on or off along the way or stay aboard for a 2-hour tour. Start at Old Town to keep history in perspective.

Ferries and water taxis can be a scenic way to reach some destinations—see page 61.

Where to stay. San Diego and its northern coastal reaches offer a wide selection of hotels, motels, and bed-and-breakfast inns. You'll find clusters of accommodations near all the city's main attractions. Make early reservations for summer and holiday weekend stays. Campers also need to reserve beachside parks well in advance (see page 121). Mission Bay's Campland on the Bay, (619) 274-6260, also fills up early.

Activities. San Diego County claims more good public beaches (70 miles) than anywhere else in the state. If you tire of swimming and sunning, you can opt for soaring, parasailing, skin diving, and deep-sea fishing—all year-round activities.

The city known as "Sports Town, U.S.A." hosts professional baseball (Padres), football (Chargers), and soccer (Sockers), as well as world-class sailing, golf, and tennis tournaments. Almost 80 courses suit golfers to a tee. Cycling and jogging routes trail along the ocean and through Balboa Park.

Clusters of stores at Seaport Village, Horton Plaza, and Old Town lure the less athletic. And Tijuana's craft-filled shops lie tantalizingly nearby.

You can see performances by local theater companies, symphony, opera, and ballet on several downtown stages. For ticket information for these and other San Diego events, call ARTS TIX, (619) 238-3810. Its office (closed Monday) is in Horton Plaza. You can save money by ordering half-price tickets on the day of performance.

For recorded information on what's happening around town, you can call (619) 239-9696.

Hotels with a Past

Good looks and longevity distinguish seven of San Diego County's hotels. Three are downtown beauties, three overlook the ocean, and one sits amid apple orchards and gold mines.

The architecture of these renovated grande dames alone makes them worthy of admiration. If you plan a stay, check current rates; several are definite splurges.

Horton Grand Hotel, 311 Island Avenue, San Diego, CA 92101; (619) 544-1886. Two Victorian hotels, once slated for demolition, were dismantled and later reassembled as this Gaslamp Quarter hostelry. Staff wear 19th-century costumes; rooms have fireplaces, four-posters, and curtain swags. Afternoon tea is served in the glass-enclosed lobby. A small museum displays mementos of the past.

Horton Plaza Hotel, 901 Fifth Avenue, San Diego, CA 92101; (619) 232-9500. A 1913 office building was converted in 1987 to this all-suites hotel. The facade still has its original Corinthian and Alaskan marble and Australian gum wood trim.

U.S. Grant Hotel, 326 Broadway, San Diego, CA 92101; (619) 232-3121. When first opened in 1910, the marble-paved U.S. Grant was downtown's most posh. After falling into disrepair over the years, it was refurbished and reopened in 1985. Take afternoon tea under the lobby's wedding cake chandeliers or dine in the elegant, wood-paneled Grant Grill.

Hotel del Coronado, 1500 Orange Avenue, Coronado, CA 92118; (619) 435-6611. This red-roofed beauty, still Coronado's focal point, celebrated her centennial in 1988. Distinguished guests over the years have included U.S. presidents, Thomas Edison, Henry Ford, Robert Todd Lincoln, the Duke of Windsor, and Wallis Simpson.

Take a self-guiding tour of the intricate corridors and cavernous rooms of this Victorian-style wooden wonder (rental cassettes available) or roam the grounds.

Colonial Inn, 910 Prospect Street, La Jolla, CA 92037; (619) 454-2181. When it opened in 1913, this clifftop hotel was La Jolla's first. Recently restored and expanded, the hotel's older section is charming.

La Valencia Hotel, 1132 Prospect Street, La Jolla, CA 92037; (619) 454-0771. Presiding over La Jolla village, this pink, Mediterranean-style hostelry was famous in the 1920s as a Hollywood hideaway. Join the locals for lunch on the Tropical Patio.

Julian Hotel, 2032 Main Street (P.O. Box 1856), Julian, CA 92036; (619) 765-0201. Set in the middle of a former ghost town, this Victorian charmer owes its past to mining and its present to tourism. The region is noted for gold-rush relics and apple pie.

The Waterfront

San Diego should be viewed from the water. The city's beautiful harbor offers parks for strolling and playing, piers and embankments for fishing, boat-launching facilities, beaches, and lots of places to watch the ships go by. And it boasts a striking convention center, marinas, bayside resort hotels, shops, and restaurants oriented to the water. Two wildlife reserves at the south end of the bay offer views of life on the marsh.

Only 1½ to 2 miles wide, San Diego Bay provides a close look at a complex assortment of military and sportfishing ships, from state-of-the-art fishing vessels to yachts of world-ranked sailors.

Getting around

Car-free options for seeing the bay include ferries, water taxis, light-rail and trackless trolleys, and bicycles.

Ferries. Ferry service was discontinued for some time after the swooping San Diego-Coronado Bridge was built in 1969, but it was resumed a few years ago. Boats carry pedestrians and cyclists between the Broadway Pier (on Harbor Drive at the foot of Broadway) and Coronado's Old Ferry Landing, a complex of shops and restaurants by Landing Park. Ferries operate daily from 10 A.M. to 10 P.M., longer on Friday and Saturday ($1.50 one way).

Water taxis. Water taxis shuttle pedestrians around the bay, making regularly scheduled stops at major waterfront hotels. For on-call service to shopping areas and restaurants, call BAY-TAXI; the tariff is a fairly steep $5.

Light-rail trolleys. An extension of the San Diego Trolley runs from downtown along Harbor Drive to the convention center. The Chula Vista Nature Interpretive Center, west of the E Street stop, can also be reached by trolley.

Trackless trolleys. The Old Town Trolley makes waterfront stops on routes around the city. The Coronado Trolley Lines links Old Ferry Landing with the Hotel del Coronado and Le Meridien.

Bicycles. Miles of bicycle paths open the bay to cyclists. One route rounds the top of the bay; another streaks from Glorietta Bay to South Bay wetlands. A favorite route starts at the parking lot of Spanish Landing Park, near the airport, heads east paralleling the waterfront, then crosses by ferry to Coronado.

Many hotels rent bikes, as does a shop at Old Ferry Landing on Coronado. To get a free San Diego cycling map, call (619) 231-2453.

Harbor tours

The best way to get your bearings is from the water. A variety of vessels depart from the well-marked dock on Harbor Drive at the foot of Broadway. Cruises loop close along the shoreline, exposing a full range of air, surface, and undersea craft and harbor activity otherwise hidden from sight.

Harbor Excursion's 2-hour cruises—past Ballast Point sub base, North Island carrier docks, the repair docks south of Coronado bridge, and Silver Strand's amphibious base—give the best look at the bay's military presence. For best viewing, stand topside, on the right facing forward. For schedule and ticket information, call (619) 234-4111.

Along the Embarcadero

To sample the waterfront scene, join the parade of walkers, joggers, and cyclists along the Embarcadero, a landscaped boardwalk that extends along the bayshore from the Coast Guard Station next to the airport all the way south to Seaport Village, about 4 miles. Special stops along the route include a floating museum and the shops and museums of a re-created seaport. Small landscaped parks offer plenty of people-watching opportunities.

Although Naval yards are off-limits, vessels moored at the Broadway Pier hold open house on weekend afternoons. Cruise ships may also be spotted at the adjacent B Street Pier. Home port for the shrinking tuna fleet is the G Street Pier, where a bay-view plaza and a restaurant at the pier's end permit good views of the sleek seiners and tubby trawlers.

Maritime Museum. The three ships of the Maritime Museum, now berthed together around a floating pier north of the excursion boat dock, are worth a half-day visit. The square-rigger *Star of India*, in service since 1863, is the world's oldest iron-hulled merchantman still under sail. Go aboard the painstakingly restored ship for a hint of sea life as it was more than a century ago. Volunteers work on rigging and sails some Sundays.

The *Berkeley*, an 1898 former San Francisco ferry, is full of exhibits and models. Visit on weekdays to see the model-building shop at its most active. Next door you can board the 1904 steam yacht *Medea*.

The museum is open daily; a moderate admission is charged.

Seaport Village. Shops and restaurants designed to evoke the past make tidy Seaport Village, at Pacific Highway and Harbor Drive, popular with bayside browsers. The shopping center's 45-foot-high tower is a re-creation of a lighthouse in the state of Washington; the refurbished turn-of-the-century carousel, operating daily, once twirled on Coney Island.

Shelter & Harbor islands

Two man-made isles in San Diego Bay accommodate boaters, sailors, anglers, and atmosphere-seekers. Once mud and sandpiles built up by dredging in the bay, Shelter and Harbor islands are now attractive resort areas studded with forests of boat masts.

Shelter Island. Really a peninsula, Shelter Island is connected to Point Loma by a salty causeway. Among the island's attractions are a fishing pier, a boat-launching ramp, marinas, restaurants, and hotels. Tropical blooms, torches, and "Polynesian" architecture lend a South Seas flavor. Winding paths provide good strolling, cycling, and bay-

Downtown San Diego buildings soar skyward to take full advantage of bayside views.
Alive with boats of all sizes, the grand natural harbor is one of the country's best
deep-water anchorages.

...Waterfront

watching spots. The Friendship Bell is a gift of Yokohama, San Diego's sister city in Japan.

Harbor Island. Opposite the airport, Harbor Island features high-rise hotels, restaurants, parks, and marinas. You can view it from a peaceful vantage point in Spanish Landing Park on Harbor Drive. On this island's western tip, a Spanish-style building houses a lighthouse and restaurant.

Coronado

Coronado's relative isolation gives it the flavor of an island. Actually it's connected to the mainland by a long, scenic sand spit and a graceful bay bridge. Low guard rails on the span open up a view stretching all the way south to Mexico.

The regal Hotel del Coronado is the focal point of the area (see page 60). Across from the hotel, a picturesque boathouse (now a restaurant) sits at the edge of Glorietta Bay, a small boat harbor with a public launching ramp. Adjoining it are a municipal golf course and a long public beach with fine sand —and occasional sound effects from planes landing at nearby North Island Naval Air Station. (Caution: Watch for stingrays on the beach early in the season.)

Although overshadowed by its more glamorous neighbor, the Glorietta Bay Inn (formerly John D. Spreckels' home) still hosts visitors. Between the complex of shops and restaurants that make up the Old Ferry Landing and Coronado's new Tidelands Park (just north of the bridge) sits Coronado's newest hotel, Le Meridien.

At the north end of the peninsula, the Naval Air Station is one of the oldest in existence. The flat island was the departure point for Charles Lindbergh's historic 1927 flight across the Atlantic. (A replica of his plane is a highlight in San Diego's Aerospace Museum in Balboa Park—see page 69.)

Southward along the narrow spit separating ocean from bay is Silver Strand State Beach, another fine stretch of shoreline.

Point Loma

The high promontory that shelters San Diego Bay from the Pacific Ocean offers grand harbor views. On a clear day you can see from the mountains of Mexico to beyond the La Jolla mesa and from the sprawling city of San Diego to the Coronado Islands and out to sea.

Cabrillo National Monument. At the tip of Point Loma stands Cabrillo National Monument, one of the smallest, most historic, and most visited monuments in the country (outdoing even the Statue of Liberty). Cabrillo's statue, a gift from Portugal (homeland of the great navigator), faces his actual 1542 landing spot at Ballast Point. The nearby visitor center explains Cabrillo's discovery of San Diego Bay and the events following it.

A glassed-in observatory at the monument permits fine views of the California gray whale migration that occurs each year from mid-December through mid-February (see page 124). The well-preserved lighthouse on the high bluff was used from 1855 until 1891, when the waterside lighthouse (still in use) was built.

Follow the nature trail to see a surprisingly unique plant community and some of the best tidepools in Southern California (you're invited to look but not touch).

The monument is open daily from 9 A.M. to sunset; there's a per-car admission charge. To reach Point Loma from downtown, take Rosecrans Street south from Harbor Drive and follow the signs. From Mission Bay, take Sunset Cliffs Boulevard and follow the signs to Catalina Boulevard. En route to the monument you'll pass through Fort Rosecrans National Cemetery, part of a U.S. Navy installation.

View Dining

Ask a dozen San Diegans about the best waterside dining places and you'll get 12 different answers. But everyone's likely to agree that any of the following restaurants will give you a fine view of the water.

The codes (I, M, E) offer some idea of the dinner tab for two (not including wine or tip): I=under $25, M=$25-$50, E=$50+. Most also serve lunch; some offer weekend brunch.

Anthony's Star of the Sea Room (E), 1360 Harbor Drive, (619) 232-7408; elegant ambience; dinner only; coat and tie.

Chart House (M), 1270 Prospect Street, La Jolla, (619) 459-8201; good chain choice; cove setting.

Fish Market and Top of the Market (I-M), 750 Harbor Drive, (619) 232-3474; mostly seafood downstairs; add tablecloths, other entrées at "Top."

George's at the Cove (E), 1250 Prospect Street, (619) 454-4244; alfresco dining; popular with locals.

Grand Island Cafe (I), Seaport Village, (619) 239-5216; patio right on the water.

Mister A's Restaurant (E), 2550 Fifth Avenue, (619) 239-1377; power lunch or dinner atop downtown high rise; continental cuisine.

Peohe's (E), 1201 First Street, Old Ferry Landing, Coronado, (619) 437-4474; views of distant city skyline; fresh seafood menu.

Reuben E. Lee (M), 880 E. Harbor Island Drive, (619) 291-1870; replicated riverboat; popular Sunday brunch.

Tom Ham's Lighthouse (I-M), 2150 Harbor Island Drive, (619) 291-9110; waterside setting; Sunday brunch; evening entertainment.

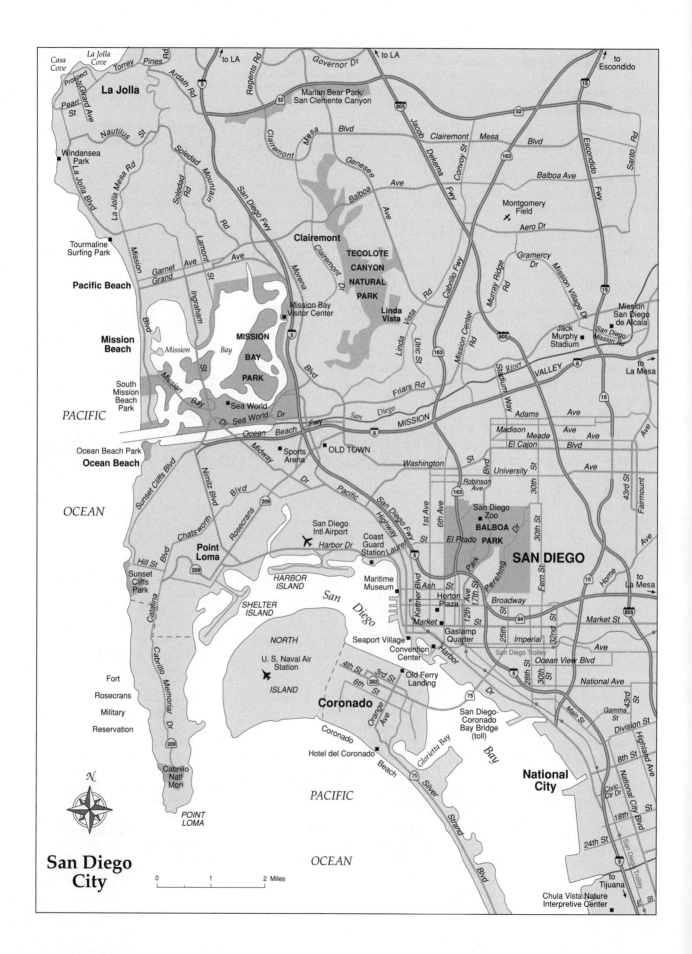

San Diego
City

0   1   2 Miles

Downtown

San Diego's first downtown was a scrabble of adobe buildings in what is now Old Town. Then Alonzo Horton, an entrepreneur from Wisconsin, decided to move the town closer to the harbor. He bought 960 acres of land in 1867 and laid out streets around a small park, Horton Plaza, which has been the city's center ever since.

After years of neglect, San Diego's downtown has undergone a face-lift. Restored historical buildings and an eye-catching shopping mall make the area attractive to both residents and visitors. Completed in 1989, the convention center (at the foot of Fifth Avenue), with its striking sail-like rooftop, helps define the urban center.

New, refurbished, and rebuilt hotels welcome guests. Restaurants top skyscrapers to take advantage of views, while atriums, breezeways, and vest-pocket parks enliven the downtown area at street level. Theater, dance, and symphony performances add life, as do sidewalk cafes, jazz bistros, and street performers.

You can get your bearings at two visitor information centers downtown, at Horton Plaza (First Avenue and F Street) and on G Street between Second and Third avenues.

Horton Plaza

With its eclectic blend of department stores, boutiques, restaurants, theaters, and markets, the gaily painted, four-block-square Horton Plaza coaxes visitors away from suburban malls. There is much to engage the senses: tantalizing smells, eye-catching banners and displays, and strolling musicians.

Bounded by Broadway, G, First, and Fourth streets, the 11½-acre complex includes more than 150 shops. At one entrance, a stairway and plaza lead down to the Lyceum, two stages that are home to the San Diego Repertory Theatre.

A multilevel parking garage makes it convenient to shop or explore the adjacent historic area.

Gaslamp Quarter

A restored area south of Horton Plaza is worth a look. Bounded by Fourth, Sixth, Broadway, and the waterfront, it's one of the country's largest national historic districts.

The onetime heart of the city was a favorite haunt of Wyatt Earp and other 19th-century notables, but it fell on hard times in the late 1890s when businesses moved north of Broadway. In later years, it became a haven for gamblers, prostitutes, and opium dealers.

Though parts of the quarter are still redolent of its past, massive redevelopment has gentrified the region with brick sidewalks, period street lamps, benches, and trees. More than 100 splendid representations of Victorian architecture now house art galleries, antique shops, hotels, restaurants, and office buildings.

The Gaslamp Quarter Theatre Company puts on contemporary plays in the intimate Elizabeth North Theatre and the larger, elegant Hahn Cosmopolitan Theatre.

Touring the area. The William Heath Davis House (410 Island Avenue) is headquarters for the Gaslamp Quarter Foundation. Built in 1850 and moved here in 1984, it's the oldest house downtown. Join a 2-hour narrated stroll every Saturday (small donation requested), or pick up a map and strike out on your own. For information, call (619) 233-5227.

The Centre City Development Corporation also sponsors free weekend bus and walking tours. For information and reservations, call (619) 696-3215.

If you're touring on your own, take special note of the historic buildings on the east side of Fifth Avenue, between E and F streets. Their detailing is typical of commercial construction in the Victorian era.

The Royal Pie Bakery (554 Fourth Avenue) makes a tempting stop and a fine historical footnote: a bakery has operated at this address since 1875, even when the second floor was a notorious brothel. Or drop into the Horton Grand Hotel (see page 60) for tea, cocktails, or a meal. The hotel restaurant, Ida Bailey's, is named for one of the city's former madams.

Around town

Walking is also a good way to take a look at downtown San Diego's large entertainment complexes, small museums, and intriguing shopping opportunities.

Arts. Downtown renaissance turned a former movie theater at Seventh and B streets into a performing hall for the San Diego Symphony. Opera, ballet, musicals, and concerts are offered at the Civic Theatre and at Golden Hall, part of the Convention and Performing Arts Center on First Avenue.

Library. San Diego's public library, at the corner of Eighth and E streets, is one of the most modern and well-stocked facilities in the country. Its collection contains 4,000-year-old Sumerian cuneiform tablets.

Shopping. Antique buffs will enjoy the Olde Cracker Factory at Kettner Boulevard and Harbor Drive. More than 40 dealers display a wide range of antiques and collectibles. For another kind of shopping experience, the Farmers Market at Horton Plaza showcases fresh produce and specialty foods.

Museums. The Firehouse Museum, located at 1572 Columbia Street, reveals a glittering array of firefighting equipment and a host of amusing oddities. The museum is open Thursday through Sunday; donations are requested.

The grand mansion at 1925 K Street, now called Villa Montezuma, is a fine museum of Victorian architecture and decorative arts, including an outstanding stained glass collection. A small admission fee is charged to visit the museum, open Wednesday through Sunday afternoon. No high-heeled shoes are permitted.

Old San Diego

In 1769, Father Junipero Serra chose a commanding site overlooking the bay for the mission that would begin the settlement of California. A fort built to protect the mission gave the place its name, Presidio Hill. Soon a town began to sprout at the foot of the hill.

Some buildings and relics of the Spanish, Mexican, and American settlements that thrived here survive; others have been reconstructed. The most interesting lie within Old Town San Diego State Historic Park, an area bounded by Wallace, Congress, Twiggs, and Juan streets.

Old Town

Old Town is no sterile museum display; many colorful shops and restaurants are tucked around patios in its historic buildings. Locals rub elbows with tourists in garden restaurants at Bazaar del Mundo, a popular shopping complex in the historic Casa de Pico hacienda between Juan and Calhoun streets at Wallace.

Old Town is near the junction of Interstate 5 and Interstate 8 north of the airport; follow signs from Interstate 5.

Getting around. Park streets are reserved for strollers. Free ranger-led walking tours take off daily at 2 P.M. Get information from park headquarters at Wallace Street and San Diego Avenue, or call (619) 237-6770. Historical society tours are offered Saturday at 1:30 P.M. from the Whaley House at San Diego and Harney.

Highlights. Most of the old houses center on the plaza, once the scene of bullfights. The flagpole has flown Spanish and Mexican flags for two centuries; the American flag was added in 1846.

Casa de Estudillo (Mason Street end of the plaza), the first Spanish casa on the plaza, was the home of the commandante of Monterey and San Diego. Nearby Seeley Stables houses horse-drawn vehicles and western artifacts. Admission to the house and stables is free, but donations are welcome.

Casa de Bandini (Mason and Calhoun streets), built by wealthy Don Juan Bandini (known for lavish fandangos and dinners), is now a Mexican restaurant. The house was Commodore Stockton's headquarters during the American occupation of California in 1846, played host to Kit Carson, and was a stagecoach station in the 1860s.

The Whaley House (corner of San Diego Avenue and Harney Street), Southern California's oldest brick structure, has served as a dairy, funeral parlor, theater, saloon, courthouse, and Sunday school (the city's first).

The restored house is open Wednesday through Sunday. Admission includes entrance to the adjacent Derby-Pendleton House, shipped around Cape Horn and put together with wooden pegs in the 1850s.

Heritage Park. Stroll through the park at Juan and Harney streets to take a look at some of the city's oldest Victorians. Seven restored 1880-era houses (one housing a charming bed-and-breakfast inn) and a venerable Jewish temple line hillside Juan Street.

Presidio Park

Five years after Father Serra dedicated Alta California's first mission, its hillside location was already too small. So the building was moved 6 miles east in 1774 into Mission Valley (see page 6).

On its former site adjacent to Old Town rises the handsome Serra Museum (open Tuesday through Saturday and Sunday afternoon; admission fee). The site of the original mission chapel is marked by a towering cross.

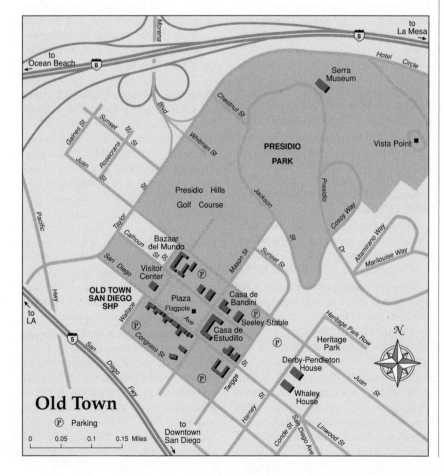

Old Town

P Parking

0   0.05   0.1   0.15 Miles

Sea World trainer introduces a young guest to one of the marine park's smiling performers, a killer whale who dazzles audiences with aquatic acrobatics.

Two City Parks

Two of San Diego's most outstanding attractions are examples of careful planning and foresight. Balboa Park, conceived in the 1860s, and Mission Bay Aquatic Park, developed a century later, attract millions of tourists yearly. They come to see one of the world's largest wild animal collections, a huge aquarium, and a raft of museums.

Balboa Park

It took more than a century for the 1,400 acres of rattlesnake-infested, hilly chaparral set aside in 1868 as a city park to become the verdant public garden you see today. And most of its impressive architecture is the result of two world fairs.

The 1915 Panama-California International Exposition contributed the Moorish and Spanish Renaissance buildings along El Prado, the central promenade, including the ornate California Tower with its 100-bell carillon, and also the world's largest outdoor organ (free concerts Sunday at 2 P.M.). The 1935 California-Pacific International Exposition added the Old Globe Theatre and the Spanish Village Arts & Crafts Center (a collection of craft shops near the zoo).

The park provides an idyllic setting for a concentration of top attractions: the world-famous San Diego Zoo, science and natural history museums, art galleries, performing arts centers, and a renowned space theater. Here, too, lie botanical gardens, playgrounds, picnic groves, a municipal golf course, a miniature railroad, and a 1910 carousel.

Getting around. The park's main entrance is from Laurel Street on the west side; it can also be reached from Park Boulevard, to the east. Parking is plentiful around El Prado's cluster of museums, the Palisades region to the south, and near the zoo.

Pick up maps and other park information at the visitor center in the House of Hospitality in the central El Prado area. Horse-drawn carriages carry visitors up and down the car-free mall.

A museum passport, available at the visitor center or participating museums, offers admission discounts. Many museums are closed Monday.

Museums of note. The rebuilt Casa de Balboa at the center of the park houses several small museums—Photographic Arts, San Diego History, Model Railroad, and Hall of Champions (sports). Next door, the Science Center's hands-on exhibits are popular with youngsters. Across the plaza, the Natural History Museum concentrates on southwestern desert and marine life.

The Museum of Man, in the California Tower at the other end of the plaza, appeals to anthropology buffs of all ages. It's noted for its American Indian research. Mummies and craft demonstrations please children.

The San Diego Museum of Art collection spans the ages, from early Asian to 20th century. The Sculpture Garden Cafe is a popular lunch spot. In the adjacent Timken Art Gallery, American and European art on display includes a number of Russian icons. The Centro Cultural de la Raza (south in the park's Pepper Grove area) focuses on contem-

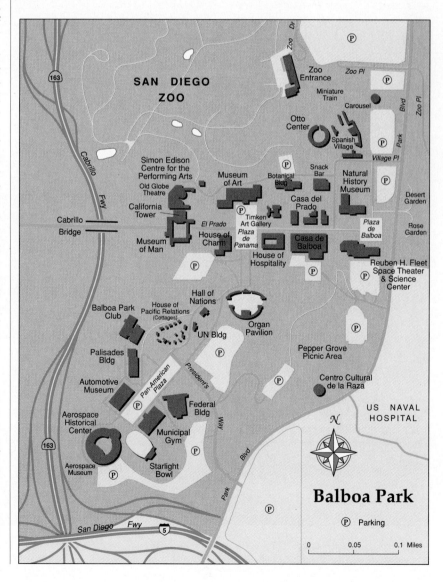

Balboa Park

Ⓟ Parking

0   0.05   0.1 Miles

porary Indian, Mexican, and Chicano art and culture.

The Aerospace Museum, a few blocks south of El Prado, greets visitors with a replica of *The Spirit of St. Louis*, Lindbergh's famous plane. Other exhibits cover the whole history of flight, from gliders to space capsules. Nearby, the Automotive Museum is another memorial to transportation.

Theaters. The 580-seat Old Globe Theatre, in a grove behind the California Tower, is part of the Simon Edison Centre for the Performing Arts. The three-theater complex includes an outdoor stage.

The Starlight Bowl, near the open-air Aerospace Museum, presents summer musicals. It's in the flight path for Lindbergh Field, so performers learn to "freeze" when planes pass overhead and resume when they can be heard.

In the Science Center building on El Prado, the Reuben H. Fleet Space Theater's huge, dome-shaped Omnimax screen was the prototype for similar theaters around the world. The screen is a tilted hemisphere; when films shot through a special fish-eye lens are projected onto it, you feel as if you're in the movie.

San Diego Zoo. Simply put, this zoo is extraordinary. More than 3,400 animals, representing some 800 species, roam its lush, 100-acre grounds. But what make this zoo unique are its cleverly designed moated enclosures simulating natural habitats, its rare and exotic inhabitants, and its endangered species breeding programs.

Cuddly koalas cling to eucalyptus branches, Malayan sun bears play in a rain forest, and majestic Sumatran tigers stride through a tropical mist. Colorful flamingos collect on the lagoons, eagles perch high overhead in a giant walk-through aviary, and peacocks strut independently through the grounds of this cageless environment.

In a separate enclosure, the Children's Zoo brings tots nose to nose with the animal kingdom's younger set. Even drinking fountains and restroom facilities are scaled down. Adults, too, crowd around the nursery and the hatchery.

Seeing the entire zoo takes time, careful planning, and plenty of walking. There's no better way to get the lay of the land than to join a guided bus tour. The 3-mile safari saves steps, travels to regions not easily reached by walkers, and introduces visitors to stage-struck animals cued by the driver.

Another way to get around is aboard the Skyfari, an aerial tramway which rises 170 feet over the zoo's grottos and mesas. When you're not spying on the animal activity below, you'll enjoy a fine overview of Balboa Park.

The zoo is open all year from 9 A.M. to dusk (later in summer). A one-price admission package is offered combining entrance fee, bus tour, and aerial tram fees (see page 122).

The zoo has food service, strollers, wheelchairs, and shops.

Mission Bay Aquatic Park

The beautiful bay right on the edge of downtown San Diego has lived through several incarnations since Cabrillo gave it the name "False Bay" after mistaking it for San Diego's harbor. It has gone from a productive estuary to a silt and trash collector to the world's largest municipal aquatic park.

But it took 20 years of community action to create the 4,600-acre playground you see today. Dredging and development transformed Mission Bay into a maze of islands and lagoons, with 27 miles of beaches, free public boat-launching ramps, picnic areas, campgrounds, playgrounds, golf courses, and miles of landscaped coves.

Along the waterfront, the sandy stretches of Mission Bay are protected from the ocean by a narrow jetty of sand. One of the lively beach communities, Pacific Beach, is often compared to the beach town of Venice near Los Angeles.

Attractions. Sea World, a huge water wonderland of aquariums, exhibits, and shows, is Mission Bay's main tourist destination, but water sports of every type are its reason for being. Marinas rent everything from paddle boats to ocean-going sloops.

Several beaches on the 1½-mile waterskiing course are set aside as pickup and landing sites. Anglers try their luck from the shore or aboard sportfishing boats. Catches within the bay include halibut, flounder, bass, croaker, and perch.

For a map of the area and information on its resort hotels, restaurants, camping choices, and recreational facilities, stop by the Mission Bay visitor center just off Interstate 5 at East Mission Bay Drive.

Sea World. This lushly landscaped, 135-acre marine life park on Mission Bay is one of the world's largest oceanariums. Outstanding aquarium exhibits and a variety of water shows make Sea World a good destination for the entire family.

One of the park's finest exhibits is the Penguin Encounter, a climate- and light-controlled environment for some 400 birds. You'll see penguins belly-flopping in the water, waddling along snowbanks, and building rock nests to raise their chicks. Your view is from a moving sidewalk on the warm side of the glass. The catchy exhibit includes a 6-minute film.

Other park "stars" include Baby Shamu—pride of the killer whale clan. At the Shark Encounter, visitors come face to snout with the world's largest collection of sharks, rays, moray eels, and other denizens of the deep.

A tram carries visitors up 70 feet over the bay. The 320-foot Sky Tower offers unobstructed views of Mission Bay and San Diego.

The park is open daily from 9 A.M. to dusk (to 11 P.M. in summer). It will take you 8 hours or more if you aim to catch all the shows and view every single exhibit. On summer nights, special shows and a laser light and fireworks display are added, and musicians, mimes, and jugglers stroll the grounds.

A one-price park admission for children and adults (see page 122) includes all shows and exhibits; parking is free. Rides, food, shops, and a guided 90-minute peek behind the scenes are extra.

Sea World is on the southern edge of Mission Bay Aquatic Park. To get there from Interstate 5, follow Sea World Drive west.

*Early morning light warms the wind-carved bluffs at Torrey Pines State Reserve, a
coastal preserve north of San Diego set aside to protect some of the world's rarest trees.*

La Jolla & the North Coast

Acres of flowers, quaint seaside communities, beaches, luxurious spas and golf courses, missions, and parks are a few of the reasons to explore San Diego's north coast.

La Jolla

A 15-minute drive north on Interstate 5 from the heart of San Diego, La Jolla is really a part of that city. But this region has always had its own personality. Although La Jolla offers a wealth of sporting, shopping, and museum-touring activities, the town does little to invite visitors—and that's part of its appeal.

Most people come to enjoy the Mediterranean-like setting of the scenic site, nestled atop cave-pocked cliffs along 7 miles of curvaceous coastline. According to Indian legend, "jolla" (pronounced hoya) means "hole" or "cave," but the Spanish translation of "jewel" or "gem" is more common.

Exploring the village. Newer high-rise developments to the north and east contrast sharply with the small-town feeling of La Jolla's heart. In the center of the village, art galleries, boutiques, and restaurants line the streets, and architecturally pleasing small hotels welcome guests.

La Jolla is best seen by walking rather than driving—parking places are hard to find, pedestrian traffic is erratic, and the layout of the village is confusing. Although Girard Avenue is the main street, it's more fun to walk along the mile or so of cliffside Prospect Street from the cottage shops and plazas at the north end to the art museum on to the south.

Restaurants along the route often occupy old houses; some offer a sea view. Locals often join visitors in the courtyard cafe of the venerable La Valencia Hotel or nearby in the refurbished Colonial Inn.

The La Jolla Museum of Contemporary Arts (700 Prospect Street) is well worth a stop to view some of California's best contemporary painting, sculpture, photography, and design. A bookstore and cafe invite loitering. The museum is open Tuesday through Sunday from 10 A.M. to 5 P.M. and Wednesday until 9 P.M. (admission free after 5).

La Jolla's curving streets are somewhat confusing. If you come north from the main part of San Diego, the quickest route to the center of town is west from the Ardath Road exit off Interstate 5.

Recreation. The area's beaches are a magnet; they vary considerably. La Jolla Shores, to the north, is long, flat, and relatively shallow out some distance, ideal for families and surfers. The private La Jolla Beach and Tennis Club marks its southern end.

Sunbathers and swimmers dot scenic La Jolla Cove (below the cliffs in the village center). Snorkelers and beachcombers explore tidepools and coral reefs. An annual Rough Water Swim in September is an exciting international competition. A cliffside walk along the cove offers grand ocean views.

South of Coast Boulevard Park (ideal for expert body surfers) lies Children's Pool, a small beach with a curving breakwater that keeps the surf gentle. At the foot of Bonair Street, Windansea Beach is a favorite with snorkelers (see page 39).

To visit one of the caves in the pock-marked cliffs, go into the curio shop at the end of Coast Boulevard. You'll pay a small admission charge to descend 133 wooden stairs into the cave (not recommended for the infirm).

Cycling is a good way to investigate the town and oceanfront. La Jolla hosts an annual Grand Prix Bicycle Race.

The Golden Triangle. A newer section of La Jolla lies off La Jolla Village Drive east of Interstate 5. Called the Golden Triangle (it's bounded on the east by Interstate 805), this is a high-rise region of offices, condominiums, hotels, restaurants, and shopping malls.

Of particular interest is the extensive collection of folk art from around the world at the Mingei International Museum in Building 1-7 of the University Towne Centre shopping complex on the south side of La Jolla Village Drive.

Torrey Pines Mesa

The northern edge of La Jolla, a former wilderness thick with groves of eucalyptus and stands of rare pine trees, is the setting for an aquarium, noted golf courses, a hang glider port, and the impressive campus of the University of California at San Diego. From the village, take Torrey Pines Road north to reach the mesa.

Scripps Institution. On the pier north of La Jolla Shores Beach sprawls Scripps Institution of Oceanography, noted for its ocean study and now part of UCSD. Their new aquarium and museum facility on Expedition Way displays intriguing aquatic flora and fauna from the ocean's depths. Children will enjoy the interactive oceanography exhibits, including a simulated submarine dive to 3,000 feet below the surface. Admission is $6.50 adults, $5.50 seniors, $4.50 teens, $3.50 ages 4 to 12.

Salk Institute. Named for the man who helped vanquish polio, this biological research center near UCSD is conspicuous for its surrealistic architecture. Tours are offered weekdays; phone (619) 453-4100 for times.

Torrey Pines State Reserve. A 1,750-acre preserve protects a gnarled and twisted grove of trees that were growing here when Cabrillo's ships first sighted California. These pines grow only here and on Santa Rosa Island, off the coast of Santa Barbara.

Well-marked trails threading the park lead to cliffs, canyons, and 6 miles of beach. To hike along the ocean, use the park's north entrance off Interstate 5 and consult a tide table to avoid being caught by rising waters.

Torrey Pines Reserve opens at 8 A.M. and closes at 10 P.M. from April to October, 5 P.M. in winter. Admission is free, but there's a charge to park. No picnicking is permitted in the reserve.

...La Jolla & the North Coast

North Coast

Along the coast between Torrey Pines and Oceanside, small towns are interspersed with state and county beaches. To poke around, leave the freeway at Del Mar and follow city streets instead. An inland side trip east of Oceanside takes you to one of California's finest missions and to the town of Fallbrook, heart of the country's avocado-growing region.

Del Mar. Visitors flock to this coastal town for the racing season (late July to mid-September) at Del Mar Thoroughbred Club, founded by Bing Crosby in the 1930s. Its famed fairgrounds are also the site of the annual county fair in June. For a bird's-eye view of some of its luxurious beachfront homes, take a balloon tour; a number of companies offer flights. Boutiques, galleries, and restaurants overflow the downtown Del Mar Plaza, Camino del Mar at 15th Street.

Rancho Santa Fe. Take Via de la Valle exit inland from Interstate 5 for a pleasant drive around Rancho Santa Fe, originally a Spanish land grant and now graced with estates and horse ranches. Douglas Fairbanks and other movie stars of the 1920s and 30s had homes in the area. Those eucalyptus trees you see everywhere were planted by the Santa Fe Railway in an unsuccessful experiment in using the wood for railroad ties.

Encinitas and Leucadia. Although suburban growth has cut into the flower fields, this region radiates color from May through September. The area is the world's leading grower of poinsettias. The Quail Botanical Gardens, east of Encinitas Boulevard, offers self-guided tours Saturday at 10 A.M.

Carlsbad. In the 19th century, this town built its reputation on its mineral waters. The spring is long gone, but Carlsbad is still noted for spas. Several small hotels have spa facilities; inland, famed La Costa is an elite retreat (see page 125).

Oceanside. Surfers, boaters, and anglers flock to this beach city, San Diego County's third largest. It's the scene of many popular regattas and races. The long wooden pier juts into the sea for 1,900 feet, attracting throngs of fisherfolk; visitors enjoy the view from a restaurant at the end of the pier. At one end of the 4-mile beach lie a large marina and Cape Cod Village, a shopping and dining complex.

Oceanside is the gateway to Camp Pendleton Marine Corps base. Visitors are welcome to drive through part of its grounds. The former ranch of Pio Pico, the last of Mexico's governors, lies within its gates.

Mission San Luis Rey. One of the most impressive restorations in the chain of California missions (see page 6) is just 5 miles east of Oceanside via State 76 (Mission Avenue). Founded in 1789, Mission San Luis Rey was the largest and most populous in the Americas. The mission, still a seminary, is open to the public Monday through Saturday and Sunday afternoon.

Fallbrook. Antique shops and avocado orchards are but two of Fallbrook's delights. Here, too, are cactus and macadamia nurseries, a koi farm, golf courses, and a handful of good restaurants. Pick up a map from the Chamber of Commerce at 300 N. Main Street weekdays, or call (619) 728-5845. From Oceanside, take State 76 east about 15 miles, then South Mission Road 6 miles north.

Border Bargains

Visitors to San Diego have long made the trek south to Tijuana in search of bargains. But now you can find them north of the border as well.

The San Diego Factory Outlet Center lies just half a mile north of the San Ysidro border crossing (14 miles south of downtown San Diego). Among its factory stores are outlets for Bass shoes, Black & Decker, Corning, Gitano, Koala Blue, Mikasa, Nike, Revere, and Van Heusen.

What is a factory outlet? Fairly new to the West, factory outlets are long-time favorites in New England and the South. They're places where name-brand manufacturers sell directly to consumers at cost or just above wholesale prices, allowing discounts of 40% to 70% off retail.

Goods are usually first-quality, surplus items identical to what you'd find in major department stores. To avoid competing with local retailers, outlets usually don't advertise, and several use names different from the familiar products they sell. Izod, Monet, and Ship 'N Shore brands, for instance, are sold at Fashion Flair; Banister Shoe is actually the U.S. Shoe Company, which makes Bandolino, Capezio, Evan Picone, Joyce, Pappagallo, and other well-known brands.

Planning your visit. Most shoppers spend at least half a day at the center, so plan to wear comfortable shoes. Pick up a center map at any store or at the mall's U.S.-Mexico visitor center.

Stores accept personal checks and credit cards. Hours are generally 10 A.M. to 7 P.M. Monday through Saturday, 11 A.M. to 6 P.M. Sunday. Tuesday is typically the lightest shopping day.

Plenty of parking is available at the center and nearby. Several food outlets offer quick dining.

To get to the center, take the last U.S. exit southwest off Interstate 5; then turn right on Camino de la Plaza. The center will be on your right. For additional details, call (619) 690-2999.

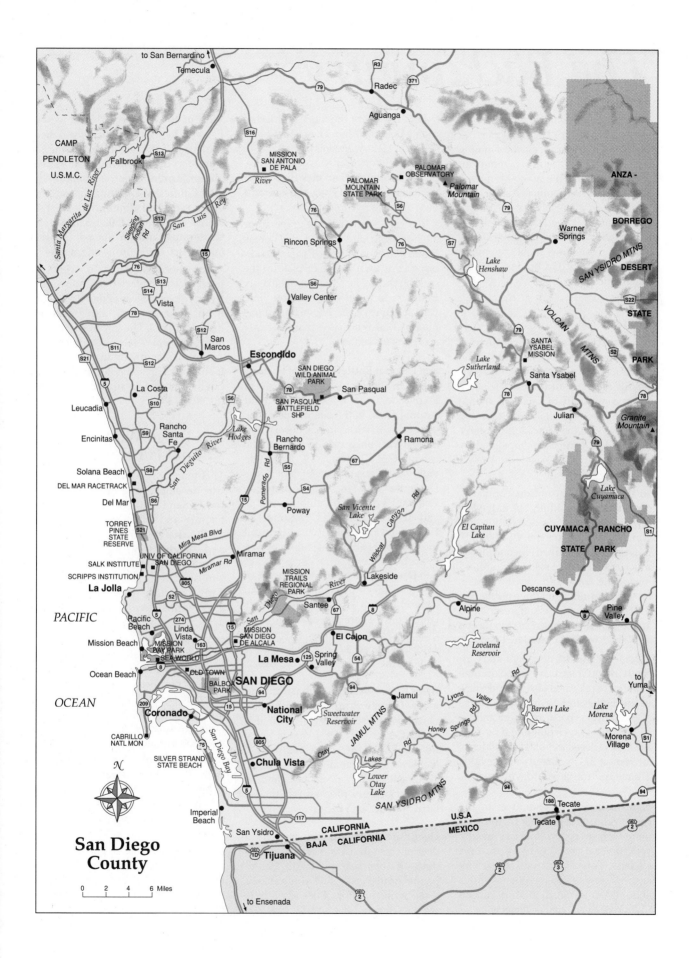

San Diego County

to San Bernardino↑
Temecula
R3
79
371
Radec
Aguanga
79
S16
MISSION
SAN ANTONIO
DE PALA
PALOMAR
OBSERVATORY
CAMP
PENDLETON
U.S.M.C.
Fallbrook
S13
PALOMAR
MOUNTAIN
STATE PARK
Palomar
Mountain
ANZA-
S13
76
River
San Luis Rey River
S6
Santa Margarita de Luz River
Sleeping Indian Rd
76
S13
S14
Vista
78
76
15
Rincon Springs
76
S7
Warner
Springs
BORREGO
Lake
Henshaw
SAN YSIDRO MTNS
DESERT
S6
Valley Center
STATE
S11
San
Marcos
S12
S22
S21
La Costa
S12
Escondido
78
SAN DIEGO
WILD ANIMAL
PARK
San Pasqual
SANTA
YSABEL
MISSION
VOLCAN MTNS
S2
PARK
Leucadia
S10
S6
SAN PASQUAL
BATTLEFIELD
SHP
Lake
Sutherland
Santa Ysabel
78
Encinitas
S9
Rancho
Santa
Fe
Lake
Hodges
Rancho
Bernardo
Ramona
Julian
S8
San Dieguito River
S5
67
Granite
Mountain
Solana Beach
DEL MAR RACETRACK
S6
S4
Poway
Pomerado Rd
79
Del Mar
15
San Vicente
Lake
Wildcat Canyon Rd
El Capitan
Lake
Lake
Cuyamaca
TORREY
PINES
STATE
RESERVE
S21
Mira Mesa Blvd
Miramar
CUYAMACA RANCHO
SALK INSTITUTE
UNIV OF CALIFORNIA
SAN DIEGO
Miramar Rd
MISSION
TRAILS
REGIONAL
PARK
River
Lakeside
STATE PARK
S1
SCRIPPS INSTITUTION
La Jolla
Descanso
805
52
Santee
67
8
Alpine
Pine
Valley
8
PACIFIC
5
Pacific
Beach
274
163
15
MISSION
SAN DIEGO
DE ALCALA
El Cajon
125
Spring
Valley
54
Loveland
Reservoir
Rd
Mission Beach
MISSION
BAY PARK
SEA WORLD
La Mesa
to
Yuma
Ocean Beach
8
OLD TOWN
BALBOA
PARK
SAN DIEGO
94
94
Jamul
Lyons Valley Rd
Barrett Lake
Lake
Morena
OCEAN
209
National
City
Sweetwater
Reservoir
JAMUL MTNS
Honey Springs Rd
Coronado
75
805
15
Otay
Lakes
S1
Morena
Village
CABRILLO
NATL MON
San Diego Bay
Chula Vista
Lower
Otay
Lake
SAN YSIDRO MTNS
94
SILVER STRAND
STATE BEACH
5
Tecate
188
94
N
Imperial
Beach
117
CALIFORNIA
U.S.A
2
MEXICO
Tecate
San Ysidro
BAJA CALIFORNIA
San Diego
County
1D
Tijuana
2
3
0 2 4 6 Miles
to Ensenada
2

The Backcountry

A land of rural charm and historical interest, San Diego's backcountry is full of surprises: wineries, ranches, mining towns, Indian museums, a mountain observatory, and the not-to-be-missed San Diego Wild Animal Park. Camp overnight in a forested state park, unwind around Escondido, or check into a time-mellowed gold-country hotel. Some of the region's highlights might be sampled in a day, but two or three days could go by rapidly.

Escondido

It's about a 40-minute drive north from San Diego on Interstate 15 to the charming city of Escondido. En route, red tile roofs are all you can see of the resort community of Rancho Bernardo from the freeway. But it's worth turning off just to visit the Mercado, an enclave of some 40 art and craft shops, studios, and restaurants. Weekends are lively.

In and around Escondido. Popularity came late to Escondido, but in the last few years the city's population has almost doubled (currently 100,000). Lawrence Welk liked Escondido so much that he built a resort here around his mobile home and added a theater, motel, restaurant, and three public golf courses. The complex is off Interstate 15 a few miles northeast of town; exit north on Mountain Meadow Road.

Near Escondido's new Civic and Cultural Center, Grape Day Park holds some of the city's relocated historic buildings: its first library (now a museum), a turn-of-the-century barn and windmill, a Victorian-era ranch house, and the 1888 Santa Fe railroad depot. The buildings, located at 321 N. Broadway, are open Thursday through Saturday afternoons.

Wine country. Escondido is in the center of a wine-growing region, and more than a dozen wineries nearby welcome visitors with tours and tastings. Three are south of the city along Interstate 15; the others cluster about 30 miles north around Rancho California Road, east of Temecula.

Ferrara Winery, the county's oldest, is a state historical site. The tasting room (1120 W. 15th Avenue) is open 9 A.M. to 5 P.M. weekdays and 10 A.M. to 5:30 P.M. on weekends. You can pick up a sandwich at the deli and enjoy the vineyard view from the patio pavilion.

You can picnic under a grape arbor after touring and tasting at Thomas Jaeger Winery (13455 San Pasqual Road); bring your own lunch, or pick up the makings here. The winery is open daily from 10 A.M. to 5 P.M. Culbertson Vineyard & Winery (32575 Rancho California Road) also boasts a charming cafe and a visitor center.

San Pasqual Battlefield State Historic Park. On State 78 about 8 miles east of Escondido (next to San Diego Wild Animal Park) is the site of one of the least-known battles in U.S. history, and almost the only one fought in the conquest of California. A 10-minute video at the visitor center depicts the December 6, 1846 struggle between General Pico's native California troops and General Kearney's U.S. Army. The U.S. troops lost in what historians call the bloodiest battle of the Mexican War.

San Diego Ostrich Ranch. Also on San Pasqual Valley Road (State 78) you can commune with an ostrich, the world's largest bird. There's no charge to view these ungainly creatures. One warning: They love to peck at objects like glasses and earrings, so don't stand too close.

Bates Bros. Nut Farm. Pack a lunch and follow County Road S6 about 8 miles north from Escondido to reach this Valley Center site (15954 Woods Valley Road). The farm's huge retail store displays nuts from all over the world, along with jams, jellies, and candies. Visitors can tour a processing plant, pet farm animals, and picnic.

Deer Park Vineyard. You won't find deer at this attraction north of Escondido off Interstate 15 (29013 Champagne Boulevard). But you can see some vintage automobiles, do a little wine tasting, or have a picnic lunch.

West of town. State 78 heads west of Escondido to reach the coast near Carlsbad. If you get hungry along the way, stop in the town of San Marcos (about 5 miles west of Interstate 15). Old California Restaurant Row here offers plenty of dining options at 12 ethnic restaurants (1020 San Marcos Boulevard), and an open-air market takes place on Saturday afternoon.

Turn north on Santa Fe Avenue in nearby Vista to reach the Southwestern Antique Gas & Steam Engine Museum in hilly Guajome Park (also the site of a historic adobe). The threshers, binders, and other early farm equipment you see on display rev up in June and October for a Threshing Bee and Antique Engine Show. For further details, call (619) 565-3600.

San Diego Wild Animal Park

This innovative wild animal preserve was developed as a breeding ground for the San Diego Zoo and a sanctuary for rare and endangered species. On 1,800 acres resembling African veldt and Asian plain, more than 2,500 animals representing 240 species roam almost as freely as they would in their native habitats. This compares with 3,400 animals on the parent zoo's 100 acres.

Visitors are kept mostly at a distance so they won't disturb the animals. A narrated monorail tour quietly skirts the park perimeter, offering glimpses of elephants, water buffaloes, lions, leopards, wildebeests, rhinos, zebras, and other creatures. The 5-mile tour takes about 50 minutes.

A couple of tips: The right side of the tram affords best viewing. Bring a pair of binoculars, and try to schedule your ride in early morning or late afternoon when the animals are most active and visible.

Another viewing opportunity is to join a photo safari and be driven right into the herds on a flat-bed truck. These caravans are expensive—about $50 per passenger.

Yesteryear's furnishings overflow an antique store's yard in bucolic downtown Julian,
a turn-of-the-century mining town noted today for its wildflowers and apple orchards.

...*Backcountry*

A 1½-mile walking trail offers spectacular vistas for animal observation and photography as well as picnicking sites. Exhibits near the park entrance include a lowland gorilla grotto, a free-flight aviary, and an animal nursery. Animal shows are scheduled throughout the day.

Gardeners will enjoy the park's landscaping. An interesting 1-acre water-wise garden displays a variety of "unthirsty" plants.

The park is open from 9 A.M. to 4 P.M. daily (to 6 P.M. in summer). Night tours take place occasionally. The ticket price includes entrance fee, monorail tours, animal shows, and exhibits (see page 122). For details, call (619) 480-0100.

To reach the park from Escondido, head east on State 78 (San Pasqual Valley Road); from San Diego, take Interstate 15 north and Via Rancho Parkway exit east onto San Pasqual Valley Road and follow the signs.

Pala Mission

In a tranquil river valley on State 76 about 5 miles east of Interstate 15 stands Mission San Antonio de Pala, a branch of Mission San Luis Rey (see page 72). This is the only original chapel building in the entire mission chain still used by American Indians as a church and chapel.

Built in 1815, the mission is adorned with frescoes and has an attractive campanile. Behind the mission rears Tourmaline Queen Mountain, once teeming with miners.

Palomar Observatory

Southeast of Pala, State 76 winds through Pauma Valley to the turnoff for Palomar Observatory, some 5 miles beyond Rincon Springs. It's a twisting but scenic 11½-mile drive up Palomar Mountain through chaparral- and rock-covered countryside.

High atop the mountain lie the great white dome of the 13-story observatory, operated by the California Institute of Technology, and a museum and exhibit hall. A self-guided tour briefs you on the workings of one of the country's largest telescopes.

The observatory is open daily from 9 A.M. to 4 P.M. You may want to wear a sweater; the interior of the dome must be kept at nighttime temperatures, since even a few degrees of variation can cause distortion.

From the road to the observatory, turn west to reach Palomar Mountain State Park (hiking, picnicking, camping). Vehicles with heavy loads should approach the observatory and park from the Lake Henshaw turnoff to the southeast, a more gradual incline.

Santa Ysabel

The white stucco chapel of Mission Santa Ysabel was rebuilt in 1924 in the style of the original 1818 mission (see page 6). Five Indian reservations still use it. A donation is suggested to tour.

Santa Ysabel's old general store, at the crossroads of State 78 and State 79, supposedly dates back to 1870. State 78 leads west into Anza-Borrego Desert State Park (see page 88).

Julian

High in the pine- and oak-covered hills, the tiny gold-rush town of Julian was once the county's second largest. A strike in 1870 briefly created a boom; at its end, the town settled comfortably into an agricultural and ranching existence. Julian is 7 miles southeast of Santa Ysabel where State 78 and State 79 again separate.

Main Street retains its original false-front buildings and wooden sidewalks. The refurbished Julian Hotel, circa 1887, and a host of bed-and-breakfast inns, many in old houses clinging to hillside sites, welcome guests. Other historic buildings house the stage stop and post office, a onetime jail, and an old-fashioned soda fountain.

Julian is famous for its apples; several bakeries and almost every restaurant in town make apple pies. Apple Day, the first weekend in October, naturally attracts crowds of visitors. But so do the Wildflower Show in spring and the autumn Weed Show. For information, contact the Julian Chamber of Commerce (see page 58).

Pioneer Museum. You can rediscover some of Julian's legendary artifacts—for starters, its first bathtub and oldest pool table—at the town's restored Pioneer Museum. The eclectic exhibits also include one of the state's finest lace collections, practical wedding gowns from the 1800s, a bookcase belonging to President Ulysses Grant, and a 1920s permanent wave machine that closely resembles an electric chair. Gold-mining equipment and a cider press are more recent additions.

The museum, located at 2811 Washington Street (off State 78/79 two blocks south of the town center) is open 10 A.M. to 4 P.M. daily (weekends only in winter). A $1 donation is suggested.

Gold mines. The George Washington Mine, the first in the area, can still be reached by a footpath from the end of Washington Street. The mine is closed, but you can look into a reconstructed assay office and blacksmith shop.

Guided 1½-hour tours of another mine, the Eagle, are offered daily from 9 A.M. to 4 P.M. ($6 adults, $4 children). To reach the mine, take C Street east from town and follow the signs.

Cuyamaca Rancho State Park

A wilderness of rugged mountain terrain and intermittent streams, Cuyamaca Rancho State Park is blessed with a wealth of seasonal wildflowers and bird and animal life. The big park (24,677 acres) about 40 miles east of urban San Diego is popular with hikers, horseback riders, and campers.

Peaks jutting 4,000 to 6,500 feet are cloaked in dense forests of ponderosa and Jeffrey pine, fir, incense cedar, and live and black oak. Views from here extend as far as the ocean to the west and the desert to the east.

Formerly an Indian gathering place and then a Spanish rancho, the park gets its name from a Spanish translation of an old Indian word for "the place where it rains." Exhibits at the park headquarters depict activities of early-day settlers.

To reach the park from San Diego, head east on Interstate 8 and turn north on State 79.

Mexico, just a few minutes away from San Diego, lures many of the city's tourists. For shopping and sports, Tijuana is a favorite day trip. Plan a longer stay to explore the border towns of Tecate and Mexicali and the charming seaport of Ensenada, south of Tijuana.

No passports are required to visit Mexico. You won't even need a tourist card unless you plan to stay longer than 72 hours or go more than 75 miles south of the border (the destinations described here are all within the limit).

Tijuana. Mexico's most-visited city has made an effort to clean up its tawdry, raffish image. Crown jewel of the new look is the Tijuana Cultural Center at Paseo de los Heroes and Avenida Independencia north of downtown.

The complex has a fine museum, shops displaying handicrafts from all over the country, and a performing arts center. A small fee admits you to the spherical Omnitheater's film on Mexican history and culture, shown in English daily at 2 P.M.

Most of Tijuana's tourist shops and restaurants are around a 7-block stretch of spruced-up Avenida Revolucion downtown. Here, too, is Fronton Palacio, home for fast-paced jai alai.

Horse and dog racing takes place at Agua Caliente Racetrack evenings and weekends; bull rings offer corridas from mid-May to mid-September. And golfers and tennis enthusiasts are welcome at Tijuana's country club. Call Tijuana Visitors Bureau, (619) 298-4105, for details on sports, or stop by an information booth at the border or on Avenida Revolucion.

Ensenada. Todos Santos Bay 66 miles south of Tijuana is the setting for Ensenada, a casually charming resort town, sportfishing center, and port for several cruise ships. Shops, small hotels, restaurants, and boat rental offices line Lopez Mateos, the main street.

For details on daily tours of Bodegas de Santo Tomas, the country's largest winery, check with the tourist office at Avenida Lopez Mateos 13-B. The government-sponsored Centro Artesanal de Ensenada next door has a good craft display.

South of town, Estero Beach attracts swimmers and surfers; La Bufadora blowhole is another 14 miles. A rustic hot springs lies 10 miles inland.

Tecate. This small, simple, clean town's primary attractions are a brewery and nearby Rancho La Puerta spa. Stop by the tourist office on the south side of the plaza on Callejon Libertad for a visitor's guide.

Mexicali. A cultural tour of Baja California's state capital might include stops at the university's regional museum (Avenida Reforma and Calle L) and the former state governor's residence (Avenida Alvaro Obregon 1209), where a gallery displays works of Mexican artists.

Most visitors come for a day to wander around shops and dine at restaurants near the border. Zona Rosa, next to the Civic Commercial Center on Calzada Independencia at the southern edge of the city, is an attractive shopping and dining area.

Mexicali hosts colorful charreadas (Mexican rodeos) once a month in the winter and twice-monthly bullfights during the winter and on holidays.

Shopping tips. From piñatas and bright paper flowers to furniture and fine silver jewelry—Mexico's handicrafts are attractive and comparatively inexpensive. Duty-free stores display European perfumes, clothing, and crystal.

U.S. currency is accepted happily anywhere along the border. Most stores offer discounts for cash. Bring small bills; getting change can be a problem. Bargaining is the name of the game in markets. Elsewhere, stores have set prices.

U.S. Customs allows each person to bring back $400 in goods without duty (including 1 liter of alcohol, if you're over 21) each 30 days. Handicrafts are usually duty free.

Driving in Mexico. Most motorists enter Mexico at the Tijuana-San Ysidro crossing. To avoid the usual long lines, returning travelers often use the less busy crossing at Otay Mesa just east of Tijuana's airport. To reach that crossing from the U.S. side, take State 17 east from Interstate 5 or 805.

Tecate's port of entry (closed midnight to 6 A.M.) is 32 miles southeast of San Diego off State 94. The Mexicali crossing is through Calexico, about 2 hours east of San Diego via Interstate 8.

Exercise caution when driving in Mexico; an automobile accident is a criminal offense for which you can be detained until claims are adjusted. Your U.S. automobile insurance is not valid in Mexico; it's a good idea to buy a short-term policy from a Mexican insurance firm on your way to the border.

If you're only going to Tijuana, you can easily park your car in San Ysidro, walk across the border, and catch a cab downtown.

Public transportation. Taking the trolley to the border is fun and inexpensive (currently $1.50). Trolleys between downtown San Diego and San Ysidro run daily from 5 A.M. to 1 A.M.

Frequent Greyhound and Mexicoach service also connect San Diego with Mexico's border towns.

Desert Destinations

outhern California's deserts are a surprise. Seemingly barren stretches of sand and cactus, they hide a wealth of plants and animals and a whole range of visitor activities. You can wind-surf on man-made lakes, rock-hunt in hidden valleys, and explore scenic old mining towns and deep underground caverns. Or you can opt for poolside sunning and rounds of golf at world-class resorts and spas, glamorous counterpoints to the sparse desert surroundings.

Throughout most of the year the desert possesses a desolate grandeur, but in spring it comes alive in an unforgettable explosion of color. The natural beauty of this blooming landscape is preserved in several state and national parks, from Antelope Valley's California Poppy Reserve to the East Mojave National Scenic Area.

Lay of the land

A collection of glittering resort communities—often called the Sunshine Strip—lines the Coachella Valley from Palm Springs southeast to Indio. The area's popularity is nothing new: the Cahuilla Indians were lured here centuries ago by its warm springs and the sheltering palm oases in the San Jacinto Mountains that rise to the west.

North and south of the valley sprawl two grand desert preserves, Joshua Tree and Anza-Borrego. Their time-carved

Resembling giant desert candles, blossoming yuccas stretch skyward against a backdrop of granite boulders at Joshua Tree National Monument. This unique high and low desert park lies northeast of Palm Springs.

canyons and wind-blown mesas reveal the subtle differences between high and low deserts.

To the southeast lies Salton Sea, a getaway for swimmers, boaters, anglers, campers, and bird-watchers. Eastward, where the Colorado River forms the California-Arizona border, the dams that tamed the river created lakes that beckon boaters and waterskiers.

The immense Mojave Desert encompasses much of southeastern California. Within this great high desert you'll find everything from ghost towns to Edwards Air Force Base, landing site for NASA space flights.

Planning a visit

Among the great virtues of this vast land is that it seems far removed from more populous regions, yet it's easy to reach from anywhere in Southern California. And it offers get-away-from-it-all experiences to suit a variety of tastes, from camping under the stars to relaxing at some of the state's finest accommodations.

When to go. The desert's magnet is its climate, especially from mid-October to mid-May. Days are generally sunny, warm, and cloudless, the air dry. Winter temperatures are comfortable, 70° to 90° during the day; nights can dip to 25°, although 40° is more usual. In summer, daytime temperatures hover around 100° or more, but low humidity makes it bearable. Rainfall is scant, falling mostly in brief storms from November through April. Spring and autumn usually have good weather, fewer people, and reduced room rates.

Getting around. Interstate 10 is L.A.'s main escape route to Palm Springs (120 miles) and other Coachella Valley oases. Interstate 15 stretches along the

northern edge of the East Mojave National Scenic Area en route to Las Vegas, and Interstate 40 skirts the southern edge on its way from Barstow to Needles. State 14 gives access to the Mojave's western edge.

Even though the desert's largest cities have commercial plane and bus service, you need a vehicle to do much exploring. Palm Springs, gateway to Coachella Valley resorts, is served by national and commuter airlines.

Lodging. Coachella Valley offers the desert's widest choice of lodging, from well-landscaped RV parks to deluxe megaresorts (see page 84). Elsewhere, you'll find the most motels and services at Lancaster/Palmdale, Victorville, Barstow, Needles, and Blythe.

Contacts

These agencies offer information on attractions and accommodations. See additional contacts throughout this chapter.

Palm Springs Desert Resorts Convention & Visitors Bureau
69-930 Highway 111, Suite 201
Rancho Mirage, CA 92270
(619) 770-9000

Desert Information Center
408 E. Fredericks St.
Barstow, CA 92311
(619) 256-8617

California Deserts Tourism Association
P.O. Box 364
Rancho Mirage, CA 92270
(619) 328-9256

The Sunshine Strip

Green golf courses and turquoise swimming pools, palm trees and tennis courts, Bob Hope and Frank Sinatra—to many, these symbolize the air-conditioned, irrigated continuum of resort communities from Palm Springs to Indio. But traces of the Coachella Valley's early days can still be found in mountain canyons and pioneer adobes, commercial date groves, and elegant old resorts.

Palm Springs may be the best known of the desert resort communities, but the 20-mile stretch of State 111 between "The Springs" and Indio boasts the valley's newest shopping and entertainment complexes as well as many of its most popular retreats. Desert Hot Springs, a few miles north of Palm Springs, has long been a spa setting.

How it all began

An ancient lake that filled the Coachella Valley for centuries began receding around 1500. The Cahuilla Indians, who had depended on the lake for fish, found other sources of food and adapted to the new environment. Some Cahuillas still live around the valley, many at nearby Morongo and Agua Caliente reservations. They also own prime valley real estate, such as the bubbling hot springs under the Spa Hotel & Mineral Springs in Palm Springs (corner of Tahquitz–McCallum Way and Indian Avenue).

The region first gained its reputation as a health spa about a century ago. Those first valley resorts were short on luxury; dry air was the elixir they promoted.

In the 1920s and 30s, the area became a refuge for the rich and famous. Hollywood celebrities like Greta Garbo, Clark Gable, and Errol Flynn patronized La Quinta Hotel when it opened in 1926. Now this hostelry 15 miles southeast of Palm Springs—the valley's oldest still in operation—has been transformed into a chic resort famous for its golf courses.

The presence of celebrities is still very much felt in these desert resort towns.

Streets, public buildings, and sports events bear their names, and tour buses patrol their neighborhoods to give visitors a glimpse of how they live.

Activities

A surprising diversity of activity welcomes valley visitors: golf, tennis, horseback riding, cycling, swimming, picnicking, hiking, ice skating, and hot-air ballooning. Spas offer extensively equipped health clubs. For a complete listing of facilities, contact the Palm Springs Desert Resorts Convention & Visitors Bureau (see page 79).

Spectators can watch California Angels spring training baseball games, polo matches, tennis tournaments, and almost 200 golf tournaments a year, including the prestigious Bob Hope Classic (January), Dinah Shore LPGA Championship (April), and Skins Game (November).

Musical and theatrical performances are presented in Palm Desert at the Bob Hope Cultural Center and the College of the Desert, and in Palm Springs at the convention center and the Walter Annenberg Theatre.

A world of shopping awaits along Palm Canyon Drive in Palm Springs and on El Paseo, 2 miles of trendy boutiques and galleries in Palm Desert.

Exploring the valley

For an all-encompassing valley view, soar aloft in a hot-air balloon or go sightseeing by helicopter or plane. Several companies offer rides; check the Yellow Pages for phone numbers.

Desert Off-Road Adventures offers a 3-hour jeep safari of the Coachella Valley backcountry, wandering some 20 miles through Indian canyons and past a bighorn sheep reserve. For information and prices, call (619) 773-3187.

Two companies offer tours past stars' homes and other attractions along the Sunshine Strip. The longer tours are a good introduction to historic landmarks, museums, parks, and shopping areas. One-hour tours focus on the most

popular sights: the huge hedged estates of Walter Annenberg and Frank Sinatra, the discreet homes of Goldie Hawn and Lena Horne, and Bob Hope's spaceship-shaped abode.

Gray Line Tours, (619) 325-0974, has daily 2½-hour bus tours at 9:30 A.M. and 1:30 P.M. from October through May 15. Celebrity Tours, (619) 325-2682, has 1- and 2-hour bus tours daily. Call for times. Both pick up at major hotels and other locations.

Palm Springs

It's easy to find your way around Palm Springs. State 111, the exit off Interstate 10 to Palm Springs, becomes Palm Canyon Drive, the city's main street (one-way heading south). Indian Avenue, a block east, runs one-way north through the central part of the "village." Tahquitz–McCallum Way is the dividing line for north and south street numbering.

Balmy winter weather often means bumper-to-bumper traffic and scarce parking in the busy downtown area. To avoid these headaches, hop aboard the Sun Trolley shuttle that loops through the village between 9 A.M. and 7 P.M. from November through May. Fare is 50 cents.

Palm Springs is also the departure point for an aerial tramway into the San Jacinto Mountains—see page 85.

Village Green Heritage Center. For a peek at Palm Springs' past, visit this collection of pioneer buildings at 221 S. Palm Canyon Drive. The center includes Cornelia White's pioneer railroad-tie house (originally part of the valley's first hotel), McCallum Adobe (home of the city founder), and Ruddy's General Store Museum (a re-creation of a typical general store of the 1930s).

Hours are noon to 3 P.M. Wednesday and Sunday, 10 A.M. to 4 P.M. Thursday, Friday, and Saturday from mid-October through May. The rest of the year, the buildings are open weekends only, noon to 6 P.M. There's a small fee to enter each building.

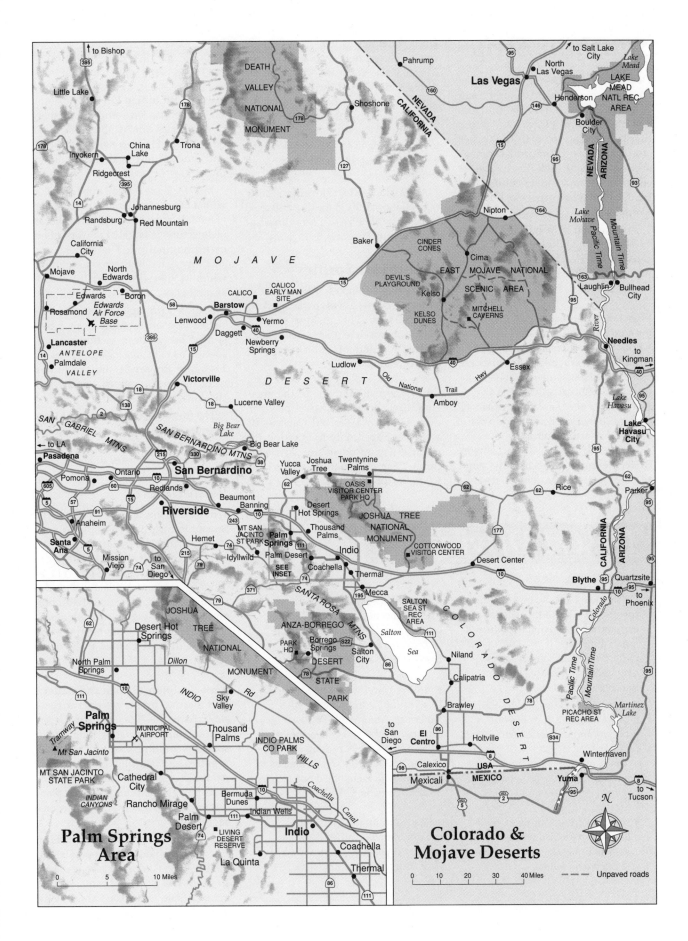

Palm Springs Area

0   5   10 Miles

Colorado & Mojave Deserts

0   10   20   30   40 Miles   ------ Unpaved roads

...Sunshine Strip

Desert Museum. Don't miss seeing the handsome museum and cultural center at 101 Museum Drive, behind the Desert Fashion Plaza. One wing displays Western art, the other contemporary. A natural sciences section concentrates on the desert environment and Indian culture. The landscaped sculpture gardens are worth a look.

The museum is open 10 A.M. to 4 P.M. Tuesday through Friday, to 5 on weekends (closed Monday and in summer). Admission is free on the first Tuesday of each month.

Moorten Botanical Garden. A stroll through this private preserve gives you a good look at desert plantings and wildlife. The 4-acre garden displays more than 2,000 unusual specimens from arid regions around the world, and some of them create surprisingly verdant spots. Benches provide a place to sit and watch the birds.

Located at 1701 S. Palm Canyon Drive, the garden is open daily from 9 A.M. to 5 P.M. (small admission fee).

Oasis Water Resort. Children of all ages combat desert heat with a visit to the 21-acre Oasis Water Resort, 1500 Gene Autry Trail. One of the biggest of the Southland's water parks, it operates daily from March through early September and on weekends through October, opening at 11 A.M. and closing at 6 P.M. in spring and autumn, 8 P.M. in summer.

Admission is $14.95 for anyone taller than 60 inches, $9.95 for those 40 to 60 inches, less after 5 P.M. There's an additional charge for parking.

Desert Hot Springs

As the name denotes, activity in this popular resort revolves around its mineral spas. The gushing springs, which can reach temperatures of 207°, are cooled to under 110° for therapeutic and recreational uses.

Spas. The most famous of the area's spas is Two Bunch Palms (see page 84), once a hideaway for Al Capone. Its waters are open only to guests at the resort, but many others are open to the public. For information, contact the Chamber of Commerce, 13560 Palm Drive, Desert Hot Springs, CA 92240; (800) 346-3347 in California, (619) 329-6403 outside the state.

Cabot's Old Indian Pueblo Museum. The desert has long attracted its share of eccentrics, and Cabot Yerxa was one of them. His unconventional home and unusual memorabilia are now a museum.

In 1913, Yerxa walked into the valley with a quart of water and a paper bag of food. His pueblo, inspired by Indian architecture, is largely the work of his own imagination. The cement and adobe maze has 35 tiny rooms with 150 windows pieced together from odd-shaped glass.

Scattered throughout the house are such exotic mementos as an 8-foot stuffed brown bear, pictures of prospector Yerxa in Alaska with his friend Theodore Roosevelt, and an Indian medicine man's vestments made from elk skin and human hair.

The museum, 67-616 E. Desert View Avenue, is open 9:30 A.M. to 4:30 P.M. daily except Tuesday. You pay a small fee and get an informal tour.

Palm Desert

This resort town midway along the Sunshine Strip is beginning to rival Palm Springs for shopping, sports, culture, and attractions. The Palm Desert Town Center (State 111 at Monterey Avenue) boasts large department stores, more than 100 shops, and an all-year indoor ice-skating rink. The College of the Desert and the Bob Hope Cultural Center host many special events.

Aerie Sculpture Garden and Gallery. Part nature preserve, part artists' showplace, this 2½-acre Palm Desert garden combines native plants with some 40 sculptures created from metal, acrylic, and stained glass. A free pamphlet maps the route along a ⅓-mile trail. The reflecting pool and plant misters attract bighorn sheep, raccoons, eagles, and ravens.

Aerie is open 1 to 4 P.M. Friday through Monday and by appointment; call (619) 568-6366. Admission is $2.50. To reach the garden, drive south 2½ miles on State 74; turn on Cahuilla Way,

---

Desert Driving

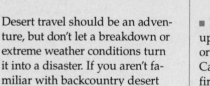

Desert travel should be an adventure, but don't let a breakdown or extreme weather conditions turn it into a disaster. If you aren't familiar with backcountry desert driving, here are some precautions you should take:

■ Give friends a copy of your itinerary and date of return.

■ Carry at least a gallon of drinking water per day per person; bring extra for vehicles.

■ Wear layered clothing. It slows dehydration and minimizes exposure in hot weather, insulates you in cold weather.

■ Don't count on being able to pick up supplies beyond the last town, or find help fast in case of trouble. Carry extra food and gas. Take first-aid gear and a sleeping bag.

■ Always travel with a good map. Desert map sources include the American Automobile Association (free to members), U.S. Geological Survey (Box 25286, Federal Center, Denver, CO 80225), and Bureau of Land Management (1695 Spruce Street, Riverside, CA 92507).

■ Road conditions can change rapidly in bad weather. Before setting out, always check with a local source such as a park ranger.

Acres of golf courses carpet the Coachella Valley between Palm Springs and Indio,
like this one at Marriott's Desert Springs Resort in Palm Desert. East of the desert play-
ground, the abruptly rising San Jacinto Mountains are often snowcapped in winter.

north on Cat Canyon Road, and west on Cholla Way to Aerie Road.

Living Desert. A 1,200-acre wild animal park and botanical garden recreates the flora and fauna of eight different desert habitats. You'll see bighorn sheep, Arabian oryx, coyotes, and reptiles. Bats and other creatures active at night inhabit a special display.

An ethnobotanical garden contains plants used by Native Americans for food, fiber, soap, and other purposes. Another section of the reserve features Joshua trees and other high-desert succulents. All areas are described in a trail guide.

The Living Desert sanctuary, at 47900 S. Portola Avenue, is about 1½ miles south of State 111. It's open 9 A.M. to 5 P.M. daily from September through mid-June. Admission is $6 for adults, $5.25 for seniors, $3 for children 3 to 15.

Indio

Early Coachella Valley date farmers envisioned a scene straight from Morocco—endless rows of date palms swaying in desert breezes. Towns were dubbed Arabia, Mecca, and Oasis. The communities that remain don't exactly present the Byzantine image their founders intended. But the date industry has thrived, and dates are such a major crop southeast of Indio that the town is often dubbed the date capital of the nation.

State 111 in western Indio is the "Date Strip." Groves alternate with date stores adorned with brightly painted plywood pavilions and Moorish cupolas. Here's your chance to buy a fancy gift pack or try a date milkshake. At Shields Date Gardens, you can watch a film on the love life of a date or wander through a fine rose garden.

National Date Festival. This popular week-long event in mid-February began in 1921 as an effort to bring tourism to the valley. Held in connection with the Riverside County Fair, festivities include a national horse show, an Arabian Nights pageant, and some hilarious ostrich and camel races.

Coachella Valley Museum. The city's tidy museum and cultural center at 82-616 Miles Avenue is housed in a small, cool adobe that was a doctor's home and office in the 1920s. Exhibits include Cahuilla Indian artifacts and old farm and household equipment.

From autumn through spring, the museum is open 10 A.M. to 4 P.M. Tuesday through Saturday, noon to 4 Sunday; in summer, it's open weekends only. Visitors pay a small fee to tour.

Desert Oases

Each new desert resort built along the Sunshine Strip (Highway 111 between Palm Springs and Indio) seems more plush than the last. Surrounded by green fairways and boasting glamorous spa, tennis, and dining facilities, these self-contained retreats might be worth an occasional splurge.

As examples of what you'll find in top-of-the-line lodging, we list one deluxe resort from each community. For a listing of all area accommodations, contact Palm Springs Desert Resorts Convention & Visitors Bureau (see page 79).

Listings below include published rates for double rooms during the peak winter season; check for latest information. Rates are usually reduced in spring and autumn; they often drop as much as 50 percent in summer.

DoubleTree Resort (formerly Desert Princess Resort), Vista Chino at Landau (P.O. Box 1644), Palm Springs, CA 92263; (619) 322-7000. Facilities: 289 units, 2 restaurants, pool and spa, 10 tennis courts, 2 racquetball courts, 18 holes golf, rental bikes. Rates: $195–$220.

Hyatt Grand Champions Resort, 44-600 Indian Wells Lane, Indian Wells, CA 92210; (619) 341-1000. Facilities: 336 units, 3 restaurants, 4 pools, health club, 12 tennis courts, tennis stadium, 36 holes golf. Rates: $220–$325.

Indian Palms Resort & Country Club, 48-630 Monroe Street, Indio, CA 92201; (619) 347-0688. Facilities: 59 units, 2 restaurants, small pool and spa, 9 tennis courts, 27 holes golf. Rates: $64–$74.

La Quinta Hotel Golf & Tennis Resort, 49-499 Eisenhower Drive (P.O. Box 69), La Quinta, CA 92253; (619) 564-4111. Facilities: 640 casitas, 5 restaurants, 25 pools and 35 spas, 30 tennis courts, 36 holes golf. Rates: $195–$285.

Marriott's Desert Springs Resort & Spa, 74-855 Country Club Drive, Palm Desert, CA 92260; (619) 341-2211. Facilities: 891 units, 5 restaurants, 3 lagoon-sized pools, health spa, 18 tennis courts, 36 holes golf. Rates: $235–$330.

Ritz-Carlton, Rancho Mirage, 68-900 Frank Sinatra Drive, Rancho Mirage, CA 92270; (619) 321-8282. Facilities: 238 units, 3 restaurants, pool, health club, 10 tennis courts. Rates: $275–$395.

Two Bunch Palms, 67-425 Two Bunch Palms Trail, Desert Hot Springs, CA 92240; (619) 329-8791. Facilities: 44 villas, restaurant, mineral springs, tanning bins, mud baths, pool, 2 tennis courts, mountain bikes. Rates: $100–$365.

Into the Mountains

When days warm up in the Coachella Valley, residents and visitors alike head for the nearby mountains to picnic in the lush canyons behind Palm Springs or ride a tram up to the cool wilderness area around Mount San Jacinto.

The craggy ramparts of the San Jacintos rise abruptly from near sea level to 10,084 feet. Although the tram is the most dramatic way to reach their upper reaches, you can also get there by way of Banning (Interstate 10 to State 243) or via Riverside and Hemet (Interstate 215 to State 74 to State 243).

Jumping-off spot for exploring the upper Jacintos by car or foot is the forested community of Idyllwild southwest of Palm Springs, where you'll find hotels, motels, restaurants, camping supplies, pack and saddle stock.

Indian canyons

The scenic canyons tucked into the folds of the mountains behind Palm Springs have been the traditional summer retreat of the Cahuilla Indians for centuries. Today the canyons attract hikers, horseback riders, bird-watchers, and photographers as well.

A toll road through the Agua Caliente Indian Reservation gives access to the canyons. Follow Palm Canyon Drive south to the reservation, about 5 miles from the heart of Palm Springs. The toll gate is open daily from 9 A.M. to 4 P.M. except in summer (usually mid-May to mid-October), when the hazard of fire is too extreme.

The road into the canyons is narrow and winding; the last half-mile requires cautious driving. For further information, call the local Bureau of Indian Affairs office, (619) 325-2086.

Palm Canyon. This 14-mile-long canyon 7 miles beyond the toll gate is noted for its fine stands of Washingtonia palms, many of them more than 1,500 years old. You can view the canyon from above at Hermit's Bench parking area (souvenirs, soft drinks, rest rooms) or from a steep trail that drops down into the canyon.

For a pleasant day's outing, bring a picnic lunch; there are tables but no drinking water. A trail, popular with horseback riders, winds through the palm groves.

Andreas Canyon. Beyond Palm Canyon, the parking area for Andreas Canyon lies half a mile off the main road in a grove of shady sycamores and cottonwoods (picnic tables, rest rooms). A particularly impressive grove of native California fan palms stands nearby. A trail follows an all-year stream about 4 miles to the head of the canyon.

Murray Canyon. Hidden between Andreas and Palm, Murray Canyon is accessible by hiking trail from Andreas Canyon. It's also popular with horseback riders. Most of the year a clear stream flows through the canyon.

Aerial tramway

To beat the heat on the valley floor, catch a tram to the top of Mount San Jacinto, where the air is pine scented and the temperatures are some 40° cooler. The trip up the mountain begins in rugged Chino Canyon at the north edge of Palm Springs. Valley views are spectacular on the 14-minute climb, but try to plan your trip for a clear day; a desert haze will obscure the view.

At the top. The two 80-passenger trams move up and down one of the sheerest mountains in North America, over granite recesses deeper than the Grand Canyon. The mountain station, 8,516 feet above the valley floor, has a restaurant (open for lunch and dinner), a gift shop, and an observation deck. A free movie shows you how the tram was built in the early 1960s.

From the mountain station, it's a 6-mile hike to the summit of Mount San Jacinto. A paved trail also leads down to Long Valley, a popular picnic site. Mules can be rented to make the trek in summer. During winter, the valley welcomes cross-country skiers.

At the base. To get to the tram, take State 111 north from Palm Springs and follow the signs. Gray Line offers bus service.

Tram rides begin at 10 A.M. Monday through Friday, 8 A.M. weekends and holidays. In summer, the last trip leaves the valley at 9 P.M. and returns at 10:45 P.M. The rest of the year, the last trip is 7:30 P.M., the return at 9:15 P.M. The tram closes for two weeks of maintenance on the first Monday in August.

Round-trip admission for the 2½-mile ride is $13.95, $8.95 for children 3 to 12. You can carry hiking or backpacking gear at no extra charge.

Mount San Jacinto State Park

This mountainous state park and wilderness area offers more than 50 miles of hiking trails. Only two state campgrounds are accessible by car, but primitive camping is available in state and federal wilderness areas.

Hikers and horseback riders alike need day-use permits to enter the wilderness section of the park. Apply in person at Long Valley Ranger Station at the top of the aerial tramway or at the state park or forest service office in Idyllwild. Backpackers need overnight permits in advance. For maps and further information, call (714) 659-2607.

San Gorgonio Pass

West of Palm Springs, Interstate 10 slices through the divide between the San Jacinto and San Bernardino mountains. The Cahuilla Indians operate the small Malki Museum on their Morongo Reservation (north side of San Gorgonio Pass). The free museum is open Tuesday through Sunday; exit north from the freeway just east of Banning on Fields Road and follow the signs.

Detour off the freeway at Beaumont and Banning for springtime views of cherry and peach orchards in bloom. From the freeway between Banning and Palm Springs, you'll see rows of power-generating wind machines sprouting up like huge, surrealistic cactus.

A showcase for spectacular wildflower productions, the vast Anza-Borrego Desert State Park sprawls grandly over a half million acres of mostly untamed desert.

Two Desert Parks

Contrast the high and low deserts on visits to two vast nature preserves: Joshua Tree National Park and Anza-Borrego Desert State Park. Both are within easy striking distance of the Palm Springs area on either side of Interstate 10, Joshua Tree to the north and Anza-Borrego to the south.

Joshua Tree National Park

This beautiful sanctuary, a transition area between the low Colorado Desert and the high Mojave Desert, is a rare preserve showcasing dramatic desert plants and wildlife. In spring, it's carpeted with wildflowers.

Although you can drive, hike, climb, picnic, and camp in its more than 850 square miles, Joshua Tree is less a playground than a showcase for a living desert so unique that government legislation has recently elevated its status from national monument to national park.

The giant desert plants that give the park its name are concentrated in the higher western half. If you travel all the way across the park, you'll see a clear delineation between the scrub vegetation and delicate wildflowers of the low desert in the eastern and southern regions and the more grandiose plants of the high desert.

You could do a day's trip from the Palm Springs area to take in scenic highlights. Plan to stay in or near the park if you want to do much hiking or scrambling over the huge granite boulders scattered about in improbable jumbles.

For more information, contact Joshua Tree National Park, 74485 National Monument Drive, Twentynine Palms, CA 92277; (619) 367-7511.

How to get there. The main entrance is from the north off state 62 at Twenty-nine Palms, about 50 miles north and east of Palm Springs (less than an hour's drive). At park headquarters south of the highway, rangers provide brochures and information on touring.

Just outside the park, Twenty-nine Palms (which has far more than 29 palms) was once a watering spot for prospectors. A small museum (6136 Adobe Road) displays mementos of early days. The free museum is open Tuesday through Sunday afternoons year-round.

You can also enter the park from the town of Joshua Tree (17 miles west of the main entrance on State 62) or, from the south, via Cottonwood Springs Road off Intersatate 10 some 25 miles east of Indio. Paved roads connect the three entrances, making loop trips possible. It's about 45 miles from the southern entrance to the main entrance, but don't expect a quick drive through the park; speed limits are low and vista turnouts frequent.

When to go. Because much of Joshua Tree is high desert, the weather is pleasant most of the year. Altitude ranges from 1,000 to 6,000 feet in the mountainous regions. Most roads are at the 3,000- to 4,000-foot level, so it seldom gets too hot for comfort even in summer. And desert nights can be cold. Occasional strong winds can whip up dust storms.

Where to stay. Black Rock Canyon campground can be reserved through Ticketron; others are first come, first served. Facilities include tables, firepits, and toilets. Bring your own water and fuel; you can fill water containers at the visitor center.

There are no motels or restaurants within the park. Limited accommodations are available in towns around the park, including Twentynine Palms and Yucca Valley to the north.

Plants and animals. Trademark plant of the high Mojave Desert, the Joshua tree (*Yucca brevifolia*) is actually a giant member of the lily family. Supposedly named by Mormon pioneers, who also called it the "praying plant" because of its upstretched arms, it grows at 3,000- to 5,000-foot elevations in the central and western parts of the park.

Joshua trees can attain heights of 40 feet. From about February to April, foot-long clusters of greenish white blossoms adorn their branches; each plant flowers only every second or third year.

The eastern half of the national park is dominated by creosote bush, spidery-branched ocotillo, and cholla cactus. Several oases within the park are shaded by stately fan palms.

The spring wildflower show depends upon winter rains, which average about 5 inches. In a normal year, a colorful display begins in lower elevations as early as March. Lost Palms Oasis Trail is one good place to spot blooms (see page 88).

Desert wildlife is abundant because of the park's variety of altitude and climate. About 250 kinds of birds and 38 species of reptiles and amphibians have been sighted.

Signs of the past. To step back a century, visit the Desert Queen Ranch. Also called Keys Ranch, this little-known landmark is better preserved than many ghost towns. Rangers lead hour-long tours to the ranch from mid-February through Memorial Day and from mid-October to mid-December. Schedules are posted at the visitor center.

You'll see traces of Indian, cattle rustling, and mining days. But the dominant presence is that of William Keys, a colorful character who homesteaded here after World War I. The tour includes the now-derelict ranch house, tiny schoolhouse, dam, and orchard. Scattered around is old-time farm gear.

Desert views. A self-guided nature trail leads to a palm oasis from park headquarters. Among numerous other trails, a walk through Cholla Cactus Garden (midway between northern and southern entrances) is interesting.

A few miles into the park from the north, Hidden Valley supposedly once sheltered cattle rustlers among its massive boulders. Keys View, at the end of the paved road south from Hidden Valley, offers vistas stretching from the

...Two Desert Parks

Salton Sea (235 feet below sea level) to the San Jacinto and San Gabriel mountains (over 10,000 feet above sea level).

The 18-mile Geology Tour Road southwest of park headquarters affords sweeping views and takes you past old mines and a fine stand of barrel cactus.

Anza-Borrego Desert State Park

Largest state park in the contiguous United States, Anza-Borrego's nearly 600,000 acres (1,000 square miles) contain fabled badlands, seasonal waterfalls, cool piney heights, natural springs, and waves of wildflowers in spring. You can't see it all in one visit.

Anza-Borrego offers an easily accessible introduction to the harsh beauty of the Colorado Desert, an extension of Mexico's vast Sonoran Desert. Its gullied badlands are its most extraordinary phenomenon, but there's far more to the park than that: subtle fragrances of sage and cottonwood, about 600 species of animals—and terrain nearly as untouched as that found by early Spanish explorers.

Juan Bautista de Anza pioneered a route through this desert in 1774, and the park name honors him. The second part of the name is a Spanish word for sheep; some desert bighorns still live in the more remote northern reaches of Anza-Borrego.

The park's visitor center (open daily from October through May, weekends only the rest of the year) is at Borrego Palm Canyon, 3 miles west of the small community of Borrego Springs on State 22. The building looks as if it was burrowed out of the desert; it's topped with cement and six feet of sand.

For additional information, contact Anza-Borrego Desert State Park, P.O. Box 299, Borrego Springs, CA 92004; (619) 767-4205.

How to get there. By car, Anza-Borrego is 1½ hours south of Palm Springs and 2 hours east of San Diego. Take State 111 east from Palm Springs, turn south on State 86, and head west on State 22 to Borrego Springs. From San Diego, take State 78 east.

When to go. The most comfortable time to visit the park is from late autumn to mid-May. Summer gets torrid, but the dry air keeps it from being unbearable. In this part of the desert, temperatures can vary as much as 50° within a 24-hour period; evenings are always cool.

Accommodations. Borrego Springs, a private enclave in the center of the park, has restaurants, trailer parks, modest motels, and two surprisingly luxurious resorts, Rams Hill Country Club (18-hole golf course) and La Casa del Zorro. For a list of lodgings, contact the Chamber of Commerce, Borrego Springs, CA 92004; (619) 767-5555.

Desert camping here varies from highly developed (Borrego Palm Canyon) to primitive (wherever you wish, with a few restrictions). Reservations for developed sites are recommended on weekends and holidays; call MISTIX, (800) 444-7275.

Around the park. More than 600 miles of roads offer a choice of scenery and terrain. Probably the most famous viewpoint in the park is Font's Point north of Borrego Palm Canyon, overlooking the spectacularly undulating Borrego Badlands. Other roads and trails lead to groves of California fan palms and stands of smoke trees (among the finest anywhere) and to clusters of the park's signature plant, the fat-boled, low-to-the-ground elephant tree (*Bursera microphylla*).

Ranger-led nature walks, auto caravans, and campfire programs are offered from the visitor center on weekends and holidays in season.

Blossom Trails

When the desert flowers, its brilliance is dazzling. Bright colors contrast vividly with the landscape's usually more subdued hues.

Several areas offer particularly extravagant spring displays. From early March through May, you can call the Wildflower Hotline, (818) 768-3533, to find out which regions have the best blossoms.

Antelope Valley. About 50 miles north of Los Angeles, a 1,745-acre California Poppy Reserve was established in 1976 on some of the state's most consistent poppy-bearing land.

The reserve (15101 West Lancaster Road, 10 miles west of Lancaster off State 138) is open daily from 10 A.M. to 4 P.M. during the blooming period (usually mid-March through May). There's a small per-car entry fee. Four loop trails let you get close to the flowers. Shelters have picnic tables.

Joshua Tree National Park. From February to April, you should find flower-filled canyons along the 4-mile Lost Palms Oasis Trail from Cottonwood Springs, a mile east of the visitor center on Interstate 10. Call (619) 367-7511 for prime viewing times.

Anza-Borrego Desert State Park. The 1½-mile trail to Palm Canyon from Borrego Palm Canyon Campground is overpopular from February to early March, but it's an excellent introduction to classic desert flora. Or you can pick up a wildflower map, updated weekly, at the visitor center.

To plan a visit around the peak period, send a stamped, self-addressed postcard (with words such as "The flowers are blooming!" written on the back) to Wildflower Notification, Visitor Center, Anza-Borrego Desert State Park, Borrego Springs, CA 92004. It will be returned when the show starts.

Salton Sea

Sandwiched between the rich farmlands of the Imperial Valley and the resorts of the Coachella Valley, the 35-mile-long Salton Sea is one of the world's largest inland bodies of salt water and a mecca for water-sports enthusiasts.

Once dry wasteland, the sea was formed in 1905 when the Colorado River overstepped its bound. Billions of gallons of floodwaters were trapped below sea level.

With no natural outlet to dilute the minerals in its waters, the shallow sea has become increasingly salty over the years. A desalinization project is now underway in an attempt to stabilize the salinity level—and prevent the Salton Sea from becoming a dead sea.

It isn't only fish who depend on the Salton Sea. This is an important link on the Pacific Flyway, host to 373 species of birds at one time or another. Spectacular skeins of Canada and snow geese shadow the skies above the sea in autumn, and a third of North America's white pelicans winter here.

When to visit. Salton Sea is a hot place in summer—temperatures can be well above 100°. Winter temperatures are in the comfortably low 50s to high 80s. Water temperatures drop as low as 50° in midwinter and climb as high as 90° in summer. Best months to visit are November and December and February through April; strong winds hamper water activity in January.

How to get there. Located 20 miles southeast of Indio, Salton Sea is ringed by good highways. State 86 runs to the west, State 111 to the east. State 78 from Anza-Borrego Desert State Park joins State 86 along the lake's southwest shore.

Recreational choices

Fishing, boating, swimming, water-skiing, bird-watching, and duck hunting are among the area's attractions. Racers consider Salton Sea one of the fastest bodies of water in the world;

because it's 235 feet below sea level, internal combustion engines run more efficiently here. A storm alert system warns boaters of occasional strong winds that can create high waves.

Although the continuing concentration of minerals in the sea has made it far saltier than the Pacific Ocean, fish introduced in the 1950s by the Department of Fish and Game have adapted and survived. And a freshwater fish, tilapia, has managed to proliferate here since it entered via the Coachella Valley canal system.

Because of the concentration of minerals, fish caught in the Salton Sea have elevated levels of selenium. Pregnant women and small children are advised not to eat them, and others should limit their consumption.

Salton Sea State Recreation Area. Headquarters of the 17,913-acre recreation area lies at the northern end of the lake about 22 miles southeast of Indio on State 111. The visitor center here is open from Labor Day to Memorial Day.

Varner Harbor is the hub for boating and fishing activities. A marina offers boat-launching facilities. The breakwater is popular with croaker fishers; corvina and sargo fishing is best from a boat.

The recreation area has both primitive and improved campsites and picnic areas. Campsites are available on a first-come, first-served basis, except for a 40-site area (25 with full hookups) that you can reserve by calling MISTIX, (800) 444-7275.

For information on facilities, contact Park Ranger, Salton Sea State Recreation Area, P.O. Box 3166, North Shore, CA 92254; (619) 393-3052.

Salton Sea National Wildlife Refuge. State 111 takes you along the sea's eastern edge for several miles before swinging away from the water. The sea then drops from sight, and you could easily miss one of its most fascinating sights: a great gathering of birds along the south shore.

A short detour gives you a close look. Turn west on Sinclair Road about 4 miles after State 111 turns south at Niland. Then it's about 4½ miles to the wildlife refuge headquarters.

Look for snowy egrets, great blue herons, and snow and Ross geese on the 2-mile nature trail along the lake. The setting is serene, but hardly quiet. In winter, when geese are present in force, their bickering makes an impressive din. A lookout tower gives a good vantage point.

Nearby desert sights

Dusty side roads and rocky trails around Salton Sea lead to hot mineral springs, Indian relics, rock-hunting grounds, ancient shell deposits, colorful canyons, and sand dunes.

From State 86 west of the sea, watch for the "bathtub ring" that marks the onetime shore of Lake Cahuilla, which covered the Salton Sink from about 900 to 1400 A.D. You'll see it along the base of the foothills west of the highway near the Imperial-Riverside county line.

Mecca Hills. Three canyons—Painted, Box, and Hidden Spring—in choice desert country just north of Salton Sea are favorites of hikers. All are off State 195, a few miles west of Mecca. Smoke trees and desert ironwood present a spring show of purple blossoms.

Travertine Rock. A mound of enormous boulders can be seen about 100 yards off State 86 some 6 miles south of its intersection with State 195. Once partially submerged by Lake Cahuilla, the mound—not a true travertine, but a calcareous tufa rock— is covered with a scaly, knobby limestone. A climb to the top (about 200 feet) affords a good view.

South of Travertine Rock, along State 86, amateur geologists and rock collectors find a happy hunting ground. Look for brightly colored quartzites, flints, granites, schists, and sandstone around the south end of the sea, the farther from the highway the better.

Along the Colorado

Once described as "too thick to drink and too thin to plow," the Colorado River forms a natural boundary between California and Arizona. It served as a canoe thoroughfare for early American Indians and, later, as a watercourse for paddle-wheel steamers.

The river today is an important water supplier for the Los Angeles Basin. But the dams that tamed it also turned it into a watery playground. Most of its 265-mile length from Hoover Dam in Nevada to the Mexican border invites recreational use. You can float an innertube down a calm stretch east of Blythe or head for the marinas that dot the shoreline at Lake Havasu.

Summers are hot in this low desert region, temperatures climbing above 100°. But July and August, with quiet and warm waters, offer outstanding boating, fishing, and waterskiing.

Around Needles

Needles sits near the junction of Interstate 40 and U.S. 95, just south of Nevada's southern tip. Established in 1869 as a steamboat landing and supply station on the Old Emigrant Trail, Needles grew with the coming of the railroad. The train depot and adjacent "Harvey House" hotel have been carefully preserved.

Good beaches line the river here; a marina and golf course add to the city's appeal. Anglers congregate downstream in the Havasu National Wildlife Refuge; a valid fishing license and a special use stamp lets you fish from the river or from the Arizona side.

Twenty-six miles upstream from Needles, the Nevada town of Laughlin is popular with Southlanders as the nearest major casino destination.

Park Moabi. This park, 11 miles southeast of Needles on Interstate 40, surrounds a lagoon that opens onto the river directly across from the wildlife refuge. Launching facilities, boat docking, and boat rentals (including houseboats) are available. Secluded inlets invite camping.

Topock Gorge. A scenic stretch of the Colorado accessible only by boat lies just below the Interstate 40 crossing. Mohave Canyon, 15 miles in length, leads south to Lake Havasu.

Neither roads nor trails approach the canyon, but boaters can explore bays, sloughs, caves, and side canyons that cut into its steep, colorful walls. While onshore camping is prohibited in many areas, houseboats may anchor overnight in sheltered bays. You can rent boats and motors at Park Moabi or across the river in Topock, Arizona.

Deep trolling may yield striped bass or trout; catfish are plentiful for bait fishers plumbing holes in warmer bays.

Lake Havasu

The intensely blue waters of sinuous Lake Havasu (3 miles across at its widest point, 45 miles long) make a refreshing break in the stark desert. This picturesque Colorado River reservoir, created by the construction of Parker Dam in 1938, fluctuates so little it has been spared the shoreline band that disfigures most reservoirs.

Lake Havasu State Park, a 13,000-acre preserve on the Arizona side of the river, has its headquarters at Pittsburgh Point on the island linked by London Bridge to Lake Havasu City.

Getting around. Lodging and facilities are centered at Lake Havasu City, Arizona. For information on the area, contact the Visitor and Convention Bureau, 1930 Mesquite Ave., Suite 3, Lake Havasu City, AZ 86403; phone (602) 453-3444.

To get to Lake Havasu City, turn south off Interstate 40 onto Arizona State 95, about 10 miles east of Topock. It's about a 20-mile drive.

From the California side, a road off U.S. 95 reaches the west side of the lake at the Chemenuevi Valley Indian Reservation (no facilities).

Boats can only be launched at a few points around the lake. More than 1,500 campsites (some accessible only by boat) are scattered along its shore.

Activities. Boaters can spend a full day exploring, often combining boating and waterskiing. You can ski for an hour in one direction, if you have the endurance. Powerful winter winds, which can turn the lake into a choppy sea, usually taper off by March. If one occurs while you're on the lake, take shelter at one of the refuges along the shore.

Anglers like Havasu for many reasons, one being that spring and autumn, most pleasant weatherwise, are also the best fishing seasons. There is no closed season, and you may fish all day and all night.

London Bridge. In 1825, the first stone of the New London Bridge was laid on the banks of England's Thames River; in 1971, the entire bridge stood on the shore of Lake Havasu. The 928-foot span manages to maintain a massive dignity despite its incongruous setting.

At one foot sits the London Bridge Resort and the English Village, with Tudor-style shops and restaurants. (Britain's union jack flies here, and the Lord Mayor of London visits on October 10 during an annual celebration.) Across the bridge lie the marina and Nautical Inn Resort. Also on the island is a busy commuter airport.

Lower Colorado

Now thoroughly tamed by a succession of dams, the lower reaches of the Colorado River attract lovers of warm-water angling, waterskiing, jetskiing, scenic cruising, and camping. Fishing is good for black bass, bluegills, crappies, and catfish.

Boats and other equipment can be rented at several places along the river at the town of Blythe. For information, contact the Blythe Chamber of Commerce, 201 S. Broadway, Blythe, CA 92225; (619) 922-8166.

Also of interest are the Blythe Intaglios about 15 miles north of town off U.S. 95. The giant figures created in the earth's surface by Indians centuries ago are the best known examples of this primitive art form in North America.

In the western reaches of the Mojave Desert, stunning spring displays of California poppies beckon visitors to the Antelope Valley.

The High Desert

The Mojave Desert stretches across southeastern California from the Nevada border to the town of Lancaster, northeast of Los Angeles. This is the high desert, ranging in elevation from 3,000 to 5,000 feet.

In spring, following winters of gentle rainfall, some 250 species of wildflowers paint an impressionistic canvas of color across the Mojave.

East Mojave National Preserve

The 1994 California Desert Protection Act designates some 1½ million acres of scenic area near the California-Nevada border as the East Mojave National Preserve. Currently managed by the Bureau of Land Management, (619) 326-3896, this vast desert encompasses mountain ranges, dry lakes, a year-round stream, and countless washes, mesas, buttes and badlands.

Among its inventory of scenic attractions, East Mojave has unique caverns (see facing page), lava beds, and sand dunes. All lie between Barstow and Needles (page 90); access is from Interstate 15 or Interstate 40.

Camping. Frontier freedom is the keynote of the present camping policy; you can pitch a tent and unroll a sleeping bag anywhere within 300 feet of a road, although you must stay more than 600 feet away from a waterhole.

Hole-in-the-Wall and Mid-Hills, two BLM camping areas with limited facilities (water, privies, fire rings, and tables), sit among piñons and junipers between 4,000 and 5,600 feet.

To get there, take Interstate 40 to Essex Road (about 100 miles east of Barstow, 40 miles west of Needles). Take Essex about 10 miles north to Black Canyon Road (good signed dirt strip). Drive north about 8 miles to Hole-in-the-Wall; Mid-Hills is 6½ miles farther.

Cinder Cones. Apollo astronauts trained for the 1969 moon landing in the blackened landscape of these 25,600 acres of lava beds and upthrust cinder cones, now a national natural landmark. Old mining roads give access; stick to them, as the cinder crumbles easily. The extinct volcanic cones are noteworthy for their petroglyphs.

From Baker (60 miles northeast of Barstow on Interstate 15), drive east on Kelbaker Road for about 10 miles. Park on the shoulder or follow a dirt road into the cones.

Kelso Dunes. The 70-square-mile Kelso Dunes are the most extensive in the West. Easily reached on a half-mile walk from the road, they're best if viewed at sunrise and sunset, when the slanting light clearly defines their shifting humps and ridges.

To reach the dunes, continue on Kelbaker Road about 22 miles beyond the cinder cones (see above). You'll pass the historic old Kelso train depot, slated to become a visitor center. A signed dirt road leads west about 3 miles to the main dunes. The dunes can also be reached by a dirt road off Interstate 40 (31 miles east of Ludlow).

Barstow area

A good base for exploring the high desert, the town of Barstow at the junction of Interstates 15 and 40 was founded in 1886 as a railroad depot for the Atchison, Topeka & Santa Fe. The train station (1611 E. Main Street) is now a shopping and dining complex.

Mojave River Valley Museum (270 E. Virginia Way) chronicles the area's history; the free museum is open daily 11 A.M. to 4 P.M.

The California Desert Information Center (831 Barstow Road) makes a good place to start backcountry exploration. Maps, exhibits, and displays on history, wildflowers, and wildlife enhance any visit. Jointly managed by the BLM and the city's Chamber of Commerce, the center is open from 9 A.M. to 5 P.M. daily; or call (619) 256-8617.

Calico Ghost Town. Founded in 1881 on the heels of one of the West's richest silver strikes, Calico once boasted more than 3,500 residents, two hotels, a church, a one-room schoolhouse, 13 saloons, and a small Chinatown. The town burned and was rebuilt twice, finally closing down when the price of silver dropped in 1896.

In 1951, Calico awoke to experience a new boom—tourists, not prospectors. The town was restored and opened to the public by Walter Knott of Knott's Berry Farm fame, whose uncle had grubstaked the original prospectors.

Today, this is a regional park where you can explore miles of tunnels at the high-producing Maggie Mine, ride the Calico-Odessa Railway, take a cable tram, and poke through buildings that are probably a bit tidier than before.

A campground (hookups) lets you spend a night in the "Old West." Motels are found nearby in Yermo and Barstow. Calico is north of Interstate 15 about 9 miles east of Barstow, 3½ miles west of Yermo.

Annual celebrations attract crowds: Calico Hullabaloo in April, Calico Spring Festival in May, Calico Days in October, and Western Fine Arts Festival in November. For information, contact Calico Ghost Town, P.O. Box 638, Yermo, CA 92398; (619) 254-2122.

Calico Early Man Site. An archeological dig 15 miles northeast of Barstow dates man's presence in North America back more than 50,000 years. The site was discovered in 1942 by an amateur archeologist. Twenty years later the National Geographic Society and the San Bernardino County Museum began excavation. To date, more than 6,000 artifacts have been discovered.

Free tours at the site off Interstate 15 are offered Wednesday through Sunday at 1:30 and 3:30 P.M., plus 9:30 and 11:30 A.M. Thursday through Sunday.

Roy Rogers/Dale Evans Museum. Southwest of Barstow at Victorville, this museum salutes the careers of the two Western stars—and equine costars Trigger, Buttermilk, and Trigger, Jr., who are stuffed and mounted for viewing along with canine pal Bullet. A video theater lets you see the whole crew in action. The museum, at 15650 Seneca Road, is open 9 A.M. to 5 P.M. daily except Thanksgiving and Christmas (moderate admission).

Northern Mojave

In the vast reaches of the northwestern Mojave Desert , the terrain ranges from high, imposing peaks to low, crystalline sinks of primeval lakes. Human history is recorded in ancient Indian petroglyphs and in 19th-century mines and mining towns.

Modern man's mark includes secluded military bases and missile sites. At Boron (on State 58 just west of U.S. 395) lies the world's largest open-pit borax mine. Its neighbor to the south is Edwards Air Force Base, offering free weekday tours; call (805) 258-3446.

Randsburg. A pleasant stop off U.S. 395 about 27 miles north of State 58, photogenic Randsburg was once a gold and silver mining center. Though the Yellow Aster Mine recently reopened and some 150 diehard prospectors work old claims nearby, it's almost a ghost town today.

Butte Street's weather-beaten buildings house antique stores, a general store and soda fountain, and a small hotel and tea room. The Floozy House, a former bordello behind the White House Saloon, is now an inn.

The Desert Museum (161 Butte Street) exhibits an impressive display of mining memorabilia. Open weekends, it's worth the small fee to tour.

China Lake. An extraordinary concentration of prehistoric petroglyphs can be seen in Renegade Canyon within the China Lake Naval Weapon Center firing range. Day-long tours are offered from the Maturango Museum in Ridgecrest. To join one, write to the museum, P.O. Box 1776, Ridgecrest, CA 93556, or call (619) 375-6900.

More than four decades of naval history are on display at China Lake Exhibit Center. Museum hours are 7:30 A.M. to 4:30 P.M. weekdays, 10 A.M. to 2 P.M. Saturday. From U.S. 395, take the Ridgecrest-China Lake exit and continue to 100 E. Las Flores.

Little Lake. About 20 miles north of China Lake, other notable Indian petroglyphs are found at Little Lake off U.S. 395. Some of the rock drawings are visible from the shore; you can rent a rowboat to see others. The greatest concentration is on the west shore and at the southeast end of the lake.

Camping fees at a private facility (tables, fireplaces, water) include bank-fishing privileges.

Western Mojave

The Antelope Valley corner of the Mojave Desert slopes gradually upward to the west as it narrows between the rolling foothills of the converging Tehachapi and San Gabriel mountains. Without its Joshua trees, the pastoral valley would not look like a desert at all. It's particularly attractive when wildflowers bloom (see page 88).

The Western Mojave has undergone a population explosion in recent years, as aerospace industries and spillover from the San Fernando Valley have brought an influx of desert dwellers. Lancaster, the largest city, is a good base for exploring, and the sprawling city park off State 14 (take the L exit) is a pleasant spot to stretch your legs.

You get more than just a scenic look at the valley if you pull off State 14 (heading north) at the lookout point a few miles south of Palmdale. A plaque shows the location of the San Andreas Fault, California's dominant rift zone. The fault line extends west across the valley to its highest elevation at Big Pines Summit (6,862 feet).

Burton's Tropico Gold Mine. The Tropico was one of the Southland's most successful gold mines, remaining in operation until 1956. On tours of the mine, visitors get a chance to see the 900-foot-deep shaft, a stamp mill, and mining equipment. Buildings on the property house collections of rocks, gems, period clothing, and old newspapers.

To reach the mine from Lancaster, take State 14 north 11 miles to Rosamond Boulevard, go west about 5 miles to Tropico Mojave Road, and follow the signs. The mine and museum are open from 10 A.M. to 4:30 P.M. Thursday through Sunday. Admission is modest. For information, call (805) 256-2644.

Exotic Feline Breeding Compound. Practically next door to the Tropico Mine, this breeding compound for exotic cats offers free tours of leopard and tiger enclosures daily except Wednesday from 10 A.M. to 4 P.M. Donations help fund research and build natural habitats for the animals. For further information, call (805) 256-3332.

A Cavern Tour

Visitors have been admiring Mitchell Caverns since prospector Jack Mitchell opened them to the public in 1932. Caverns such as these that combine all three types of cave formations—dripstone (stalagmites, stalactites), flowstone (ribbons, draperies), and erratics (helictites, shields)—occur only once in 40,000 caves.

Now a natural preserve in the Providence Mountains State Recreation Area, the caverns are open from mid-September through mid-June. Ranger-led 1½-hour tours (small fee) depart the visitor center at 1:30 P.M. weekdays and 10 A.M., 1:30 P.M., and 3 P.M. weekends and holidays. Bring a sweater; year-round temperature inside the caverns is 65°.

The caverns are reached from a 17-mile paved road off Interstate 40, about 100 miles east of Barstow and 40 miles west of Needles. Views from the visitor center, some 4,300 feet above the desert floor, are stunning. A few short trails and six primitive campsites (limited water) complete the facilities.

South Sierra Country

Superlatives come easy when you're talking about the region in and around the southern part of the Sierra Nevada. This area encompasses a legendary desert, the tallest peak in the lower continental United States, the Southlanders' favorite ski destination, some of the country's oldest and most massive trees, and much more.

To the west of the towering mountain range lies the southern half of the vast Central Valley, acre for acre the world's richest agricultural region.

A few of the places described in this chapter hardly seem part of Southern California when you locate them on a map. But such northerly attractions as Mammoth Mountain are much more aligned to the Southland by virtue of access and economy than they are to the northern part of the state.

Highs & lows

Two adjacent national parks—Sequoia and Kings Canyon—contain several thousand acres of giant sequoias (*Sequoiadendron giganteum*) within their combined area of 1,300 square miles. On the eastern edge of Sequoia National Park, majestic Mount Whitney's 14,495-foot peak looms above other magnificent granite mountains.

The rugged backcountry of both parks is a hiker's domain of peaks and canyons, threaded with an intricate trail system that includes the southern end of the famed John Muir Trail. Camp-

Like massive sentinels from the past, Sequoia National Park's groves of ancient giants dwarf—and awe—visitors. Some of the trees are more than 2,500 years old.

grounds in the heart of the parks are cool summertime retreats.

To the east of the Sierra, Death Valley National Park is an ideal winter destination. Nowhere else in California is nature's palette more vividly displayed than on this wind-carved landscape. Badwater, on the valley floor 282 feet below sea level, is the lowest point in the Western Hemisphere.

Between Death Valley and the Sierra is the Owens Valley, where wanderers will discover ghostly remains of mining communities and a 4,000-year-old bristlecone pine forest.

Planning a visit

There's air service to the region's larger cities (American and America West to Bakersfield, commuter lines elsewhere). But you'll need a car to thoroughly explore the area. Interstate 5 and U.S. 99 are the major north-south arteries west of the mountains. U.S. 395 through the Owens Valley offers access to the mountains from the east.

When to go. Sequoia and Kings Canyon are year-round playgrounds, though the more remote areas are not accessible in winter. The road connecting the two parks may be closed by snow at times. For recorded weather information, call (209) 565-3351.

Mammoth Mountain, north of Kings Canyon, is one of the state's longest-operating ski areas, sometimes open as late as the Fourth of July weekend. From spring through summer, the region plays host to hikers, backpackers, anglers, and mountain climbers.

The best time to visit the desert is February to May, after winter rains but before the intense heat of summer. In spring, the desert blushes with thousands of square miles of wildflowers.

The Central Valley, too, sizzles in summer. Residents escape then to nearby lakes and mountain parks.

Where to stay. Accommodations range from campgrounds, cabins, and lodges to resorts, roadside motels, and city hotels. Visalia and Bakersfield offer the greatest choice of lodging in the southern part of the Central Valley. Death Valley and Mammoth have both modern resort facilities and campgrounds. Some accommodations and camping areas in Sequoia and Kings Canyon are open all year.

Contacts

These agencies offer information on attractions and accommodations. See additional contacts throughout this chapter.

National Park Service
Sequoia and Kings Canyon
National Parks
Three Rivers, CA 93271
(209) 565-3456

Mammoth Lakes Visitor Information Center
P.O. Box 48
Mammoth Lakes, CA 93546
(800) 367-6572

Death Valley National Park
Death Valley, CA 92328
(619) 786-2331

Greater Bakersfield Convention & Visitors Bureau
P.O. Box 1947
Bakersfield, CA 93303
(805) 325-5051

Sequoia & Kings Canyon

Giant trees, awesome canyons, cascading streams, and sparkling lakes greet visitors to two spectacular national parks in the southern Sierra. Much of their natural beauty can be explored by road or trail. Bus tours, self-guided nature trails, naturalist-conducted walks, and pack trips allow everyone to sample this unspoiled mountain country.

Developed visitor amenities are concentrated in the western reaches of the parks, primarily along the 46-mile Generals Highway connecting Sequoia and Kings Canyon national parks. You can pick up maps and other material at visitor centers in the Ash Mountain, Giant Forest, Lodgepole, and Grant Grove areas—all reached via the winding Generals Highway.

Vast expanses of the two parks are road-free high country. Inhabited only by wildlife for nine months out of the year, this backcountry invites hikers and backpackers in summer. The main traffic arterial is the John Muir Trail, which begins to the north in Yosemite National Park and runs south for 225 miles. From the east side of Sequoia, the Whitney Portal Trail joins the John Muir Trail near Mount Whitney's summit (see Lone Pine, page 99).

Activities. Summer is the time for hikers and backpackers. For backcountry travel, wilderness permits and reservations (with a trail-entry date) must be obtained in advance. For information, call (209) 565-3307.

Horseback riders can hire mounts at Grant Grove in Kings Canyon for day-long trail rides. Guided day and overnight rides into the backcountry depart from Lodgepole, Cedar Grove, and Mineral King areas of the parks.

Fishing is good for brook, brown, rainbow, and golden trout. Most anglers head for the South Fork of the Kings River in Kings Canyon park. In Sequoia, the best fishing accessible by road is along the Kaweah River's Middle Fork. A California fishing license, available in both parks, is required for anyone 16 or older.

In winter, cross-country skiers head for the small Wolverton Ski Area (near Giant Forest) and Grant Grove.

How to get there. Sequoia and Kings Canyon, joined end to end along the Sierra ridge and administered jointly, can be reached easily from the west. State 198 runs 70 miles from Visalia to Sequoia, entering at Ash Mountain—headquarters for both parks. The KOA Campground in Visalia offers guided day-long bus tours of the parks; call (800) 322-2336.

From Fresno, it's 55 miles on State 180 to the Big Stump entrance of Kings Canyon.

Generals Highway, the connector between the two parks, offers dramatic views. It's a difficult drive for motor homes and large trailers, especially the 16 miles between Ash Mountain (southern entry) and Giant Forest.

The scenic highway was completed in 1934. A hint of the care taken to preserve the natural beauty along its route is Tunnel Rock, a great boulder left in the path of the road.

Where to stay. At altitudes ranging from 2,100 to 7,500 feet, more than 1,300 campsites in the two parks offer a choice of scenery and geology. Some campgrounds allow trailers (no hookups available). All except Sequoia's Lodgepole are on a first-come, first-served basis. You can reserve Lodgepole sites through Ticketron; this campground and a few others at lower elevations are open all year.

Giant Forest Lodge in Sequoia offers motel-type rooms, tent cabins, and two-room cabins, as well as a cafeteria and a summer-only restaurant and lounge; by the mid-90s, overnight facilities will be moved out of Giant Forest to the new Clover Creek area 5 miles beyond Lodgepole. The smaller Stony Creek Lodge, midway between Grant Grove Village and Giant Forest Village, has a restaurant.

Grant Grove Lodge in Kings Canyon (open all year) has modest roofed or canvas-topped cabins without baths in a pine forest; there's also a coffee shop. Cedar Grove, along the banks of the Kings River, offers limited lodging from mid-May to mid-September. Bearpaw Meadow Camp offers tent camping, dining facilities, and hot showers from the end of June until Labor Day.

To make reservations for lodges and cabins, write to Reservations Manager, Sequoia & Kings Canyon Guest Services, Sequoia National Park, CA 93262. You can also call (209) 561-3314 all year for information and reservations.

Sequoia spectacles

The first national park in California and the second in the entire national park system, Sequoia was established in 1890 to protect groves of giant sequoias. More of the huge trees grow here than anywhere else in California—their only native habitat. In 1978, the park was enlarged with the addition of the Mineral King area.

Giant Forest. Crowning the park's sequoia groves is the largest living thing in the world—the General Sherman Tree. The massive sequoia is 102 feet in base circumference, 36½ feet thick, and 275 feet tall; some 140 feet above ground, a limb almost 7 feet in diameter extends from the trunk.

The General Sherman Tree stands in the Giant Forest, the most developed area of the park. The 2-mile Congress Trail, which begins near the General Sherman Tree, takes you to yet other spectacular specimens: Senate, House, and Founder's groves, as well as President McKinley and Chief Sequoyah trees. Booklets at the trailhead explain what you'll see along the way.

Moro Rock. Walk or drive 2 miles from Giant Forest to ascend this massive boulder more than 6,000 feet above the valley floor. Steps lead 300 feet to its summit—and a 360° view.

Crystal Cave. This stalactite-hung cavern 9 miles west of Giant Forest is open daily in summer for guided tours ($3 for adults, $1.50 for children 6 to 12).

Heather Lake. Sequoia's most accessible alpine lake lies 4 miles by trail from Wolverton Ski Area. Pear Lake, 2 miles beyond, is cradled in a barren granite basin.

Mineral King. Once a silver-mining area, this rugged region in the park's southern reaches is now a peaceful retreat for summer campers and hikers. A high valley set amid a rugged mass of spectacular peaks and canyons, Mineral King lies at the end of a narrow road that winds 29 miles east from Three Rivers (southwest of the park on State 198). Inaccessible in winter, the road is not recommended for trailers or RVs anytime.

Kings Canyon highlights

To the north of Sequoia, Kings Canyon has the distinction of being both one of the oldest and one of the newest national parks. When established in 1940, it absorbed tiny General Grant National Park, a sanctuary set up shortly after Sequoia was created in 1890.

Now the old section of the park is known as the General Grant Grove.

Kings Canyon is actually two entirely separate areas. The smaller west side contains the most developed section—General Grant Grove. Much of the rest is a bewildering maze of jagged peaks and rugged canyons. Densely forested, with an elevation that varies from 4,600 to 6,600 feet, the park is usually comfortably cool.

General Grant Grove. Most visitors head for General Grant Grove, which contains almost all the park's facilities and also the world's second largest tree. The General Grant sequoia has a base circumference of 108 feet—actually 6 feet larger than the General Sherman Tree in Sequoia National Park, though the General Grant has a smaller total volume. Both trees were standing in the Bronze Age more than 3,000 years ago. General Grant has been designated as the nation's official Christmas tree, and an impressive yuletide ceremony is held here every year on the Sunday before Christmas.

Informative campfire programs are given every summer night in the nearby amphitheater. For park lore, join one of the trips led daily by rangers; schedules are posted in the village.

Kings Canyon region. The park's other developed area is reached by a 30-mile stretch of State 180 from Grant Grove. The road, closed in winter, drops 2,000 feet before attaining its destination. Parking overlooks on sweeping curves allow far-reaching views of the deep canyons of the Middle and South forks of the Kings River and the peaks that rise beyond.

About 20 miles beyond Grant Grove is marble-walled Boyden Cavern; guided tours are conducted daily in summer and early autumn.

Cedar Grove, in a canyon along the South Fork of the river, is the popular base point for trail rides into the high country. The level valley floor is good for cycling. Rangers lead a variety of walks during the day and present nightly campfire programs in summer.

Big, Bad Bodie

"Goodbye, God, I'm going to Bodie," wrote a little girl in her diary in 1881 when her family moved to what was then one of the wildest mining camps in the West. Her dismay was not unfounded; there was allegedly at least one murder a day in "big, bad Bodie." A busy red light district and 65 saloons kept the town jumping day and night.

Bodie's boom was short-lived, but since 1964, the 486 acres that make up the town have been a state historic park—one of the best preserved Western mining ghost towns in existence.

Recently, controversy has again surrounded Bodie as drilling rigs once more bore into the bluffs around town. Efforts by a large mining corporation to search for

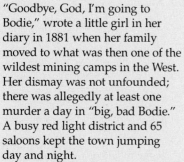

gold on the ridge above town, using modern equipment and methods, have park people worried about damage to structures and to the visitor experience. As one ranger put it, "It's ironic. Gold made Bodie, and gold could unmake Bodie."

Booms and busts. The town was named for a prospector who discovered gold here in 1859 and died in a blizzard soon after. Its heyday really began in the late 1870s with the discovery of several rich veins of gold. By 1879, 10,000 people called Bodie home, making it the largest settlement between Sacramento and Salt Lake City.

The boom was over by 1882, though some sporadic activity occurred in the 1890s and again in the 1920s and 30s.

Today, the 170 weathered buildings that remain are maintained in a condition of "arrested decay." A detailed park map with a self-guided walking tour to some 69 sites costs $1. Rangers offer free history talks at 3 P.M. daily except Monday and Thursday. On weekends and holidays from Memorial Day to Labor Day, free tours of the old Standard Mine take place at 11 A.M. and 2 P.M.

How to get there. To reach Bodie (open all year), take U.S. 395 to State 270 (north of Mono Lake and east of Yosemite National Park); the last 3 miles are unpaved and often inaccessible in winter. A modest day-use fee is charged per vehicle. Bring your own lunch; there are no stores or overnight facilities.

Just beyond the jumbled rocks of the Alabama Hills in Owens Valley, a trail ascends mighty Mount Whitney, tallest peak in the contiguous United States.

East of the Sierra

The full impact of the Sierra Nevada is rarely appreciated until you see its abrupt east face, the one it turns toward the desert. This side of the range, to the east of Sequoia and Kings Canyon and west of Death Valley, has much to offer vacationers: high desert country, spectacular mountain scenery, uncrowded trails, good fishing, ghost towns, spring wildflowers, and excellent skiing in winter.

U.S. 395 leads north and south through the whole section, linking a chain of little towns. From this arterial highway, you can go east into Death Valley or west a short distance into the towering mountains.

Travelers to the Owens Valley will find motels and restaurants in Lone Pine, Independence, and Big Pine. Bishop, at the top of the valley, provides the widest selection. The Mammoth region has a variety of lodgings.

Owens Valley

The bending and cracking of the earth's surface that created the Sierra Nevada and the parallel White, Panamint, and Inyo ranges also sank a long, deep trough between them—Owens Valley, a place of hot springs, craters, lava flows, and earthquake faults.

Lone Pine. Gateway to the Owens Valley, the small town of Lone Pine has long been a favorite site for filming movies and commercials. Many early Westerns were shot west and northwest of town on Movie Flat Road.

Thirteen miles west of Lone Pine is the start of the Whitney Portal Trail, a steep, 10¾-mile path to the summit of Mount Whitney. Hikers need permits; write to the U.S. Forest Service, P.O. Box 8, Lone Pine, CA 93545.

The Eastern Sierra Interagency Visitor Center, south of town at the junction of U.S. 395 and State 136, has maps and information on the whole area.

Independence. Turnoff for the Kearsarge Pass entrance to the Sierra high country, tiny Independence is the home of the excellent Eastern California Museum (155 N. Grant Street). The historical museum is open Wednesday through Monday from 10 A.M. to 4 P.M.; donations are requested.

One block north of Center Street on U.S. 395 stands the restored mansion known as Commander's House. Open weekends during summer (donations requested), this 11-room structure is the only survivor of Camp Independence, established in 1862 to protect early Owens Valley residents.

Seven miles south of Independence are the remains of the World War II Japanese-American internment camp of Manzanar.

Ancient Bristlecone Pine Forest. The world's largest bristlecone forest grows in a 28,000-acre area of the White Mountains. Stunted and twisted by the harsh forces of nature, the ancient trees—some more than 4,000 years old—resemble pieces of driftwood decorated with green needles.

The pines are about 20 miles from U.S. 395. Turn east onto State 168 (Westgard Pass Road) just north of Big Pine; a winding but well-marked side road (usually open late June through October) climbs up to the Schulman Memorial Grove. Take warm clothing, food, and water, and make sure your gas tank is full; there are no services after Big Pine.

Bishop. The valley's most bustling metropolis, Bishop (population 3,500) is at its most vibrant in autumn, when groves of cottonwood and aspen are ablaze. The town stages a colorful Mule Days celebration on Memorial Day weekend and a rodeo on Labor Day. The Chamber of Commerce (690 N. Main Street) has information on area attractions.

Laws. The once-active railroad town of Laws makes a worthwhile break from the long drive through Owens Valley. It's just off U.S. 6 about 5 miles northeast of Bishop.

The 11-acre Laws Railroad Museum and Historical Exhibit displays period buildings daily, weather permitting, from March through mid-November, and on weekends the rest of the year; donations are encouraged.

Mammoth & more

One of the country's largest ski areas, Mammoth Mountain has some 30 lifts, 150 trails, and 30,000 vertical feet of ski runs. Summer visitors hike and backpack into the John Muir Wilderness and fish and boat in area lakes.

Mammoth draws most of its winter crowd from Southern California—it's easily reached from the south over U.S. 395 (about 300 miles from Los Angeles) but cut off from the west when passes are closed by snow.

The resort town of Mammoth Lakes, about 42 miles northwest of Bishop, makes a good base for exploring the 200,000-acre region promoted as Mammoth Lakes Recreational Area. A visitor center, an aerial tram, and cozy mountain lodges welcome visitors. Trails lead to such unusual geologic formations as Devils Postpile National Monument, a sheer wall of basaltic columns more than 60 feet high. Forest Service campgrounds, usually crowded in summer, are virtually deserted after September.

Hot Creek. Soaking in Hot Creek's mineral springs is a popular pastime. The water in the 4-foot-deep pool is unusually buoyant—and very hot. Ask for directions at the U.S. Forest Service Visitor Center on State 203, about 3 miles off U.S. 395.

Mono Lake. Ancient Mono Lake, 60 square miles of salty, alkaline water in a lunarlike setting, is a breeding ground for gulls and a resting spot for millions of migratory waterfowl. To learn about the birds and the lake's spectacular tufa formations, stop by the state reserve on the south shore. Mono Lake lies off U.S. 395 at Lee Vining, 26 miles north of Mammoth.

Death Valley

The forbidding name given to this desert valley doesn't ring true after you have spent a spring day here. It's actually a valley of light, color, and life. You can drive, hike, and camp for weeks among its 14 square miles of dunes, 200 square miles of salt flats, and 11,000-foot mountains.

The valley probably got its name in January 1850 when one 49er is known to have died here—but not from heat or thirst. A party of nine others may also have perished, and pioneers crossing the area certainly suffered extreme hardships. But measured against the rest of the western desert, Death Valley's record of human lives lost is reassuringly low.

Administered as a national monument since 1933, Death Valley is distinguished from other desert valleys by its great size, diverse scenery, and colorful history. It's also unique among deserts for its great extremes of temperature and topography. A record high of 134° was set in 1913. Elevations range from 282 feet below sea level near Badwater to 11,049 feet above sea level at nearby Telescope Peak.

Desert geology. Fossils of prehistoric mammals discovered here show that the arid salt flats and gravel desert of Death Valley were once a fertile plain. As the climate became drier, ancient lakes evaporated into salt deposits and mud playas. Wind reduced granite to sand and blew it into dunes. Since the wind blows from all directions, the dunes remained intact.

Plants and animals. The popular belief that nothing lives or grows in Death Valley is discounted by the diverse animal and plant life that has tenaciously adapted to the burning heat and dryness. Only the central salt flats are barren.

Nearly 1,000 species of plants and trees, including ferns, lilies, and orchids, flourish in the monument. Twenty or more flowering plants—including the yellow Panamint daisy, the blue-flowered Death Valley sage, and the small-blossomed goldcarpet—grow nowhere else in the world. Ancient bristlecone pines live high on Telescope Peak.

You're not likely to see many animals—most emerge only at night. But many creatures, including bighorn sheep and wild burros, do live in a 2-mile area between Telescope Peak and Badwater.

Even fish exist in this desert. Descended from Ice Age ancestors, the rare pupfish or "desert sardine" thrives in Salt Creek, Saratoga Springs, and Devil's Hole—an astonishing example of rapid evolutionary adaptation.

Planning a visit

From November through mid-April, Death Valley's tourist facilities are in full operation and the climate is mild. It's only in summer that visitors experience the blazing sun and intense heat usually associated with desert climes. If you must cross the valley in summer, make sure your car is in good condition, carry extra water, and travel at night when temperatures drop.

How to get there. The national park hugs the California-Nevada border and spills over into Nevada at its northeast corner. The closest major air terminal is at Las Vegas, Nevada, 160 miles southeast of the monument. Light planes can land at Furnace Creek and Stove Pipe Wells.

From U.S. 395, it's 60 miles from Lone Pine to Towne's Pass on State 136/State 190, the most spectacular and best route from the west into Death Valley. From the southwest, State 178 runs 75 miles from U.S. 395 into the park, entering just west of Wildrose campground; there's a high-clearance gravel section for about 6 miles before Wildrose.

Another approach is from the southeast on State 127, which meets State 190 to the east of the monument at Death Valley Junction.

Where to stay. Accommodations are rarely a problem in Death Valley, but reservations are suggested, particularly around President's Day, Easter, Thanksgiving, Christmas, and the annual Death Valley 49ers Encampment in early November.

Lodging within the park runs from rustic to resort. Rates at the luxurious Furnace Creek Inn (swimming pool, tennis courts, stables, and 18-hole golf course) include meals. The Furnace Creek Ranch, a mile down the road, has more modest motel-style rooms or cabins. The inn is open from October through mid-May; the ranch remains open year-round. For information and reservations, contact Furnace Creek Inn and Ranch Resort, P.O. Box 1, Death Valley, CA 92328; phone (619) 786-2345.

Stovepipe Wells Village, on State 190 about 25 miles northwest of Furnace Creek, has motel-style rooms, swimming pool, restaurant (closed in summer), grocery store, and service station. The mailing address for information and reservations is Death Valley, CA 92328; you can call (619) 786-2387.

Camping. Most of the park campgrounds have scenic backdrops ranging from whispering sand dunes to sweeping mountain views. The most improved campgrounds are in the valley. Texas Spring and Furnace Creek (the latter open all year but very hot in summer) are both close to the visitor center; Ticketron reservations are accepted for Furnace Creek.

Campgrounds at higher elevations are open in summer. Campers must furnish their own firewood, and backcountry campers should come prepared to boil the water they use. At some campgrounds, you must provide your own water.

In the frequented parts of the valley, camping is strictly confined to established campgrounds. Backcountry camping is permitted if you don't litter or have ground fires.

The Wildrose campsites, open year-round, provide a nice change of pace from other campgrounds. Located at 3,500 feet on the west side of the Pan-

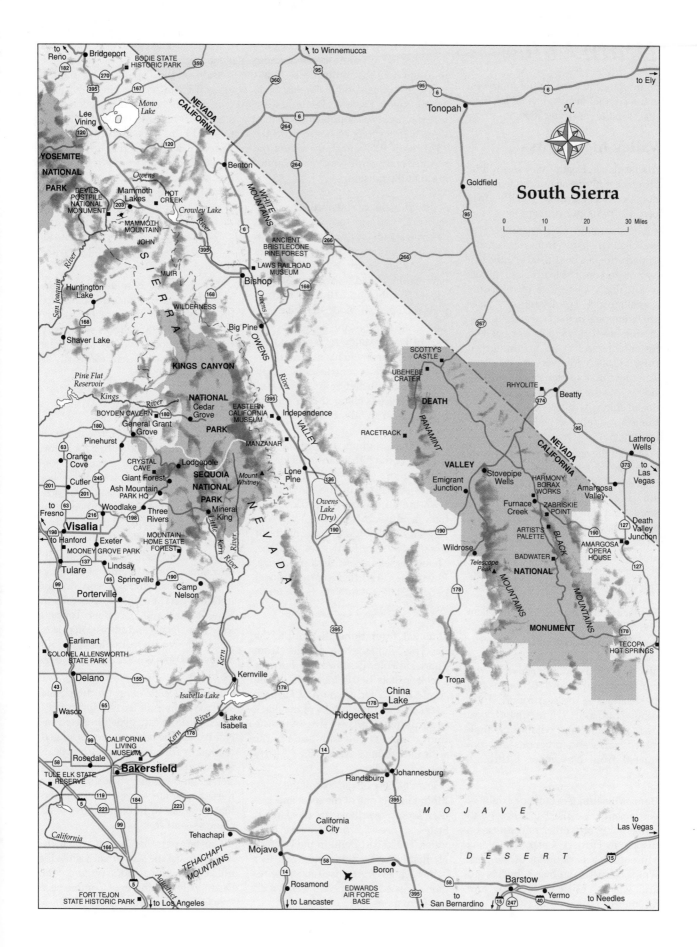

...Death Valley

amint Range just inside the southwest entrance, this facility has tables, fireplaces, pit toilets (no water).

Valley highlights

At first glance, Death Valley seems little different from the surrounding desert. But upon closer scrutiny, you'll begin to perceive its unique dimensions.

The mountain face, seemingly unbreached when seen from afar, is really slotted with fascinating labyrinths that lead on and on. The featureless salt flat is actually a vast maze of miniature crystalline alps. The distant sand ridges are mountains in their own right—but mountains that yield underfoot and restore themselves to an unmarked pristine state with every fresh breeze. The unnatural splotch on the far hillside is a waste pile marking an abandoned mine, its tunnels, shafts, headframes, and railroad beds still more or less intact.

Death Valley can be explored on more than 500 miles of well-maintained roadways. Most of the area's unique attractions lie no more than an easy stroll from one of them. This area is also well suited for cycling, as major attractions are concentrated in a few areas near relatively flat paved roads. A four-wheel-drive vehicle opens up still more backcountry.

Furnace Creek. Because of an excellent and dependable water supply from nearby springs, this popular region near the center of the park on State 190 has always been the hub of activity. You can buy maps and other useful publications at the year-round visitor center and tour a museum of local geology, plants, and wildlife. Naturalist-led walks and programs are conducted from November 1 through Easter.

Borax Museum. An outdoor exhibit of equipment once used to extract and refine borax and other minerals is on display in Furnace Creek. The Borax Museum is a parking lot of the past, with stagecoach and buggy, buckboard and wagon, railroad handcar and locomotive.

Also on the grounds are a crude mining machine, a hand-operated stamp mill, and the 1883 mining office-bunkhouse that once stood in Twenty Mule Team Canyon. The great 20-mule-team wagons, nearly as sound as when they were hauling tons of borax from the 1880s until 1907, mark the site of the restored Harmony Borax Works 2 miles north of the museum.

Scotty's Castle. At the northern end of the park, you can tour an incredible desert mansion built in the 1920s by a locally legendary character known as Death Valley Scotty. Walter Scott and his wealthy friend Alfred M. Johnson spent $2 million and 10 years to complete the Spanish-Moorish house.

Scotty's flamboyant escapades are part of Death Valley folklore, and the castle is testimony to his natural showmanship and eccentric personality. Tours are conducted daily; a moderate admission fee is charged. You can use the picnic area without charge.

Rhyolite. A booming city of 12,000 at the start of the 20th century, Rhyolite is now a ghost town. Among the surviving structures of the old mining town are an elaborate railroad depot (now a museum and store) and the Rhyolite Bottle House, its walls built from 51,000 beer bottles set in adobe. The owner sells desert glass and curios. Rhyolite is just northeast of the national park on State 374 in Nevada, 2½ miles west of Beatty.

Unusual formations. To sample the desert's color, view a sunrise from Zabriskie Point (southeast of Furnace Creek on State 190) or follow the 9-mile scenic Artist's Drive south of Furnace Creek among the foothills of the Black Mountains. Halfway through the canyon, Artist's Palette hillside burns with intense hues when viewed early or late in the day.

Dante's View, on the crest of the Black Mountains, is one of the most spectacular scenic overlooks in the United States. It rises 5,775 feet above Badwater. The lowest point in the Western Hemisphere, Badwater lies 282 feet below sea level. At close range, the region's crusted pools reveal weird rock salt formations.

Charcoal kilns that look like giant stone beehives almost blend into the hillside of the Panamint Mountains. Once used to reduce pines and junipers to charcoal for the Modoc Mine smelter 25 miles to the west, the century-old kilns appear as good as new. To reach them, take the Upper Wildrose Canyon road from Wildrose Ranger Station.

In the northern part of the park 16 miles west of Scotty's Castle, you can view a crater created 3,000 years ago by a volcanic explosion. The Ubehebe Crater is half a mile wide and 500 feet deep.

The Racetrack, 27 miles south of the crater, is a mud flat that's the setting for the "mystery of the moving rocks." When wet, the Racetrack is so slippery that high-velocity winds skid great boulders across its surface as easily as if they were pebbles.

West of the park

The Amargosa Opera House in Death Valley Junction is the setting for Marta Becket's one-woman dance performances. The ballerina even painted her own "audience," a realistic, wall-size mural depicting 260 members of a Spanish court, ranging from bawdy commoners to sedate nobles.

Performances are held Monday, Friday, and Saturday nights at 8:15 P.M. from November through April (except in December) and on Saturday only in May, October, and December. For performance details and admission prices, write Amargosa Opera House, Death Valley Junction, CA 92328, or call (619) 852-4316.

South of Death Valley Junction, State 127 passes through Tecopa Hot Springs, where visitors can splash in free mineral baths. The springs once belonged to Indians who believed they had healing powers and brought their lame and sick to bathe. When they turned over the site to white settlers, it was agreed that the water would remain free to all comers—and so it has.

Clusters of trailers around the bathhouses make the settlement visible for miles. For information, write to the Death Valley Chamber of Commerce, 2 Post Office Row, Tecopa, CA 92389.

Amid the picturesque ruins of Death Valley's Harmony Borax Works stands an original 20-mule-team rig. Above the other-era scene, snow dusts the national park's 11,049-foot Telescope Peak.

San Joaquin Valley

Encompassing the southern half of California's great Central Valley, the San Joaquin Valley to the west of the Sierra ranks high among the nation's producers of food, fuel, and fiber. Sunshine, fertile soil, a long growing season, and water from surrounding mountains create ideal conditions for cotton, citrus fruits, grapes, nuts, and many other fruits and vegetables. The valley is also the state's top oil-producing region; you're likely to see an oil well pumping in the midst of a vineyard or potato field.

For the traveler, sunshine and the vast reservoir system that irrigates the valley make for good boating, swimming, and rafting. Valley towns can also be pleasant places to break a trip. Unexpected treats such as Wasco, the world's top rose-growing area, lie a short distance off main highways. In summer, millions of blooms line State 43 west of Bakersfield.

How to get there. Airlines, Amtrak, and bus lines serve larger valley cities. Interstate 5 skirts the sparsely populated western edge of the valley, and State 99 cuts through the valley's center; both offer easy north-south access. State 58 and State 178 are major east-west routes across the bottom of the Sierra range.

From Los Angeles, motorists enter the valley on the "Grapevine" route over the Tehachapis. Today's smooth freeway gives no indication of the troubles experienced by earlier travelers over this pass. Winter storms do sometimes cause temporary road closures due to icing. Throughout the valley, low-lying dense winter fog can be a problem for motorists at times.

Where to stay. Valley cities such as Bakersfield and Visalia, and Fresno farther north, are gateways to national parks and the high country of the Sierra Nevada. Nearby lakes and rivers offer added recreational opportunities. Motor inns and motels are only an offramp away from State 99, more infrequent along Interstate 5.

Bakersfield

Situated on the south bank of the Kern River at the southern end of the San Joaquin Valley, Bakersfield is county seat for Kern County and a major highway junction. Not only is Bakersfield a center for agriculture, petroleum, and tourism; it's also recognized as the state's country music capital.

The city has a host of playgrounds, parks, golf courses, and tennis courts. Lake Ming and Hart Park lie due east of town. Southern California's largest man-made lake, Isabella, lies about 45 miles east in the Sierra foothills. The nearby Kern River provides a natural setting for fishing, white-water rafting, hiking, camping, picnicking, and horseback riding.

The Basque influence is still felt in Bakersfield, legacy of sheepherders who came here a century ago. Several restaurants, including Matia's, Wool Growers Cafe, and the Noriega Hotel (established in 1897), offer traditional meals. Most are located in the east side of the city near the railroad station. You can buy a sourdough sheepherder loaf at Bakersfield's century-old Pyrenees Bakery (717 E. 21st Street).

Kern County Museum's Pioneer Village. Frontier history comes alive at a 14-acre museum at 3801 Chester Avenue. Some 56 buildings (originals and restorations) are laid out as a vintage model town of the 1860-1930 era. Indoors, the main museum building houses fossils from nearby McKittrick oil field, a diorama of birds and mammals, Indian relics, and a most unusual curiosity—a dog-powered butter churn.

The museum and village are open weekdays from 8 A.M. to 5 P.M., weekends and holidays from 10 A.M. to 5 P.M. (closed New Year's, Thanksgiving, and Christmas). Museum admission is free; there's a small fee to explore the village.

California Living Museum. Thirteen miles northeast of Bakersfield off State 178, this combination natural history museum and zoo displays hundreds of California desert animals in their native habitats. Included are a reptile house, one of the state's largest walk-in aviaries, a desert tortoise enclosure, and a children's petting zoo. Located at 14000 Old Alfred Harrell Highway, the museum is open Tuesday through Sunday from 10 A.M. to sunset. A small admission fee is charged.

Tule Elk State Reserve. At Buttonwillow, 22 miles west of Bakersfield via State 58, you can view a small band of tule elk at a 965-acre sanctuary. Now an endangered species, these animals once roamed the Central Valley's vast marshland. The reserve is 3 miles west of Interstate 5.

Fort Tejon State Historic Park. An old military post south of Bakersfield once quartered the Army's most unusual unit, the First Dragoons and Camel Corps. Established by the U.S. Army in 1854, the park is handily situated off Interstate 5 near Lebec (30 miles south of Bakersfield).

The post is open daily year-round. After touring its museum, reconstructed barracks, and officers' quarters, you can picnic on the grounds in the shade of some lovely old trees. A living history program is presented the first Sunday of each month. On the third Sunday of each month from April through October, a mock Civil War skirmish is staged for visitors at 10 A.M., noon, and 2 P.M.

Visalia vicinity

Founded in 1852, Visalia is the oldest city in the southern San Joaquin Valley. Self-guiding walking tour maps of its historic district can be picked up weekdays from the Chamber of Commerce, 720 W. Mineral King Avenue.

State 198 heads east from Visalia to Sequoia National Park. During the peak summer season, many travelers use the city as a base for exploring the nearby mountain area.

Mooney Grove Park. Acres of oaks and date palms shade this pleasant park 5 miles south of Visalia, open daily in summer, Thursday through Monday the rest of the year. Detour from the highway to picnic and enjoy lake scenery; a small per-car fee is charged.

Tulare Historical Museum. A museum in the onetime railroad town of Tulare, about 8 miles south of Visalia, traces county history from a century or so ago, when much of the area lay beneath one of the largest bodies of water west of the Mississippi. Tulare Lake today is a ghost that reappears only in the wettest years.

To visit the museum, located at 444 W. Tulare Avenue, take State 137 west 1¼ miles from State 99. It's open Thursday through Saturday and Sunday afternoons (small admission charge).

Colonel Allensworth State Park. A fascinating detour off State 99 about 30 miles south of Visalia, this historic park was once a town settled and governed entirely by blacks. Seven buildings, including a library and private homes, have been restored.

The town was founded in 1908 by Allen Allensworth, a former slave from Kentucky who was once sold because he tried to learn to read. The park is open daily, but you can only go inside the buildings on weekends. The small campground (water, rest rooms) is seldom filled. Turn off State 99 at Earlimart; drive west 7 miles on County J22, then south a mile on State 43.

Mountain Home State Demonstration Forest. John Muir's favorite grove of sequoias is enshrined about 8 crow-flying miles from the southern border of Sequoia National Park. This 4,500-acre forest and Balch Park, the 160-acre park that it surrounds, receive less attention than their famous neighbor; summer weekdays can be downright quiet.

The giant sequoias in the 53-acre Adams Memorial Redwood Grove are the main draw, but the whole area is interesting. The Yaudanchi Yokuts made their summer home here near the Tule River, leaving numerous bedrock mortars. Hedrick Pond, once the site of a lumber mill, is stocked with rainbow trout. Campgrounds offer some 200 spaces (no hookups, no reservations); you pay only in Balch Park.

Gateway to Mountain Home is Porterville, about 15 miles east of State 99 via State 190. From there, drive 17 miles east on State 190 past Springville, then north on County J37 for 3½ miles and east 18 miles on Bear Creek Road.

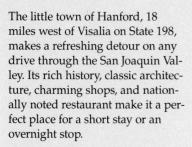

Detour to Hanford

The little town of Hanford, 18 miles west of Visalia on State 198, makes a refreshing detour on any drive through the San Joaquin Valley. Its rich history, classic architecture, charming shops, and nationally noted restaurant make it a perfect place for a short stay or an overnight stop.

Founded by the Southern Pacific Railroad in 1877, Hanford was named for its popular paymaster, James Hanford, who paid workers millions of dollars in gold and was alleged to have signed more checks than any other person in American history.

Pick up a self-guiding tour map at the Chamber of Commerce office (213 W. Seventh Street; open 8 A.M. to 5 P.M. weekdays) or at the Amtrak station 2 blocks down the street.

Cozy Irwin Street Inn near Courthouse Square heads the short list of accommodations. For lodging information, call the Chamber of Commerce at (209) 582-0483.

Courthouse Square. Built in the late 1800s, the courthouse fronting on the picture-perfect town square has been restored in recent times. Today it houses gift shops, boutiques, and a bar and restaurant. In good weather, flower and fruit stands and an antique carousel attract residents and tourists outside the building.

Behind the courthouse, the dark red building called La Bastille served as the city jail before its transformation into a restaurant. Nearby stand other architectural gems. The Superior Dairy, an old-fashioned ice cream parlor, has been in business for more than 60 years.

China Alley. Hanford's more exotic historical buildings are found in China Alley, a few blocks east of downtown. At the end of the last century, when jobs on railroads and farms brought as many as 800 Chinese families to Hanford (including future Chinese statesman Sun Yat-sen), China Alley was home to boardinghouses, gambling dens, and herbalist shops.

In those early days, the Taoist Temple, built in 1893, served as the Chinese community center. The temple can be toured by request; call (209) 584-3236. The wooden structure nearby that houses King's Hand Laundry started life as a hotel for immigrants.

Hanford's name turns up in more than a few out-of-town address books thanks to the Imperial Dynasty Restaurant, owned and operated by the Wing family for more than a century. Chef Richard Wing pioneered the Chinese-accented French fare that has become so trendy elsewhere.

For a splendid nine-course splurge, make reservations three or four days in advance by calling (209) 582-0196.

Central Coast

Stretching between Ventura County and the Monterey Peninsula, California's Central Coast embraces some of the state's loveliest beaches and a series of intriguing seaside communities. Tucked into inland valleys are resorts and inns, celebrity retreats, wineries, apple farms, and Arabian horse ranches. Six old Spanish missions—at Ventura, Santa Barbara, Solvang, Lompoc, San Luis Obispo, and San Miguel—welcome visitors.

Offshore, the Channel Islands offer glimpses of unique wildlife at one of the country's newest national parks. Cruises from Oxnard, Ventura, and Santa Barbara allow you to explore this beautiful marine sanctuary (see page 117). Other ocean-going opportunities include coastal deep-sea fishing and whale watching.

Coastal highlights

Santa Barbara, 90 miles north of Los Angeles, is one of the oldest and prettiest cities along the coast. Spreading along a wide and gently curving beach, it lies on a sunny sheltered plain backed by the rugged mountains of the Santa Ynez range. The city's stunning setting, lush landscaping, and distinctive Spanish architecture have lured generations of vacationers.

The wide beaches of Ventura and Oxnard to the south offer choice surfing and fishing sites. Inland around the resort town of Ojai, hikers, cyclists, and horseback riders find miles of trails.

Up the coast lie the Danish village of Solvang, the flower fields around

The state's own "Rock of Gibraltar," a 576-foot volcanic remnant, rises above the fishing port of Morro Bay and provides nesting for peregrine falcons.

Lompoc, gracious Santa Maria, and the clam beds of Pismo Beach. Beyond San Luis Obispo, State 1 hugs the coast from Morro Bay to San Simeon, site of the incredible Hearst Castle.

Planning a visit

With its ideal climate, easy accessibility, varied attractions, and wealth of activities, the Central Coast is popular year-round. Summer attracts the most visitors, though fog can be a factor then. If you visit in summer, make reservations well ahead for Hearst Castle tours. Hotels, seaside motels and inns, guest ranches, and beach campsites are also booked well in advance during the summer.

Some of the area's warmest and sunniest days occur in spring and autumn. It's easier to find accommodations then, and rates are significantly lower than during the summer. Fishing holds up well into autumn, and ocean temperatures, though cool in early spring, remain warm enough for swimming into November.

Winter days can be sparkling along this section of coast. All attractions are open, the crowds are gone, and surf-viewing is at its best.

How to get there. American, United, and smaller commuter airlines serve Santa Barbara. Commuter airlines also fly to Santa Maria and San Luis Obispo. Amtrak has service to Santa Barbara and San Luis Obispo. Greyhound offers daily bus service.

Driving is the best way to see the area. Look for rental car agencies in larger towns. A combination of U.S. 101 and the narrower and somewhat more meandering State 1 skirts much of the coast. Other highways give access to the region's inland destinations.

Where to stay. You'll find a wealth of lodging choices all along the Central Coast, including deluxe resorts, guest ranches, city hotels, bed and breakfasts, and budget-priced motels.

In the 1930s and 40s, movie stars made famous such deluxe retreats as the Ojai Valley Inn, the Alisal guest ranch near Solvang, and Santa Barbara's Biltmore Hotel, El Encanto Hotel, Montecito Inn, and San Ysidro Ranch—all of which still welcome guests.

Camping is permitted at some state beaches and state parks. Private campgrounds are sprinkled throughout the area. Reserve far in advance for weekends throughout the year and anytime in summer.

Contacts

These agencies offer information on attractions and accommodations. See additional contacts throughout this chapter.

Santa Barbara Visitor Information Center
One Santa Barbara St.
(P.O. Box 299)
Santa Barbara, CA 93102
(805) 965-3021

Solvang Visitors Bureau
1511 Mission Dr.
(P.O. Box 70)
Solvang, CA 93463
(800) 468-6765

San Luis Obispo Chamber of Commerce
1039 Chorro St.
San Luis Obispo, CA 93401
(805) 781-2777

Santa Barbara

Santa Barbara's colorful history dates back to the Chumash Indians, who settled the region in large numbers thousands of years ago. When the Spanish arrived in the 1700s, they called this place *La Tierra Adorada*—the beloved land. Today's visitors, beguiled by the city's climate and setting, find it hard not to share the enchantment.

When a 1925 earthquake destroyed many post-Victorian structures and forced the early demolition of others, it opened the way for Santa Barbara to express its heritage in the course of rebuilding. Today, the city reflects that history in its Spanish and mission-style architecture—adobe construction, tile roofs, bell towers, and the Mediterranean love of colorful accents. To ensure the perpetuation of this style, an architectural review board approves the design of every commercial and public building.

Not all of Santa Barbara's urban charm is man-made, however; nature contributes a gentle lushness that enhances the traditional-looking buildings. Stately palms ring many buildings, bougainvillea tumbles down whitewashed walls, and fir trees (decorated at Christmastime) mark pedestrian crossings downtown.

Santa Barbara's cultural calendar is testimony to the city's love for plants—the International Orchid Show is held here every spring, and the Santa Barbara Fair & Expo in April includes a flower show. The city pays homage to its past during the colorful Old Spanish Days Fiesta in August.

Visitors are often puzzled by Santa Barbara's layout. Streets have the unsettling habit of bending abruptly and taking off in another direction, or of ending at U.S. 101, which divides downtown's historic section from the beach. To decipher the street system, pick up a map at the Visitor Information Center along the waterfront near Stearns Wharf (corner of Santa Barbara Street and Cabrillo Boulevard). Other useful brochures on attractions around the city are also available.

Heart of the city

Downtown Santa Barbara is designed for strolling. With few exceptions, buildings are no taller than four stories, the result of a strictly enforced height ordinance that can't be varied without voter approval. New construction is designed to blend with existing buildings. Convenient city lots and garages make it easy to park; and the first 90 minutes are free.

State Street, the city's landscaped main artery, provides an entrée to the historic area bounded by Victoria, Chapala, Ortega, and Santa Barbara streets—the original core of the city that surrounded the Spanish Presidio. Plaques and markers identify the early buildings; a few of them are open to visitors. Pick up a free map of the self-guided walking tour at the visitor center or county courthouse. Or join Heritage Tours of Santa Barbara for a narrated walk through history; tours leave Plaza de la Guerra Monday through Saturday at 10 A.M. and Sunday at 1 P.M.; there is a fee. For information, call (805) 962-8578.

Santa Barbara Museum of Art. One of the country's finest small museums is located at the corner of State and Anapamu streets.

The museum building is bright, airy, and—unlike other city landmarks—modern. Soft, natural light falls on Greek, Roman, and Egyptian sculptures and priceless glassware. An encircling gallery and adjacent halls contain impressive collections of Asian, European, and American art.

The museum is open Tuesday through Sunday, except major holidays; admission is charged. Guided tours are offered daily at 2 P.M.

Santa Barbara County Courthouse. Built in 1929, the courthouse resembles a Spanish-Moorish castle. Its buildings and grounds cover a square block bounded by Santa Barbara, Anacapa, Anapamu, and Figueroa streets. An English translation of the motto above the entrance arch on Anacapa Street reads, "God gave us the country. The skill of man hath built this town."

Two-story murals in the Assembly Room colorfully depict Santa Barbara history, including the arrival of Juan Rodriguez Cabrillo in 1542, the founding of Mission Santa Barbara in 1786, and Colonel John C. Fremont's 1846 heralding of American rule in California. For an unequalled view of the city, take the elevator to the top.

The courthouse is open daily; free guided tours are offered Tuesday through Saturday at 2 P.M., with additional tours Wednesday and Friday at 10:30 A.M.

Historical Society Museum. Many of the city's historic treasures are housed in this museum, situated at the corner of De la Guerra and Santa Barbara streets. One wing is a library; the other is devoted to exhibits of the Mexican, Spanish, and Early American periods. On display are a carved statue of Saint Barbara, intriguing letters, early costumes, and relics of writer Richard Henry Dana's visits to the city.

The museum is open afternoons Tuesday through Sunday, except major holidays. Donations are requested.

Casa de Covarrubias. Built in 1817, the L-shaped adobe at 715 Santa Barbara was the site of the last meeting of the Mexican Assembly. Adjoining it is the adobe that served as Colonel John C. Fremont's headquarters after the American takeover in 1846. Both are open to visitors.

Lobero Theatre. On the site of the city's first theater (at the corner of Anacapa and Cañon Perdido streets), this showpiece was built in 1873 by Italian musician Jose Lobero. It's now the setting for contemporary productions.

Arlington Center for Performing Arts. Another palatial movie theater from a different era is worth a look. The Arlington, at 1317 State Street, is home to the city's symphony orchestra.

El Presidio de Santa Barbara State Historic Park. Ongoing restoration is bringing back some of the city's oldest structures at this park at 122 and 123 E. Cañon Perdido. El Cuartel (Guards House) and La Cañeda Adobe are part of the original Spanish fort on the site blessed by Father Serra in 1782. The padre's quarters and the chapel are reconstructions on original foundations. The park, including a museum shop in El Cuartel, is open 10 A.M. to 5 P.M. Monday through Saturday, noon to 4 P.M. Sunday.

El Paseo. A delightful shopping arcade reminiscent of Old Spain has been built in and around the adobe home of the De la Guerra family, begun in 1819 by mission Indians. A brick in the passageway bears the date of completion, 1826. Casa de la Guerra was the setting for a Spanish wedding fiesta in Dana's *Two Years Before the Mast.*

Import and specialty shops are now located here at 814 State Street. Across the street is the plaza where the first City Council met in 1850 and where the first City Hall was located.

The Waterfront

Santa Barbara boasts one of the most inviting stretches of coastline anywhere. Miles of wide, gently curving beaches, fringed with palms, offer space for swimmers, surfers, picnickers, scuba divers, anglers, and grunion-hunters. A picturesque 92-acre yacht harbor, protected by a long breakwater, shelters the local fishing fleet as well as hundreds of pleasure craft.

Attractive hotels and motels face the beach along Cabrillo Boulevard, an oceanfront drive popular with strollers, cyclists, and roller skaters. A Sunday arts and crafts show at Palm Park along the waterfront overflows for a mile along the boulevard.

Stearns Wharf. Constructed in 1872 and restored in 1981, Stearns Wharf is California's oldest working pier. Fishing is still popular, but the 3-block-long wharf at the foot of State Street is also the site of restaurants, shops, and a seafood market. The Santa Barbara Winery tasting room at the wharf is open daily from 10 A.M. to sunset for the sampling of area wines.

From the pier, harbor cruises depart several times a day. Or you can board the Santa Barbara Trolley here for a 90-minute tour of the town.

Sea Center. A small marine museum and aquarium at Stearns Wharf offers winter whale-watching cruises and field trips to the Channel Islands (see page 117). The museum is open daily; there is a small admission charge. A relief map of Santa Cruz Island highlights the displays at the Nature Conservancy Center next door.

Water sports. Motorboats and sailboats in several classes can be rented at the yacht harbor. A boat-launching ramp and a large parking area for boat trailers lie at the foot of Bath Street. Most waterskiing takes place between the wharf and East Beach. If the water is choppy, stay inside the breakwater.

Some of the area's best surfing and snorkeling can be found a few blocks north or south of the wharf. Arroyo Burro and Leadbetter beaches, both west of the breakwater, offer rough but inviting surf.

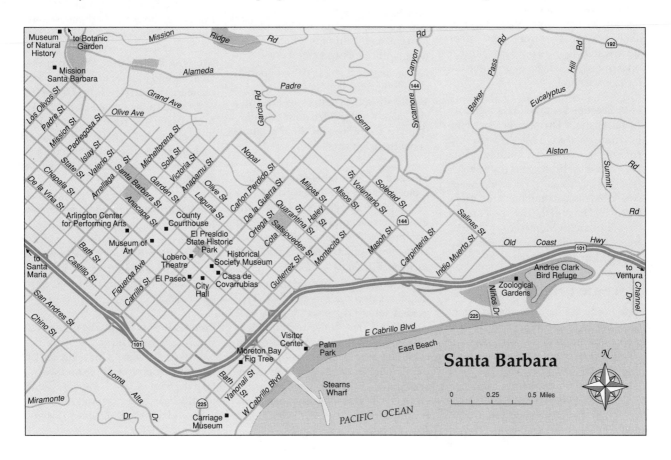

...Santa Barbara

No license is necessary for pier fishing; still-fishing with shrimp for bait may produce a nice haul of tasty perch. Offshore fishing is about as productive here as anywhere along the California coast. Charter boats from Sea Landing west of the wharf take anglers out for half-day and full-day fishing excursions in pursuit of albacore, marlin, and sailfish.

Zoological Gardens. In a charming garden setting just north of the ocean and E. Cabrillo Boulevard are some 200 elephants, lions, monkeys, sea lions, exotic birds, and other animals. A miniature train takes visitors on a tour of the zoo ($4 adults, $2 children). In the farmyard area, children can pet and feed domestic animals. Athletic seals show off in a sealarium with viewing portholes to accommodate visitors of any height. The zoo, at 500 Niños Drive, is open daily; an admission fee is charged.

Andree Clark Bird Refuge. On E. Cabrillo Boulevard next door to the zoo, a beautifully landscaped preserve gives shelter to geese, swans, and other freshwater fowl. Footpaths and a bikeway skirt a lagoon. Feeding the birds is discouraged.

Four Seasons Santa Barbara Biltmore Hotel. Channel Drive, to the east of the bird refuge, leads past the lush and colorful gardens surrounding Santa Barbara's most prestigious resort hotel. It also provides an entrée to the exclusive residential community of Montecito. Two more of the city's best known hostelries are in Montecito—the Montecito Inn (built by Charlie Chaplin) and the San Ysidro Ranch.

A scenic drive

Many of Santa Barbara's major attractions are highlighted along a 24-mile scenic drive around the city. You can obtain a map of the route at the Visitor Information Center near Stearns Wharf (One Santa Barbara Street).

One of the prettiest parts of the drive leads into the hills behind town. Mission Canyon Road begins at Mission Santa Barbara and heads north to the Museum of Natural History and the Santa Barbara Botanic Garden. Alameda Padre Serra winds southeast from the mission through the 500-foot-high foothills known as The Riviera. This pleasant residential area (the location of El Encanto Hotel) offers beautiful views of the city and the ocean beyond. To return to the downtown area, take Gutierrez Street.

Mission Santa Barbara. Overlooking the city from a knoll at the end of Laguna Street sits the tenth of the 21 missions founded by the Spanish in California. Established in 1786 by Father Fermin Lasuén, Santa Barbara is the only mission to remain continuously in the hands of the Franciscans.

Its unique stone facade makes the "Queen of the Missions" a popular subject for photographers. The two-towered design was copied from a Roman book on architecture written by Vitruvius in 27 B.C. (The book is still in the mission archives.)

Three of the mission's original rooms remain, one a primitive kitchen. The chapel, curio room, and library contain relics of mission life. Entrance to the cemetery is through a Roman arch hung with skulls and crossbones.

The mission is still in use as a parish church; its altar light has burned constantly since the chapel was built. You can take a self-guided tour Monday through Saturday and Sunday afternoon; there is a small fee.

Museum of Natural History. Located 2 blocks north of Mission Santa Barbara, at 2559 Puesta del Sol Road, the museum is set amid 2 acres of wooded grounds. Well-conceived exhibits focus on regional plants and animals and prehistoric Indians.

The museum is open daily except major holidays (admission fee). Free guided tours take place Sunday at 2 P.M. Within the museum complex, Gladwin Planetarium's closed-circuit television lets groups of people view the skies together. Shows are Saturday and Sunday afternoons and Saturday evening; a Wednesday afternoon show is added in summer. Call (805) 682-4334 for information.

Santa Barbara Botanic Garden. Indigenous California plants, from wildflowers to redwoods, grow in natural settings on 65 acres in Mission Canyon, just 1½ miles above the mission. More than 5 miles of trails wind through sections representing canyon, desert, Channel Island, arroyo, and redwood forest plant life, following historic Mission Creek to the dam and aqueduct built in 1806 to supply water to the mission.

The garden bursts with color in spring and summer. Flowering shrubs and brilliant wildflowers blaze in the meadow section, ceanothus (wild lilac) contributes white and blue shades to the landscape, and cacti and yucca bloom in the desert. The garden, at 1212 Mission Canyon Road, is open daily all year from 8 A.M. to dusk. Guided tours are offered Thursday at 10:30 A.M. and Sunday at 11 A.M. Admission is charged.

Earl Warren Showgrounds. Horse shows are popular events in Santa Barbara. The Earl Warren Showgrounds on the west side of town (Las Positas Road at U.S. 101) hosts most of them, including the Santa Barbara National Horse Show in August.

Moreton Bay fig tree. At the corner of Chapala and Montecito streets just west of Stearns Wharf stands the largest tree of its kind in the United States. Native to Australia, the fig was planted by a little girl in 1877. Today, it's reckoned that 10,000 people could stand in its shade; its branch spread is estimated at 160 feet.

Carriage Museum. Vintage surreys, hansoms, and buggies are on display in this free museum (hours vary) at 129 Castillo Street, a few blocks west of the wharf. Look sharp for the building; it sits back from the street next to an open field.

Polo Grounds. The public is invited to watch polo matches at the Santa Barbara Polo & Raquet Club, just east of the city at Carpinteria. From U.S. 101, take the Santa Claus Lane exit. Games usually take place Sunday afternoon from April through October. There is an admission fee.

For many vacationers, Santa Barbara is the pot of gold at the end of a rainbow. Its stunning setting, handsome Spanish architecture, and wealth of cultural and recreational offerings make it a good base for exploring California's Central Coast.

Into the Valleys

For a change of pace from the ocean scene, poke about in the valleys around Santa Barbara and Ventura. Just a few minutes away from vacation-packed beaches, you can enjoy peaceful back-country driving, pleasant wine tasting, and uncrowded lakeside camping. Rolling hills and soft meadows dominate the inland landscape, and quiet little communities fit right in with the leisurely atmosphere.

Santa Clara Valley

From the coastal cities of Ventura and Oxnard, southbound travelers have several alternatives to U.S. 101. State 126 heads east through the fertile Santa Clara Valley, eventually meeting Interstate 5 just north of Six Flags Magic Mountain amusement park. State 1 follows the coast south.

Ventura. A stop in Ventura can be rewarding. Miles of broad beaches, a great fishing pier, and a well-developed harbor appeal to swimmers, surfers, anglers, and boaters. From October to March, monarch butterflies winter in and around the city. Ventura's harbor is the year-round embarkation point for cruises to the Channel Islands.

Pick up a touring map of the area from the Ventura Visitors and Convention Bureau (89-C S. California Street). The county's handsome Museum of History and Art, 100 E. Main Street, houses Chumash Indian, Spanish, and early pioneer artifacts. Hours are from 10 A.M. to 5 P.M. Tuesday through Sunday; admission is free.

Across the street is modest Mission San Buenaventura, the last mission founded by Father Serra. Fascinating relics turned up by archeologists digging next to the mission are on display at the free Albinger Archaeologial Museum (closed Monday).

Picnickers can head for Plaza Park at Santa Clara and Chestnut streets or the beach promenade at the southern end of California Street. The promenade and the western end of Surfer's Point Park are good places to watch beach activity.

Follow signs from U.S. 101 to reach the harbor. En route, you pass the historic Olivas Adobe. The grounds are open daily; house tours are given on weekends from 10 A.M. to 3 P.M.

Hotels, restaurants, and shops are part of the harbor scene. The tidy building at the end of Spinnaker Drive is the visitor center for Channel Islands National Park. Exhibits and a film describe the islands, visible from the center on a clear day. The office of Island Packers, tour operator for the islands, is next door. For more information on trips to the park, see page 117.

Oxnard area. South of Ventura on State 1, Oxnard started life as a farming community, became a Navy town, and is now developing into a tourist destination. From the city's Channel Islands Harbor, charter companies run fishing and whale-watching cruises; in summer, boats take visitors to Channel Islands National Park. A public boat-launching ramp lies just south of Channel Islands Boulevard. Fisherman's Wharf, a New England–style village at the harbor, welcomes browsers, shoppers, and diners.

South at Port Hueneme, a free museum pays tribute to the Civil Engineer Corps and the Seabees. Displayed in Building 99 of the Naval Construction Battalion Center are cultural artifacts from around the world. Located at Ventura Road and Sunkist Avenue, the museum is open Monday through Saturday from 9 A.M. to 4:30 P.M. and Sunday from 12:30 to 4:30 P.M., except on national holidays. Visitors obtain a pass at the gate; children under 16 must be accompanied by an adult.

Santa Paula. The little town at the junction of State 150 and State 126 is a shipping center for lemon-rich Santa Clara Valley. One of California's earliest oil booms took place here, a fact memorialized in the free museum at Tenth and Main streets.

Six Flags Magic Mountain. At the eastern end of the Santa Clara Valley,

State 126 intersects Interstate 5. Just south lies Six Flags Magic Mountain, a 260-acre theme park where rides let the adventuresome try white-water rafting, take a splashing dash through a water flume, race through a mine in a runaway car, ride a jet boat, and go skydiving. Yosemite Sam Sierra Falls, a new water ride, plunges down a 760-foot slide. An arsenal of roller coasters, including the world's fastest and tallest looper, guarantee thrills.

Other attractions include an amphitheater with live entertainment, restaurants, and craft shows. Small fry love Bugs Bunny World and the petting zoo. You can visit the park daily in summer, on weekends and holidays (except Christmas) the rest of the year. Gates open at 10 A.M. The gate price (see page 122) covers rides and entertainment.

Ojai Valley

For a pleasant lake and mountain side trip between Ventura and Santa Barbara, use State 33 and State 150 to reach Ojai. Tucked among hillsides covered with citrus and avocado groves, this little resort town has long been a retreat for well-to-do Los Angelenos.

Some say that Ojai (pronounced o-high) comes from an Indian word meaning "nest." Certainly the moon-shaped valley is well insulated against fog, wind, and smog by both its altitude and the Topa and Sulphur mountain ranges.

Lake Casitas. The lake west of town hosted the rowing competition of the 1984 Olympics. It's a favorite spot for campers, boaters, and anglers (swimming and waterskiing are prohibited). Activities are concentrated at the upper end of the reservoir; boat rentals are available at the landing. Campsites are numerous and spacious, though few are tree shaded; trailers are permitted. Day-use and overnight camping fees are moderate. An observation point at the dam on the southeastern end of the lake is reached from State 33 or Santa Ana Road.

Ojai and beyond. A tennis and golf resort, a haven for horseback riders, and a refuge for artists, the community of Ojai maintains a leisurely pace reminiscent of early Spanish days. Even its architecture is vaguely Spanish in feel. The handsome Ojai Valley Inn and Country Club, the area's premier resort, is open to the public.

Cultural activities share the spotlight with sports. A music festival in June and a Mexican Fiesta in September are but two of the yearly highlights. The country's oldest tennis tournament is held here in April.

Beyond the serene little valley stretch miles of wild and rugged mountain terrain with creeks, campsites, and pleasant picnic sites. North on State 33, Wheeler Gorge is the largest and most popular of the public camping parks. En route, note scenic Matilija Dam. Farther north, a side road leads to Piedra Blanca, a spectacular outcrop of white sandstone rocks.

Goleta Valley

Bordered by the luxurious residential development of Hope Ranch to the east and squeezed between the Santa Ynez Mountains and the Pacific, Goleta Valley just northwest of Santa Barbara boasts some of the coast's best beach parks—Goleta, El Capitan, Refugio, and Gaviota—and several notable attractions. One quick trip off U.S. 101 is to the seaside campus of the University of California at Santa Barbara—actually at Goleta, not Santa Barbara.

Cycling is popular with area residents and visitors alike; rentals are available, and bikeways are well marked. An easy ride leads past historic landmarks, along the beach, and into the university campus.

Goleta Depot Railroad Museum. In Lake Los Carneros Park, a restored Victorian railroad station has become a museum. Tours of the grounds (Wednesday through Sunday afternoons) give visitors a nostalgic look at the era of steam locomotives. You can ride miniature trains in summer and at the annual Depot Day celebration on the third Sunday of October. To reach the depot, take Los Carneros Road exit north from U.S. 101.

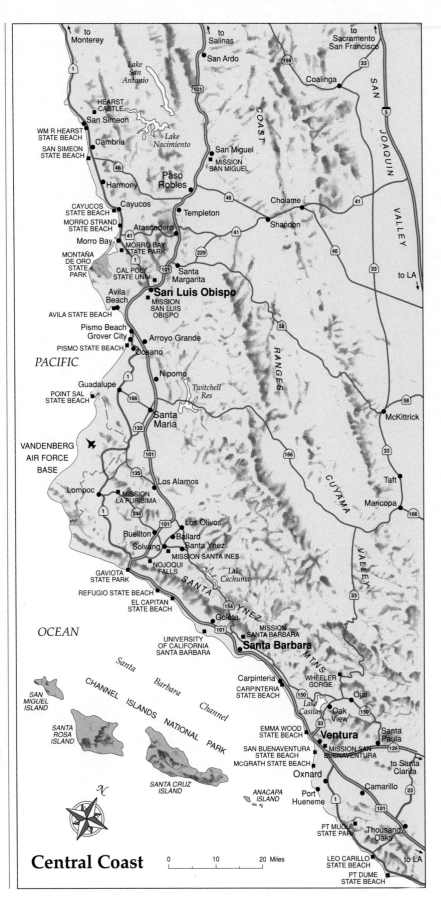

Central Coast

Quaint Santa Ynez Valley town of Solvang celebrates its Scandinavian roots during an annual Danish Days festival held in September. Traditionally attired women prepare aebleskiver, a puffy pancake.

...Into the Valleys

Stow House. This gracious country home, built in 1872, was once the heart of a vast ranch. Wide verandas and gingerbread detailing adorn the exterior; inside, rooms are furnished with period antiques. Next door, the Howard Sexton Memorial Museum features a blacksmith shop and farm implements.

Both structures, located near the Goleta Depot north of U.S. 101, are open Sunday afternoon from 2 to 4 P.M. (closed in January); admission is free.

Santa Ynez Valley

Snuggled between mountain ranges behind Santa Barbara is the Santa Ynez Valley, where stagecoach-era towns provide a scenic contrast to Vandenberg Air Force Base at the western end of the lush basin. The valley's equine residents graze along whitewashed fences that demarcate the many horse ranches; some ranches welcome visitors.

A happy blend of climate and geology has turned the valley into one of the state's best wine regions. Tours and tasting are offered at a couple dozen wineries. Pick up a wine-touring map at the visitor center in Santa Barbara, or contact the Santa Barbara County Vintners' Association, P.O. Box 1558, Santa Ynez, CA 93460; (805) 688-0881.

State 246 enters the valley through the Danish community of Solvang. State 154, a former stagecoach route from Santa Barbara, traverses the length of the valley, rejoining U.S. 101 just beyond Los Olivos.

Lake Cachuma. Along State 154 about 11 miles west of the San Marcos summit sprawls Lake Cachuma Recreation Area, a 9,000-acre county park. Along the shoreline, oaks shade camping and trailer spaces, fire pits, and picnic tables; shower and laundry facilities are available.

In winter, the lake is stocked with fingerling rainbow trout and Kamloops trout from British Columbia. Cool spring and autumn months provide the best fishing; angling slows in summer. Tackle and boat rentals are available. No swimming or waterskiing is allowed, but three swimming pools are open from April through October.

The year-round recreation area charges for admission, parking, and overnight camping. It's crowded in summer, so plan to arrive early.

Valley towns. Scattered around the valley are picturesque small towns that seem little affected by the state's growth.

Santa Ynez deliberately maintains its Old West atmosphere with high-front buildings and a "Western Town" complex. The white-steepled church at the corner of Tivola and Lincoln streets, built in 1897, is one of the valley's oldest. At 3596 Sagunto Street, a museum and carriage house offer insights into 19th-century life. Both are open Friday through Sunday from 1 to 4 P.M.; the carriage house is also open Tuesday through Thursday from 10 A.M. to 4 P.M.

Los Olivos, once a stop for the Butterfield Stage Lines, still serves food to travelers at Mattei's Tavern, the old inn. Also of interest around town are galleries, tasting rooms, and the elegant little Los Olivos Grand Hotel.

Nearby Ballard, established in 1880, was the valley's first settlement. The little red schoolhouse (2425 School Street) is now a historic landmark.

Buellton, at the crossroads of U.S. 101 and State 246, offers access to Santa Ynez Valley and Solvang 3 miles to the west. Buellton got on the map as the "home of split pea soup," a specialty of Andersen's Restaurant.

Solvang. Solvang's windmill structures, copper and thatched roofs crowned with artificial nesting storks, gas lights, cobblestone walkways, and horse-drawn trolley suggest a quaint environment manufactured solely for the tourists who throng its streets. But this town is solidly Scandinavian in heritage, food, and customs.

About two-thirds of the 3,500 or so residents are of Danish descent. Danish educators from Minnesota selected the area as the site for a folk school in 1911, when the only building in town was the Mission Santa Ines.

Patterned after a typical rural Danish meetinghouse, the Bethania Lutheran Church on Atterdag Road contains a scale model of a fully rigged ship hanging from its ceiling, a common Scandinavian tradition. The pulpit is hand carved. Danish-language services are held the first Sunday of each month.

Solvang's fine bakeries have made the town famous. Look for Danish pancakes, too—thin ones, or the puffy balls called *aebleskiver*. Eat them with *medisterpølse*—pale, thick sausages. Several restaurants serve the traditional *smørrebrød*.

Shopping leans toward Scandinavian imports, with an emphasis on gourmet and delicatessen foods, housewares, toys, apparel, and gifts.

Tourists flock to the colorful Danish Days celebration in mid-September and to the summer Theaterfest. For information, stop at the Visitors Bureau, 1571 Mission Drive (open daily).

Mission Santa Ines, the old Spanish mission still in use today, is just east of Solvang's main business district. Founded in 1804, it's one of the best restored of all the missions. The chapel, museum, and cemetery are open daily.

Nojoqui Falls. One of the state's most graceful waterfalls highlights a drive between Solvang and the coast. From Solvang, drive south on Alisal Road for about 6½ miles. If you're coming from U.S. 101, turn off about 5 miles north of Gaviota Pass on a road marked "To Nojoqui Falls County Park." A short walk along a woodsy path brings you to the waterfall, best in spring.

Mission La Purisima. If you visit just one mission—especially if you're traveling with children—it should be Mission La Purisima Concepcion, 15 miles west of Buellton and 5 miles east of Lompoc in a quiet rural setting off State 246. Carefully restored and operated as a state historic park, the mission presents a row of simple facades: church, craft workshops, and padres' living quarters. A colorful fiesta is held here the third Sunday in May.

Lompoc. Lompoc Valley produces more than half the world's flower seeds. From May to September, thousands of acres of fields are in bloom; you can catch glimpses from the roads. A festival in late June includes a floral parade.

Up the Coast

The Spanish and Indian influence in this part of the Central Coast is revealed in such musical place names as Guadalupe, Santa Maria, Oceano, Nipomo, Arroyo Grande, San Luis Obispo, Morro Bay, Cayucos, and Cambria.

Take your choice of routes: U.S. 101 is faster but bypasses most of the historic and recreational spots; State 1 takes a more rural direction along the ocean. At San Luis Obispo, the highways diverge, State 1 heading north to the shore at Morro Bay and U.S. 101 veering inland toward Paso Robles and nearby Mission San Miguel (see page 6).

Explorations from U.S. 101 lead to ranching and wine-growing valleys around the Santa Lucia Mountains. Most of the wineries are clustered around Paso Robles, though a few in the Edna Valley region south of San Luis Obispo on State 227 offer tasting rooms. Stop at Templeton Corner, a tasting outlet for dozens of boutique wineries, on the main street of the tiny town of Templeton.

Nipomo (off U.S. 101 just north of State 166) was a private ranch before becoming an important stopover on the old El Camino Real between the Santa Barbara and San Luis Obispo missions. Although most of its historic structures are gone, the adobe ranch house still stands. Jocko's restaurant draws crowds for spicy beans and big steaks.

A few miles north in Arroyo Grande you'll find Western storefronts, an old jail, and other historic remnants. Attractive Lopez Lake, 10 miles inland, has camping sites (full hookups), boat rentals, a sandy shore, and a water slide.

If you drive State 1, Guadalupe offers the first look at the coast's most extensive sand dunes. Follow Main Street west to Rancho Guadalupe County Park; occasional high winds shift sands and force some road closures. On the town's lone street, Basque House is but one of the restaurants serving good food, not atmosphere.

Around Pismo Beach. The town of Pismo Beach was named for its resident mollusk, the Pismo clam. The bay's broad, surf-swept arc provides an ideal environment for clams; but because the shore is too accessible to clam-loving humans, the greater part of the clam beds has been made into a preserve.

Monarch butterflies brighten the town from November through March. Fishing is good from the end of the long pier, where you can charter deep-sea boats.

Pismo State Beach. Some 6 miles of shoreline from the town of Pismo Beach south to the Santa Maria River make up one of the state's finest beach parks; you'll find campgrounds, picnic areas, rest rooms, and showers here. The park's southern reaches include the vast expanse of Pismo Dunes Preserve, where visitors picnic, hike, and slither up and down the sandy slopes. Vehicles are prohibited in the preserve.

The southern entrance to the park is through Oceano, once an aspiring seaside resort. A few Victorian-era gingerbread houses still stand.

Avila State Beach. Popular with locals, Avila State Beach nestles within the northern arc of San Luis Obispo Bay. Warm water makes the ocean ideal for swimming. Facilities include a pier, charter boats, a launching ramp, and rental concessions for gear.

Above the quiet bay, luxurious San Luis Bay Inn offers great views and a golf course. A detour off San Luis Bay Drive leads through oak-lined See Canyon, a major apple-producing area. You can buy apple varieties here that you won't find in supermarkets.

San Luis Obispo

Cupped in a small valley, San Luis Obispo, the region's focal point, makes a good base for exploring the countryside. The town grew up around Mission San Luis Obispo de Tolosa, established in 1772. Among local lodgings are the colorful and curlicued Madonna Inn, the modern Victorian-style Apple Farm Inn, and the country's first motel (Motel Inn). Good restaurants and shops abound.

Detouring off the freeway that slices through San Luis Obispo, you'll discover a surprising showcase of California architectual history. A brochure available from the Chamber of Commerce (1039 Chorro Street) describes some 20 attractions along a 2-mile walking or driving tour. Highlighted are the mission, the County Historical Museum, and the 1874 Ah Louis store, which once served as a bank and post office for Chinese railroad workers.

San Luis is livelier than you might expect a museum town to be, hosting a Spanish Fiesta in May, a Jazzfest over the Fourth of July weekend, and a Mozart Festival in August.

Every Thursday the town throws a party. Higuera Street is blocked off near the mission, and local farmers truck in their produce. By 6 P.M. the downtown spills over with people buying, selling, eating, browsing, or swapping gossip.

Mission Plaza. Located in the heart of town at Chorro and Monterey streets, the mission was the first to be built with a tile roof. Today the restored building is a parish church and museum. The mission is open daily; a minimum donation is requested.

Across the street from the mission, the county's historical museum, housed in a 1905 Carnegie library, keeps an eclectic collection of regional memorabilia dating back to the Chumash and Salinian Indian periods. It's open 10 A.M. to 4 P.M. Wednesday through Sunday; admission is free.

The well-landscaped plaza fronting the mission was designed by Cal Poly students. Footbridges span the creek that meanders through town, leading to shops and restaurants.

Cal Poly. California Polytechnic State University, famous for its schools of architecture and agriculture, sits on rolling hills overlooking the city from the northeast. Students at Cal Poly, no ordinary campus, learn by doing—at the campus nursery, chicken farm, or printing press. Campus-produced jams, milk, and a very popular salsa are sold

Channel Islands National Park

Scattered off the coast between Santa Barbara and San Diego lie the eight volcanic islets that make up the Channel Islands, among the first parts of California to be explored by Europeans. Cabrillo anchored near Anacapa Island in 1542; in 1769, Portola made reference to it in his log.

Once home to thousands of Chumash Indians and later a destination for hunters, the islands are mainly nature preserves now where boaters, hikers, and campers can view a kind of American Galapagos. Windswept canyons and meadows support plants and wildlife found nowhere else.

On clear days, the islands are visible from the mainland. The closest, Anacapa (actually three tiny islands), lies 11 miles from shore. The popular tourist destination of Santa Catalina Island is also part of the Channel Islands (see page 37).

Natural wonders. To ensure the preservation of rare and endangered plants and wildlife, five of the islands—Anacapa, San Miguel, Santa Rosa, Santa Barbara, and privately owned Santa Cruz—were designated as the Channel Islands National Park in 1980. The rich waters surrounding the park are a national marine sanctuary.

Beaches and rocky inlets are refuges for seals, sea lions, and sea elephants. Other local residents include island foxes, cormorants, and California brown pelicans.

Tidepools teem with activity, and giant kelp forests in the offshore waters shelter more than 1,000 species of marine life, visible to scuba divers and snorkelers. Migrating gray whales are sighted from December through April.

Plant enthusiasts won't be disappointed with the unique trees, shrubs, and wildflowers. The vivid blooms of the giant coreopsis steal the show in late winter, painting the islands with splashes of brilliant yellow.

An island visit. Island Packers, the park concessioner, offers trips to Santa Barbara, Santa Cruz, Santa Rosa, and San Miguel islands in summer. Service to Anacapa is available year-round. Boats leave the harbor at Ventura at 9 A.M. daily in summer and during the winter whale migration, returning at 5 P.M. Island Packers also makes daily summer runs for campers and, in April and May, half-day non-landing trips.

For reservations, write to Island Packers, 1867 Spinnaker Drive, Ventura, CA 93001; phone (805) 642-1393. For information and prices, call (805) 642-7688.

Channel Islands Adventures provides air tours to Santa Cruz and Santa Rosa islands all year from Camarillo. Day trips include a picnic lunch. From April through October, a four-day weekend or five-day midweek package includes airfare, meals, and island accommodations in a two-story adobe ranchhouse dating back to 1864.

For information and reservations, contact Channel Islands Adventures, 305 Durley Avenue, Camarillo, CA 93010; phone (805) 987-1678.

Primitive camping (no food or water is provided) is permitted on Anacapa, San Miguel, Santa Rosa, and Santa Barbara. Reserve ahead for camping sites and for ranger-guided walks on San Miguel and Santa Rosa.

For information, write to the Superintendent, Channel Islands National Park, 1901 Spinnaker Drive, Ventura, CA 93001, or stop at the visitor center at the tip of Ventura's harbor. Photographs, displays, an indoor tidepool, and a 25-minute film make this a worthwhile stop.

The Nature Conservancy operates 90 percent of Santa Cruz Island as a preserve; the other 10 percent has been owned by the Gherini family since the 1800s. Permission to visit the island is strictly limited. Island Adventures (308 Lion Street, Ojai, CA 93023) offers day trips and overnights. Visitors camp or stay at a ranch on the east end of the island. For details, phone (805) 646-2573.

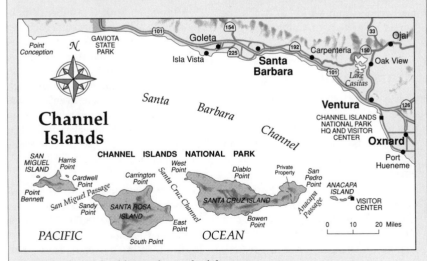

Santa Barbara Island lies to the south of the map area.

...Up the Coast

at the student store (closed Sunday) near the visitors parking area.

North on State 1

From San Luis Obispo, State 1 cuts through photogenic hills and rolling farmlands, wending its way northwest to Morro Bay. In summer, the valley's blue skies are usually blanketed by fog, and temperatures drop abruptly.

Montaña de Oro State Park. Los Osos, 12 miles west of San Luis Obispo, is the gateway to one of the state's most beautiful parks. Unlimited ocean vistas are a part of its lure. Hikers explore Valencia Peak and other hills that overlook the nearly 100 miles of coastline from Point Sal in the south to Piedras Blancas in the north.

Made up largely of rugged cliffs and headlands, the 5,600-acre park contains little coves with relatively secluded sandy beaches. Spring wildflowers abound; the predominantly yellow color inspired the park's name, which means "mountain of gold" in Spanish. About 50 campsites are located near the old Rancho Montaña de Oro headquarters beside Islay Creek.

Morro Bay. The fishing town of Morro Bay 12 miles northwest of San Luis Obispo spreads along the eastern shore of the estuary that gives it its name. Motels, shops, and seafood restaurants ring the waterfront. Sightseeing boats cruise around the harbor; a clam taxi shuttles hikers, picnickers, and birdwatchers to the 4-mile-long spit separating bay and ocean.

Chess players congregate around the giant board at the foot of the centennial stairway that leads from Harbor Street to the waterfront. Boats dock right behind the fish markets; a battalion of pelicans awaits one false move.

Morro Rock, which separates Estero Bay (to the north) from the harbor, was a landmark for Spanish explorers. The 576-foot-high rock, westernmost in a chain of long-extinct volcanoes that form the picturesque backbone of San Luis Obispo County, is a protected nesting site for peregrine falcons.

Morro Bay State Park. Spacious and verdant, the inviting park a mile south of town spills over the hillside and down to the bay. It's a good place to camp, picnic, rent a boat, or play golf.

On the way to the park, stop by the Museum of Natural History for a view of the bay and Morro Rock. Fascinating displays and movies feature local wildlife and area history. Open daily, the museum charges a modest fee.

Cayucos. Take the Ocean Avenue exit off State 1 to visit Cayucos, a funky beach town with a pier long enough to get anglers out beyond the surf line. The town was once known for abalone, but overfishing killed the industry; only some shell decorations around town serve as a reminder. Several antique shops, some modest restaurants, and a few other stores line the main street.

Harmony. Don't blink or you might miss this former dairy town, population 18, several miles south of Cambria. About a block long, it has a pottery shop, a couple of design studios, a glassblower, a restaurant, and a wedding chapel made from a wine cask.

Cambria. Fine galleries, restaurants, and shops line artsy Cambria's Main Street, the link between the two villages that make up the town. Although a number of intimate inns are sprinkled around town, reservations are at a premium on weekends and in the summer. Coastal parks are good vantage points from which to watch the winter migration of California's gray whales.

Hearst Castle

Media tycoon William Randolph Hearst called his San Simeon estate "the ranch," an understatement if ever there was one. The opulent grandeur of his hilltop hideaway might have drawn the envy of Kublai Khan.

Some 40 miles up the coast from San Luis Obispo, the gilded towers of Hearst Castle glitter like gems among a strangely eclectic but glamorous collection of mansions, terraced gardens, pools, art objects, bunkhouses, and garages. The estate that crowns La Cuesta Encantada—Hearst's Enchanted Hill—cost nearly three million Depression-era dollars and took Hearst and architect Julia Morgan from 1919 to 1947 to build.

In 1957, the Hearst family turned the palatial residence over to the state. It's now a state historic monument toured by more than 1 million visitors annually—second only to Disneyland as California's most popular attraction.

Tours. Guided tours give glimpses of a way of life that rivaled the most extravagant fantasies enacted by Hearst's movie-star guests. Because of the vastness of the estate—123 acres of grounds, three guest houses, and a main house with 38 bedrooms, 14 sitting rooms, 2 libraries, a kitchen, and a theater—four tours are offered.

Tour 1 takes in the gardens, a guest house, the pools, and the main floor of the mansion. Tour 2 covers the upper floors of the main building, including Hearst's private quarters and personal libraries, guest rooms, and kitchen. Tour 3 includes the guest wing of the main building, a guest house, gardens, pools, and a home movie theater. Tour 4, available only from April through October, visits the wine cellar, pools, underground vaults, and bowling alley.

Each tour lasts about 2 hours and requires considerable walking and climbing. Comfortable shoes and a sweater or jacket are advised, as part of each tour is outdoors. Tour 1 is the best introduction to the property.

Although a limited number of tickets are sold at the visitor center each day on a first-come, first-served basis, advance reservations for the tours, which cost $14 adults, $8 ages 6 to 12, are recommended. Reserve through MISTIX, (800) 444-7275. Evening tours ($25 adults, $13 children take place on spring and autumn weekends. Hearst Castle is open daily, except New Year's Day, Thanksgiving, and Christmas.

Lodging. For information on accommodations, contact San Simeon Chamber of Commerce at (805) 927-3500 or Cambria Chamber of Commerce at (805) 927-3624. You can reserve San Simeon State Beach campsites through MISTIX two months ahead.

On a tour of Hearst Castle in San Simeon, visitors pause at the Neptune Pool fronting the mansion. William Randolph Hearst's former estate took three million Depression-era dollars and almost three decades to build.

An Activity Guide

Camping at National Parks

Advance planning will help you get the most out of a camping trip to one of California's national parks or monuments. For information and fees (currently $6 to $10 per night), contact the individual areas listed below or the National Park Service Information Office, 30401 Agoura Rd., Agoura Hills, CA 91301, phone (818) 597-9192.

Three campgrounds (in Sequoia National Park and in Death Valley and Joshua Tree national parks) accept reservations up to 8 weeks in advance through MISTIX. To charge reservations, call (800) 365-2267.

Maximum RV length varies from campground to campground—be sure to check ahead of time.

Channel Islands National Park (see page 117). Information: (805) 644-8157. Primitive camping is permitted on Anacapa, San Miguel, Santa Barbara, and Santa Rosa islands; reservations are required. You must bring your own food and water.

Island Packers provides transportation to the islands (see page 117); make boat reservations at least 2 weeks in advance. Various ecological organizations also lead trips; contact park headquarters.

Death Valley National Park (see page 100). Information: (619) 786-2331. All-year campgrounds include *Furnace Creek,* near park headquarters (34 tent and 136 tent/RV sites, disposal station, disabled facilities, elevation -196 feet; reservations accepted) and unimproved *Wildrose,* near the State 178 entrance (30 tent/RV sites, no water, pit toilets, elevation 4,100 feet).

Open from November to April are *Sunset,* near Furnace Creek (1000 tent/RV sites, disposal station, disabled facilities, elevation -190 feet); nearby *Texas Spring* (40 tent and 53 tent/RV sites, disposal station, elevation 0 feet); and *Stovepipe Wells* (24 tent and 175 tent/RV sites, disposal station, elevation 0 feet).

Emigrant, 9 miles southwest of Stovepipe Wells (10 tent/RV sites, elevation 2,100 feet), is open April to October. Two unimproved, high-altitude camping areas farther south are open March through November.

Devils Postpile National Monument (see page 99). Information: (619) 934-2289. Located 13 miles west of Mammoth Lakes off State 203, Devils Postpile has one campground (24 tent/RV sites, elevation 7,600 feet), open June to October.

East Mojave National Preserve (see page 92). Information: (619) 326-3896. Developed Bureau of Land Management campgrounds are open all year at *Mid-Hills* (26 tent/RV sites, elevation 5,600 feet), 15½ miles southeast of Cima off Cedar Canyon Road, and *Hole-in-the-Wall* (9 tent/RV sites, elevation 4,200 feet), 25½ miles northwest of Essex off Interstate 40. *Providence Mountains State Recreation Area,* 21 miles northwest of Interstate 40 on Essex Road, is also open year-round (6 tent/RV sites, elevation 4,300 feet).

Joshua Tree National Park (see page 87). Information: (619) 367-7511. Open October to April is *Black Rock Canyon,* 5 miles southeast of Yucca Valley off State 62 (100 tent/RV sites, disposal station, elevation 4,000 feet; reservations recommended). Open all year is *Cottonwood,* 32 miles northeast of Indio off Interstate 10 (62 tent/RV sites, disposal station, elevation 3,000 feet).

Other undeveloped campgrounds (pit toilets but no water), all free, are on side roads south of State 62. Open year-round are *Hidden Valley* (62 tent/RV sites, elevation 4,200 feet); *Indian Cove* (114 tent/RV sites, elevation 3,200 feet); *Belle* (20 tent/RV sites, elevation 3,800 feet); and *Jumbo Rocks* (130 tent/RV sites, elevation 4,400 feet). Open October to May are *White Tank* (20 tent/RV sites, elevation 3,800 feet) and *Ryan* (27 tent/RV sites, elevation 4,300 feet).

Kings Canyon National Park (see page 96). Information: (209) 565-3456. Six campgrounds are clustered in two areas along State 180: north of Wilsonia near Grant Grove Village (6,600-foot elevation) and along the South Fork of the Kings

River near Cedar Grove (4,600-foot elevation). All have tables, fire rings, water, flush toilets, and showers; camping limit is 14 days from mid-June to mid-September, 30 days the rest of the year.

Near Grant Grove Village, *Azalea* is open year-round (30 tent and 87 RV sites, disposal station, disabled facilities). Open May to September are *Sunset* (30 tent and 154 tent/RV sites) and *Crystal Springs* (25 tent and 42 tent/RV sites).

Near Cedar Grove, *Sentinel* is open May to October (83 tent/RV sites, disabled facilities). Open June to October are *Sheep Creek* (111 tent/RV sites, disposal station) and *Moraine* (120 tent/RV sites).

Santa Monica Mountains National Recreation Area (see page 24). Information: (818) 888-3770. Encompassing some 150,000 acres of federal, state, county, and city lands, the NRA includes state-operated coastal campgrounds at *Leo Carillo State Beach* and *Point Mugu State Park* (page 121). North of State 1 off Las Virgenes Road is *Malibu Creek State Park* (64 tent/RV sites, elevation 500 feet).

Sequoia National Park (see page 96). Information: (209) 565-3456. Campgrounds have tables, fire rings, toilets, and water; most have a 14-day camping limit from mid-June to mid-September, 30 days otherwise.

Along the General's Highway (State 198) are three all-year campgrounds: *Dorst* (190 tent/RV sites, elevation 6,720 feet); *Lodgepole* (163 tent and 98 RV sites, disposal station, showers, disabled facilities, elevation 6,700 feet; reservations accepted); and *Potwisha* (44 tent/RV sites, disposal station, disabled facilities, elevation 2,100 feet). Open April to October is *Buckeye Flat* (28 tent sites, elevation 2,800 feet). Some campgrounds are to be relocated in the mid-90s.

In the Mineral King area, open May to September, are *Atwell Mill* (23 tent sites, elevation 6,645 feet) and *Cold Springs* (37 tent sites, elevation 7,500 feet). Open all year (limited winter access) is *South Fork* (13 tent/RV sites, elevation 3,650 feet).

Camping at State Beaches

 Camping at state beaches and coastal parks gives you easy access to surfing, swimming, surf fishing, clamming, skin diving, and other fun along the Pacific. The following listings capsulize camping facilities south to north. A detailed guide of state park facilities is available for a fee—contact the Publications Section, California Department of Parks & Recreation, P.O. Box 942896, Sacramento, CA 94296-0838; phone 916/322-7000.

Campsite reservations can be made between 48 hours and eight weeks before date of arrival through the MISTIX reservation system. To charge reservations to a Visa or MasterCard number, phone (800) 444-7275 (California only) or (619) 452-1950 (out of state) on weekdays from 8 A.M. to 5 P.M., on Saturday and Sunday from 8 A.M. to 3 P.M.

Camping fees generally range from $7 to $20 per campsite per night, plus a $3.95 non-refundable reservation fee. RV hookups may be slightly higher. Reduced fees apply for anyone 62 years or older. Self-contained recreational vehicles can overnight at several state beaches on a first-come, first-served basis. Regular fees apply for "en route" sites.

SAN DIEGO COUNTY

Silver Strand State Beach, 4½ miles south of Coronado; en route camping, food service. Surfing, swimming, sailboarding, fishing. Contact: (619) 435-5184.

San Elijo State Beach, ½ mile northwest of Cardiff-by-the-Sea (Birmingham Drive off Interstate 5); 171 campsites, disposal station, store. Surfing, swimming, skin diving, fishing. Contact: (619) 753-5091 or (619) 729-8947.

South Carlsbad State Beach, 3 miles south of Carlsbad; 222 campsites, disposal station, store. Surfing, swimming, skin diving, fishing. Contact: (619) 438-3143 or (619) 729-8947.

San Onofre State Beach South, 3 miles south of San Clemente off Interstate 5 (Basilone Road); 221 campsites, disposal station, store, hike-in 20-site primitive campground (summer), en route camping

(summer). Swimming, fishing, hiking trails. Information: (714) 492-4872 or (714) 492-0802.

ORANGE COUNTY

San Clemente State Beach, 2 miles south of San Clemente off Interstate 5; 160 campsites, 72 with hookups for vehicles to 30 feet. Surfing, swimming, fishing, hiking. Check conditions—ocean has rip currents. Contact: (714) 492-3156.

Doheny State Beach, 2 miles south of San Juan Capistrano on State 1; 121 campsites, disposal station, food service. Surfing, swimming, fishing, marine life refuge and diving area offshore, interpretive center. Contact: (714) 496-6171.

Bolsa Chica State Beach, 3 miles north of Huntington Beach; en route camping only, cold showers, fire rings, dressing rooms, food service. Swimming, fishing, nature trail. Contact: (714) 846-3460.

LOS ANGELES COUNTY

Dockweiler State Beach, west of L.A. Airport at the west end of the Imperial Highway; 158-site RV campground (hookups), disposal station, store. Swimming, fishing, volleyball. Contact: (213) 305-9503.

Leo Carillo State Beach, 28 miles west of Santa Monica on State 1; 138 campsites (50 near beach accessible only to vehicles less than 8 feet in height), disposal station, store (weekends only in winter). Surfing, swimming, skin diving, fishing, tidepools, nature trail. Migrating whales visible November–May. Contact: (818) 706-1310.

VENTURA COUNTY

Point Mugu State Park, 15 miles south of Oxnard; 50 developed and 100 primitive campsites, disposal station. Swimming, fishing, hiking, exhibits. Contact: (818) 706-1310.

McGrath State Beach, 3½ miles south of Ventura; 174 campsites, disposal station. Swimming, fishing, nature trail, wildlife area. Contact: (805) 654-4744 or (805) 654-4611.

Emma Wood State Beach, 3 miles north of Ventura; 61 campsites operated by Ventura County, (805) 643-3951; en route camping. Group camp, campsites for hikers and bicyclists operated by state. Swimming, fishing, bike path. Contact: (805) 643-7532 or (805) 654-4611.

SANTA BARBARA COUNTY

Carpinteria State Beach, 12 miles south of Santa Barbara; 174 campsites (119 with hookups), disposal station. Surfing, swimming, fishing, interpretive display. Contact: (805) 684-2811 or (805) 654-4611.

El Capitan State Beach, 20 miles northwest of Santa Barbara; 140 campsites, disposal station, store; en route camping. Surfing, swimming, fishing, nature trail, bike path. Rocky shore with tidepools. Contact: (805) 968-3294.

Refugio State Beach, 23 miles northwest of Santa Barbara; 85 campsites, store. Swimming, fishing, bike path. Contact: (805) 968-3294.

Gaviota State Park, 33 miles west of Santa Barbara; 59 campsites, store (weekends only in winter). Bring drinking water. Swimming, fishing, boating, hiking and equestrian trails. Contact: (805) 567-5013.

SAN LUIS OBISPO COUNTY

Pismo State Beach, 2 miles south of Pismo Beach; Oceano Campground has 82 sites (42 with hookups), North Beach Campground 106 sites, disposal station. Fishing, hiking trails, monarch butterfly preserve (winter season). Contact: (805) 489-2684.

Montaña de Oro State Park, 12 miles west of San Luis Obispo; 50 undeveloped sites; en route camping. Fishing, hiking and equestrian trails, nature trail. Contact: (805) 528-0513 (summer only) or (805) 772-2560.

Morro Bay State Park, Morro Bay; 115 campsites, 20 sites with hookups, disposal station, food service; en route camping. Fishing, boating, nature walks and programs, 18-hole golf course. Outstanding marine area, shore bird habitat. Exhibits on natural history, wildlife, ecology, Native American life. Contact: (805) 772-2560.

Morro Strand State Beach, Morro Bay; 104 campsites. Swimming, fishing. Contact: (805) 772-2560.

San Simeon State Beach, 5 miles south of San Simeon; 132 developed, 115 primitive campsites, disposal station. Fishing, hiking trails. Contact: (805) 927-2010.

Theme Parks & Zoos

From San Diego in the south to Bakersfield in the north, Southern California is dotted with elaborate amusement parks and vast zoological gardens.

THEME PARKS

Disneyland, Harbor Boulevard exit off Interstate 5, Anaheim; (714) 999-4565. See page 50 for description. *Hours:* 10 A.M. to 6 P.M. weekdays, 9 A.M. to midnight weekends (9 A.M. to midnight weekdays in summer, 8 A.M. to 1 A.M. summer weekends). *Admission:* $28.75 adults, $23 children 3 to 11. *Other costs:* Parking, food, souvenirs, wheelchair/stroller rental, kennels.

Knott's Berry Farm, Beach Boulevard exit off Interstate 5, Buena Park; (714) 220-5200. See page 49 for description. *Hours:* Daily except Christmas, 10 A.M. to 6 P.M. weekdays, to 10 P.M. Saturday and 7 P.M. Sunday (10 A.M. to midnight daily in summer). *Admission:* $25.95 adults, $17.95 seniors, $15.95 children under 54 inches. *Other costs:* Parking, food, souvenirs, headliner performances, wheelchair/stroller rental.

Baby giraffe enjoys a handout at San Diego Wild Animal Park.

Oasis Water Resort, 1500 Gene Autry Trail, Palm Springs; (619) 325-SURF. Inner-tube river ride, free-fall and speed slides, splash pools, wave pool. *Hours:* 11 A.M. to 6 or 8 P.M. daily March through Labor Day, weekends through October. *Admission:* $16.95 anyone over 60 inches, $11.95 for those 40 to 60 inches, $10.95 seniors. *Other costs:* Parking, food, surfboards, lockers.

Raging Waters, Raging Waters Drive off Interstate 210, San Dimas (near Pomona); (714) 592-6453. Forty-four acres of get-wet attractions, including 10 slides, wave pool. *Hours:* Open mid-May to mid-October, 10 A.M. to 7 P.M. weekends only in spring and fall, daily in summer (varying extended hours). *Admission:* $18.50 anyone 48 inches or taller, $9.95 for children 42 to 48 inches, $10.50 seniors. *Other costs:* Parking, lockers, rafts, snacks.

Santa's Village, State 18, Sky Forest, San Bernardino Mountains; (714) 337-2481. Santa's workplace with shops, rides, and petting zoo. *Hours:* Daily, 10 A.M. to 5 P.M. mid-June through mid-September and mid-November through December; call for other times. *Admission:* $9 ages 3 to adult, $4.50 seniors. *Other costs:* Food.

Sea World, Sea World Drive off Interstate 5, Mission Bay, San Diego; (619) 226-3901. See page 69 for description. *Hours:* 9 A.M. to 5 P.M. in winter, to 6 P.M. spring and fall, to 11 P.M. summer. *Admission:* $24.95 over 11, $18.95 children 3 to 11. *Other costs:* Food, wheelchair/stroller rental.

Six Flags Magic Mountain, Magic Mountain Parkway off Interstate 5, Valencia; (805) 255-4111. See page 112 for description. *Hours:* Daily, 10 A.M. to 10 P.M. or later, in summer; weekends and school vacations rest of year, 10 A.M. to 6 P.M. *Admission:* $26 adults and children over 4 feet, $17 seniors, $15 children under 4 feet (free under 2 years). *Other costs:* Parking, food, souvenirs, some concerts, wheelchair/stroller rental.

Universal Studios, Lankershim Boulevard off U.S. 101, Universal City; (818) 508-9600. See page 20 for description. *Hours:* Daily except Thanksgiving and Christmas; call for seasonal hours. *Admission:* $27 adults, $21 seniors and children 3 to 11. *Other costs:* Parking, food, wheelchair/stroller rental.

Wild Rivers Waterpark, Irvine Center Drive off Interstate 405, Laguna Hills; (714) 768-WILD. See page 52 for description. *Hours:* Open mid-May through September; call for seasonal hours. *Admission:*

$15.95 ages 10 and older, $8.95 seniors, $12.95 children 3 to 9. *Other costs:* Parking, bodyboards, lockers, snacks.

ZOOS

California Living Museum, 14000 Old Alfred Harrell Highway, 13 miles east of Bakersfield off State 178; (805) 872-CALM. Botanical gardens and native wildlife zoo, with reptile house, walk-in aviary, desert tortoise enclosure, petting park. *Hours:* Tuesday through Sunday, 10 A.M. to sunset. *Admission:* $3.50 adults, $2.50 seniors, $2 children 4 through 17.

Los Angeles Zoo, Zoo Drive, Griffith Park, near the junction of Interstate 5 and State 134; (213) 666-4090. See page 29 for description. *Hours:* Daily except Christmas, 10 A.M. to 5 P.M. (6 P.M. in summer). *Admission:* $6 adults, $5 seniors, $2.75 children 2 to 12. *Other costs:* Food, souvenirs, elephant or camel rides, wheelchair/stroller rental.

Moonridge Animal Park, Moonridge Road, Big Bear Lake, San Bernardino Mountains; (714) 866-3652. Small mountain wildlife complex. *Hours:* 8 A.M. to 4 P.M. daily in summer. *Admission:* Free.

San Diego Zoo, Balboa Park; (619) 234-3153. See page 69 for description. *Hours:* Daily, 9 A.M. to 4 P.M. (to 5 P.M. July through Labor Day). *Admission:* Deluxe tour (bus tour, aerial tram, children's zoo) $15 adults, $6.50 ages 3 to 15. *Other costs:* Food, souvenirs, wheelchair/stroller rental.

San Diego Wild Animal Park, Rancho Parkway exit off Interstate 15 to San Pasqual Valley Road, Escondido; (619) 747-8702. See page 74 for description. *Hours:* Daily, 9 A.M. to 5 or 6 P.M., to 11 P.M. in summer. *Admission:* $16.50 adults, $9.50 ages 3 to 15. *Other costs:* Parking, wheelchair/stroller rental.

Santa Ana Zoo at Prentice Park, 1801 E. Chestnut Ave., Santa Ana; (714) 835-7484. Primate collection, petting zoo, playground. *Hours:* Daily except Christmas and New Year's, 10 A.M. to 5 P.M. *Admission:* $2 adults, 75 cents seniors and children 3 to 12. *Other costs:* Wagon rental.

Santa Barbara Zoological Gardens, 500 Niños Drive, west of U.S. 101; (805) 962-6310. See page 110 for description. *Hours:* Daily, 10 A.M. to 5 P.M. in winter, 9 A.M. to 6 P.M. in summer. *Admission:* $5 adults, $3 seniors and children 2 to 12. *Other costs:* Snacks, souvenirs, carousel and train rides, wagon/stroller rental.

Golf Courses

If you take your golf game on the road, you'll find an ever-increasing choice of places to play in Southern California. Because of their popularity you need to reserve tee times well in advance. Our sample of public and resort courses gives some idea of what's available. For a more complete roundup, contact local visitor bureaus and chambers of commerce. Yardage listed is from the regular tees.

GREATER LOS ANGELES AREA

Brookside Golf Course, 1133 N. Rosemont Ave., Pasadena; (818) 796-0177. Flat public courses with lots of trees; near Rose Bowl. *Koiner:* 18 holes, par 72; 6,661 yards; rating 71.6, slope 117. *Eonay:* 18 holes, par 70; 5,689 yards; rating 66.3, slope 104.

Griffith Golf Courses, 4730 Crystal Springs Dr., Los Angeles; (213) 663-2555. Two championship public courses in Griffith Park next to the zoo. *Harding:* 18 holes, par 72, 6,488 yards; rating 69.1, slope 108. *Wilson:* 18 holes, par 72; 6,802 yards; rating 70.9, slope 109.

Industry Hills Golf Club, 1 Industry Hills Pkwy., City of Industry; (818) 965-0861. Two championship public courses. *Dwight D. Eisenhower:* 18 holes, par 72; 7,192 yards; rating 70.9, slope 130. *Babe Zaharias:* 18 holes, par 72; 6,735 yards; rating 70.3, slope 130.

Rancho Park Golf Course, 10460 W. Pico Blvd., Beverly Hills; (213) 838-7373. Popular flat public course; usually lush fairways; 18 holes, par 71; 6,585 yards; rating 71.2, slope 108.

ORANGE COUNTY

Anaheim Hills Public Country Club, 6501 E. Nohl Ranch Rd., Anaheim; (714) 637-7311. Hilly, challenging Richard Bigler public course near Disneyland; 18 holes, par 71; 6,180 yards; rating 68.4, slope 116.

Costa Mesa Golf Course, 1701 Golf Course Dr., Costa Mesa; (714) 754-5267. Lush public club and facilities with vast practice area. *Los Lagos:* 18 holes, par 72; 6,542 yards; rating 69.0, slope 110. *Mesa Linda:* 18 holes, par 70; 5,486 yards; rating 63.3, slope 96.

Newport Beach Golf Course, 3100 Irvine Ave., Newport Beach; (714) 852-8681. Premier executive public course; 18 holes, par 59; 3,490 yards; rating 51.7, slope 83.

The Links at Monarch Beach, 33080 Niguel Rd., Laguna Niguel; (714) 240-8247. Challenging Scottish link–style resort/public course designed by Robert Trent Jones, Jr.; 18 holes, par 70; 5,900 yards; rating 67.2, slope 117.

SAN DIEGO AREA

Balboa Park Municipal Golf Course, Golf Course Dr., San Diego; (619) 232-2470. Two-tier public courses in parklike setting. *18-hole course:* par 72; 6,300 yards; rating 68.3, slope 110. *9-hole course:* par 32; 2,197 yards.

La Costa Country Club, Costa del Mar Rd., Carlsbad; (619) 438-9111, (800) 854-5000. Renowned resort hotel and spa. Dick Wilson/Joe Lee–designed resort courses. *North:* 18 holes, par 72; 6,983 yards; rating 69.8, slope 117. *South:* 18 holes, par 72; 6,896 yards; rating 69.3, slope 117.

Mission Bay Golf Center, 2702 N. Mission Bay Dr., San Diego; (619) 273-1221. Popular flat public course; 18 holes, par 58; 3,175 yards.

Pala Mesa Resort, 2001 State 395, Fallbrook; (619) 728-5881. Championship resort course has distinctly different 9s—one is hilly, the other wooded; 18 holes, par 72; 6,472 yards; rating 69.4, slope 117.

Rancho Bernardo Inn & Country Club, 17550 Bernardo Oaks Dr., Rancho Bernardo; (619) 277-2146. Resort course located in long, winding valley; 18 holes, par 72; 6,388 yards; rating 69.5, slope 118.

Torrey Pines Inn & Golf Club, 11480 N. Torrey Pines Rd., La Jolla; (619) 452-3226. Outstanding public facility; choice of two challenging Billy Bell courses. *North*: 18 holes, par 72; 6,659 yards; rating 69.6, slope 116. *South:* 18 holes, par 72; 7,021 yards; rating 72.2, slope 124.

PALM SPRINGS AREA

Indian Wells Golf Resort, Grand Champions Hotel, Indian Wells; (619) 346-GOLF. Two excellent resort courses. *East:* 18 holes, par 72; 6,686 yards; rating 69.4, slope 110. *West:* 18 holes, par 72; 6,478 yards; rating 68.7, slope 109.

La Quinta Hotel Golf & Tennis Resort, La Quinta; (619) 345-2549. Stark rocks of Santa Rosa Mountains frame distinctive Pete Dye resort courses; 54 holes, each 18-hole course par 72. *Dunes:* 6,874 yards; rating 70.6, slope 129. *Mountain:* 6,834 yards; rating 71.4, slope 136. *Citrus:* 7,135 yards; rating 70.9, slope 123. Dunes and Citrus courses open only to resort guests.

Mission Hills Resort Hotel & Golf Club, Rancho Mirage; (619) 328-3198. Pete Dye championship resort course open to hotel guests and public; 18 holes, par 70; 6,743 yards; rating 70.3, slope 126.

Palm Springs Municipal Golf Course, 1885 Golf Club Dr., Palm Springs; (619) 328-1956. Outstanding city public course; 18 holes, par 72; 6,701 yards; rating 69.6, slope 102.

PGA West, 56150 PGA Blvd., La Quinta; (619) 564-7170. Call a day ahead for tee times. Pete Dye–designed resort course. *TPC Stadium:* 18 holes, par 72; 7,261 yards; rating 71.2, slope 130. *Nicklaus:* 18 holes, par 72; 7,264 yards; rating 69.2, slope 122.

SANTA BARBARA AREA

Alisal Golf Course, 1054 Alisal Rd., Solvang; (805) 688-4215. Excellent ranch-hotel facility. Designed by Billy Bell, resort course meanders along a seasonal creek; 18 holes, par 72; 6,286 yards; rating 68.5, slope 114.

La Purisima Golf Course, 3455 State 246, Lompoc; (805) 735-8395. Designed by Robert Muir Graves and Damian Pascuzzo, public course incorporates ideas derived from golf design seminars; 18 holes, par 72; 7,105 yards; rating 72.5, slope 132.

Ojai Valley Inn & Country Club, 1203 Country Club Rd., Ojai; (805) 646-5511. World-class resort course designed by George Thomas and Billy Bell has contrasting 9s—one flat, the other rolling hills; 18 holes, par 70; 5,909 yards; rating 68.9, slope 117.

Sandpiper Golf Course, 7925 Hollister Ave., Santa Barbara (near Goleta); (805) 968-1541. Reminiscent of Scotland, outstanding Billy Bell seaside public course has sweeping fairways and spacious greens; 18 holes, par 72; 7,053 yards; rating 71.3, slope 126.

Boat Cruises

 Viewing Southern California's coast from the deck of a boat is usually the best way, and certainly the most scenic, to get your bearings. From south to north, the following operators all offer boat tours.

SAN DIEGO

Bahia Belle, 998 W. Mission Bay Dr.; (619) 488-0551. Mission Bay cruises aboard sternwheeler.

Classic Yacht Charters, 555 W. Beech St. #518; (619) 234-0306. Bay cruises.

Harbor Excursions, 1050 N. Harbor Dr.; (619) 234-4111. Two-hour look at military presence on the bay.

Invader Cruises, 1066 N. Harbor Dr.; (619) 234-8687. Bay cruises on schooner, sternwheeler, or motor yacht.

San Diego-Coronado Ferry, Broadway and Harbor Drive; (619) 233-6872. Fifteen-minute shuttles.

San Diego Harbor Excursion, 570 N. Harbor Dr.; (619) 234-4111. Daily bay cruises.

NEWPORT/BALBOA

Cannery Cruises, Cannery Restaurant, Balboa Peninsula; (714) 675-5777. Weekend brunch and dinner cruises.

Catalina Passenger Service, Balboa Pavilion; (714) 673-5245. Year-round 45- and 90-minute harbor tours.

Hornblower Yacht Cruises, Newport Harbor; (714) 631-2469. Sunday brunch and dinner cruises.

Pavilion Queen, Balboa Pavilion; (714) 673-5245. Sunday buffet cruises.

LONG BEACH/SAN PEDRO

Buccaneer/MardiGras Cruises, San Pedro; (213) 548-1085. Harbor and dinner cruises on schooner or paddlewheeler.

Catalina Channel Express, P.O. Box 1391, San Pedro, CA 90733; (213) 519-1212. Channel crossings to Catalina Island.

Catalina Cruises, Shoreline Village & Queen Mary, Long Beach; (213) 410-1062. Narrated harbor cruises, shoreline cocktail cruises.

Los Angeles Harbor Cruises, Village Boat House, Ports O'Call; (213) 831-0996. Daily one-hour harbor tours.

Spirit Cruises, Ports O'Call, Berth 76, San Pedro; (213) 831-1073. Harbor cruises, summer weekend cocktail cruises.

Spirit of Los Angeles, Ports O'Call, San Pedro; (213) 514-2999. Lunch and dinner daily, weekend moonlight cruises.

MARINA DEL REY

Hornblower Dining Yacht, Dock 52, Fisherman's Village; (213) 301-9900. Harbor tours, Sunday champagne brunch cruises on Mississippi-style riverboat.

SANTA BARBARA

Capt. Don's Harbour Cruises, Stearns Wharf; (805) 969-5217. One-hour cruises May–October.

MORRO BAY

Clam Taxi, 699 Embarcadero; (805) 772-8085. Sandspit shuttle and tour boat.

Tiger's Folly, 1205 Embarcadero; (805) 772-2257. Paddlewheeler.

Whale Watching

 After summers spent feeding in the Bering Sea and Arctic Ocean, California gray whales head south each winter to birthing and breeding grounds 4,000 miles away in Baja California.

This December-through-January migration brings the large mammals so near to shore that they can be seen from land at several points. Males and noncalving females begin trickling north again in March. Cows with calves appear outside the surf line from April on into May.

One of the best places from which to watch the passing parade is the whale-watching station at San Diego's Cabrillo National Monument on Point Loma. Sightseeing boats offer even closer looks. The following cruise operators are grouped from south to north.

OCEANSIDE/SAN DIEGO

Baja Expeditions Inc., P.O. Box 3725, San Diego, CA 92103; (619) 581-3311. January–March trips to Baja California.

Biological Adventures, Fisherman's Landing, 2838 Garrison, San Diego, CA 92106; (619) 222-0391. December–March.

H&M Landing, 2803 Emerson St., San Diego, CA 92106; (619) 222-1144. December–February.

Helgren's Oceanside Sportfishing Trips, 315 Harbor Dr., Oceanside, CA 92054; (619) 722-2123. December–April.

Islandia Sportfishing, 1511 W. Mission Bay Dr., San Diego, CA 92109; (619) 222-1164. December–January.

San Diego Natural History Museum, P.O. Box 1390, San Diego, CA 92112; (619) 232-3821. December–February.

DANA POINT/ NEWPORT BEACH

Burns Charters, 2602 Newport Blvd., Newport Beach, CA 92663; (714) 675-2867. December to season's end.

Catalina Passenger Service, Davey's Locker, 400 Main St., Balboa, CA 92661; (714) 673-5245. December–March.

Dana Wharf Sport Fishing, 34675 Golden Lantern, Dana Point, CA 92629; (714) 496-5794. October–February.

Orange County Marine Institute, 24200 Dana Point Harbor Dr., Dana Point, CA 92629; (714) 831-3850. November–March.

LONG BEACH/SAN PEDRO

Catalina Cruises, P.O. Box 1948, Catalina Terminal, San Pedro, CA 90733; (213) 410-1062. December–March.

Queen's Wharf, 555 Pico Ave., Long Beach, CA 90802; (213) 432-8993. December–April.

Spirit Cruises, Berth 76, Ports O'Call, San Pedro, CA 90731; (213) 831-1073. January–March.

VENTURA/ SANTA BARBARA

Capt. Don's Harbour Cruises, P.O. Box 1134, Summerland, CA 93067; (805) 969-5217. February–March.

Island Packers, 1867 Spinnaker Dr., Ventura, CA 93001; (805) 642-1393. December–March.

Santa Barbara Museum of Natural History, 2559 Puesta del Sol Rd., Santa Barbara, CA 93105; (805) 962-0885. November–March.

Sea Landing Sportfishing, Breakwater, Santa Barbara, CA 93109; (805) 963-3564. February–April.

MORRO BAY

Virg's Fish'n Inc., 1215 Embarcadero, Morro Bay, CA 93442; (805) 772-1223. December–March.

Wine Touring

 You'll see vineyards throughout the Southland, but the majority of wineries and tasting rooms are in three widely separated districts: Temecula, the Santa Ynez Valley, and Paso Robles.

The elaborate Robert Mondavi Wine & Food Center in Orange County (1570 Scenic Avenue, Costa Mesa) stages a variety of wine tastings, concerts, art shows, and cooking demonstrations that are open to the public. For details on upcoming events, call (714) 979-4510.

Not far from Old Town in Los Angeles is that city's oldest winery, San Antonio (737 Lamar Street), open daily from 8 A.M. to 6 P.M. for touring and tasting. From Interstate 5, take the Main Street exit west, continue 5 blocks to Lamar, and drive south 2 blocks.

TEMECULA

Tucked into the southwest corner of Riverside County about 60 miles north of San Diego, the hilly Temecula area is known for fruity white wines. Reds such as Petite Sirah have also gained attention.

Almost a dozen wineries provide tours and tastings. Most can be reached from the Rancho California Road exit off Interstate 15. Cafe Champagne (open 11 A.M. to 9 P.M. daily), at the John Culbertson Winery, offers a delicious alternative to picnicking.

For a complete list of wineries, contact the Temecula Valley Chamber of Commerce, 40945 County Center Dr., Suite C, Temecula, CA 92390; (714) 676-5090.

SANTA YNEZ VALLEY

The wineries in the scenic valley near Santa Barbara are easy to reach from main highways—U.S. 101, State 246, and State

154. For a list of 22 wineries welcoming guests, write to the Santa Barbara County Vintners' Association, P.O. Box 1558, Santa Ynez, CA 93460, or call (805) 688-0881. Maps can also be picked up at wineries.

"One-stop" tasting rooms offer a chance to compare wines from a number of sources. Los Olivos Tasting Room, 2905 Grand Avenue, Los Olivos, is open 11 A.M. to 8 P.M. daily (small charge for tasting). Stearns Wharf Vintners, on the pier in Santa Barbara, offers free tasting from 10 A.M. to 5 P.M. daily.

PASO ROBLES

Two dozen Paso Robles wineries are open for tasting, most from 10 A.M. to 5 P.M. daily. Almost all lie along U.S. 101 (the north-south route) or State 46 (the east-west corridor). Many wineries have pleasant picnic sites.

Start your tour on the main street of the tiny town of Templeton a few miles south of Paso Robles. Templeton Corner serves as a central tasting room for boutique wineries. Pick up a winery map here, or contact the Paso Robles Chamber of Commerce, 548 Spring St., Paso Robles, CA 93446; (805) 238-0506.

A popular wine festival is held the third Saturday in May in Paso Robles' downtown City Park.

Health Spas

 If you're worried about staying fit on vacation, take heart. Southern California—particularly San Diego County—is noted for its fine spas. They come in as many sizes and shapes as their patrons.

A dictionary definition of a spa is "any locality frequented for its mineral springs." So our directory samples modest, therapeutic settings where people still "take the waters" as well as exclusive, beauty-oriented retreats. Advance reservations are required almost everywhere; some spas offer day-use facilities.

SAN DIEGO AREA

Cal-A-Vie, P.O. Box 1567, Vista, CA 92084; (619) 945-2055. Week-long health and beauty programs include fitness training, massage, and exercise.

The Golden Door, P.O. Box 1567, Escondido, CA 92033; (619) 744-5777. Expensive week-long health and beauty programs, luxurious lodging.

La Costa Hotel & Spa, 2100 Costa del Mar Rd., Carlsbad, CA 92009; (619) 438-9111. Large resort with variety of fitness and basic spa programs for men and women, pools, jogging trail, 23 tennis courts, 2 golf courses, 8 noted restaurants (open to public).

Murrieta Hot Springs Resort, 28779 Via las Flores, Murrieta, CA 92362; (800) 458-4393. Hot springs with mud and mineral baths, 3 pools, 14 tennis courts, and fitness facilities; 2-day packages with accommodations in lodge and cottages.

Rancho La Puerta, P.O. Box 2548, Escondido, San Diego, CA 92033; (800) 443-7565. Just over the border in Tecate, this was the modest first version of Golden Door (see preceding); week-long packages include meals and exercise classes (massage and beauty services extra).

DESERT AREA

Bermuda Resort, 43019 Sierra Highway, Lancaster, CA 93534; (805) 942-1493. Fitness and weight-loss plans, extra-cost massage and beauty treatments.

Desert Hot Springs Hotel & Spa, 10805 Palm Dr., Desert Hot Springs, CA 92240; (619) 329-6495. Motor inn with cluster of hot mineral pools, dining room, massage.

The Palms at Palm Springs, 572 N. Indian Ave., Palm Springs, CA 92262; (619) 325-1111. Individually tailored fitness programs; packages include low-calorie meals (2-day minimum).

Spa Hotel & Mineral Springs, 100 N. Indian Ave., Palm Springs, CA 92262; (619) 325-1461. Palm Springs grew up around these Indian-owned mineral springs; hotel offers 2-night and 7-night spa packages, day-use rates.

CENTRAL COAST

The Ashram, P.O. Box 8009, Calabasas, CA 91372; (818) 888-0232. Exclusive star retreat for shape-up breaks, focusing on fitness, vegetarian cuisine.

The Oaks at Ojai, 122 E. Ojai Ave., Ojai, CA 93023; (805) 646-5573. Fun-and-fitness spa with overnight packages that include low-calorie meals, exercise classes, evening programs.

Sycamore Mineral Springs Resort, 1215 Avila Beach Dr., San Luis Obispo, CA 93401; (805) 595-7302. Small motor inn 1 mile from beach, in-room spas, outdoor hot springs.

Cycling

Unlike Southern California's freeways, its bicycle routes are uncrowded. Many offer a different view of the region than you'll see from a car, and in some cases two wheels simply provide the best way to tour an area. We highlight a few particularly inviting routes. Rental bikes are available in most areas.

GREATER L.A.

Stretching from the Santa Monica Pier to the bluffs at Palos Verdes, the 19-mile paved South Bay Bike Trail passes Venice's bizarre bazaar of street vendors and entertainers, Marina del Rey (leave the path at Fiji Way to reach Fisherman's Village), and the rest of beach-town row.

ORANGE COUNTY

Bikeways parallel the shore at Bolsa Chica State Beach in Huntington Beach and stretch the length of Balboa Peninsula in Newport Beach. The ferry to Balboa Island lets you take your bike along.

SAN DIEGO

Bicycle paths open up miles of waterside cycling along the harbor. Other routes show off inland terrain. For a map of all bike trails, call (619) 231-2453. Many hotels rent bikes, as does a shop at Coronado's Old Ferry Landing.

Waterfront. A 4½-mile pathway shared by cyclists, pedestrians, and joggers runs along the waterfront from the west end of Spanish Landing Park (west of the airport along Harbor Drive) to the south arm of Embarcadero Marina Park. From here, you can cross by ferry to explore Coronado and Silver Strand State Beach (8 level miles of unimpeded views).

DESERT

In winter, the sun-washed desert is an excellent place for cycling. A number of bikeways in the Palm Springs area offer routes especially suited to families with young children, and Death Valley's level terrain and stunning scenery are best seen at a bike's pace.

Palm Springs Area. Tahquitz Bikeway, a 10-mile route between Palm Springs and Rancho Mirage, skirts two golf courses before leaving landscaped neighborhoods for a desert wash. You can pick it up at the corner of Sunny Dunes Drive and Sunrise Way. If you don't want to go the whole way, a 1½-mile ride takes you to DeMuth Park, a good place for a picnic.

Free maps and rentals are available at bike shops such as Mac's Bike Rentals (700 E. Palm Canyon Drive).

Death Valley. Cycling in the national monument requires special considerations. Check weather conditions with a ranger, be prepared for flats, carry liquids and snacks, and dress in layers for changing temperature conditions. You'll need to provide your own wheels—the monument has no bike rentals.

The following are round-trip mileages, difficulty ratings, and best times to visit six attractions around Furnace Creek by bike.

Badwater: 36 miles; some long, gradual climbs; moderately strenuous; go in the morning.

Artists Palette: 13 miles, 2½-mile climb, then rolling; moderately strenuous; best in late afternoon.

Golden Canyon: 6¼ miles plus 2- to 3-mile hike up to Zabriskie Point or Red Cathedral; level, easy; afternoon ride.

Zabriskie Point: 9 miles; 888-foot climb; moderate; go at first light to watch the illumination of Golden Canyon and Manly Beacon peak.

Twenty Mule Team Canyon: 16 miles southeast (2¾ unpaved); steady climb; moderate; late afternoon.

Mustard Canyon (turn left from State 190 at Harmony Borax Works): 4½ miles (1½ unpaved); flat, easy; morning or afternoon.

CENTRAL COAST

Though cycling in the cities during rush hours should be avoided, several coastal routes are rewarding. Check with the Ventura Visitors and Convention Bureau (address on page 112) for designated bike tours. One takes you to the Channel Islands National Monument headquarters, another through the historical downtown.

Santa Barbara is full of beautiful cycling paths. You can bike from the city to Goleta via Cathedral Oaks Road; paths explore the University of California campus at Santa Barbara.

At Morro Bay, you can cycle north from downtown on Embarcadero to Morro Rock; another recommended route takes you along Main Street and out State Park Road to the Museum of Natural History and Morro Bay State Park.

Skiing

L.A.-area skiers head up to the nearby San Bernardino and San Gabriel mountains for non-taxing fun. Serious sport means an all-day drive north to Mammoth Mountain.

GREATER L.A. AREA

Bear Mountain, Big Bear Lake off Big Bear Blvd.; (714) 585-2519. Lifts: 1 quad chair, 5 double chairs, 3 triple chairs, 2 pomas. Summit: 8,805 feet.

Mount Baldy, Mount Baldy Rd., San Gabriels; (714) 981-3344. Lifts: 4 double chairs. Summit: 8,600 feet.

Mountain High East and West, State 2, Wrightwood; (619) 249-5471. Lifts: 2 quad, 9 double, 3 surface chairs. Summit: 8,200 feet.

Mount Waterman, State 2, La Cañada Flintridge; (818) 440-1041. Lifts: 3 double chairs. Summit: 8,023 feet.

Ski Sunrise, State 2, Wrightwood; (619) 249-6150. Lifts: 1 quad, 3 surface chairs. Summit: 7,600 feet.

Snow Forest, south of Big Bear Village; (714) 866-8891. Lifts: 1 triple, 3 surface chairs. Summit: 8,000 feet.

Snow Summit, State 18 east of Big Bear, Big Bear Lake, CA 92315; (714) 866-5766. Lifts: 2 quad, 2 triple, 6 double chairs. Summit: 8,200 feet.

Snow Valley, State 18, Running Springs; (714) 867-2751.Lifts: 8 double, 5 triple chairs. Summit: 7,440 feet.

MAMMOTH

June Mountain, State 158, June Lake; (619) 648-7733. Lifts: 5 doubles, 2 quad, 1 minipoma, 1 tram. Summit: 10,200 feet.

Mammoth Mountain, north of Bishop off State 395, Mammoth Lakes; (619) 934-2571. Lifts: 5 quad, 7 triple, 14 double chairs; 2 gondola, 2 surface. Summit: 11,053 feet.

SOUTHERN SIERRA

Montecito-Sequoia Nordic Resort, contact 472 Deodara, Los Altos, CA 94024; (800) 227-9900. Groomed and backcountry touring trails, ski school, and rentals in Sequoia National Forest between Sequoia and Kings Canyon national parks.

Index

Mammoth Mountain skier